van Gogh

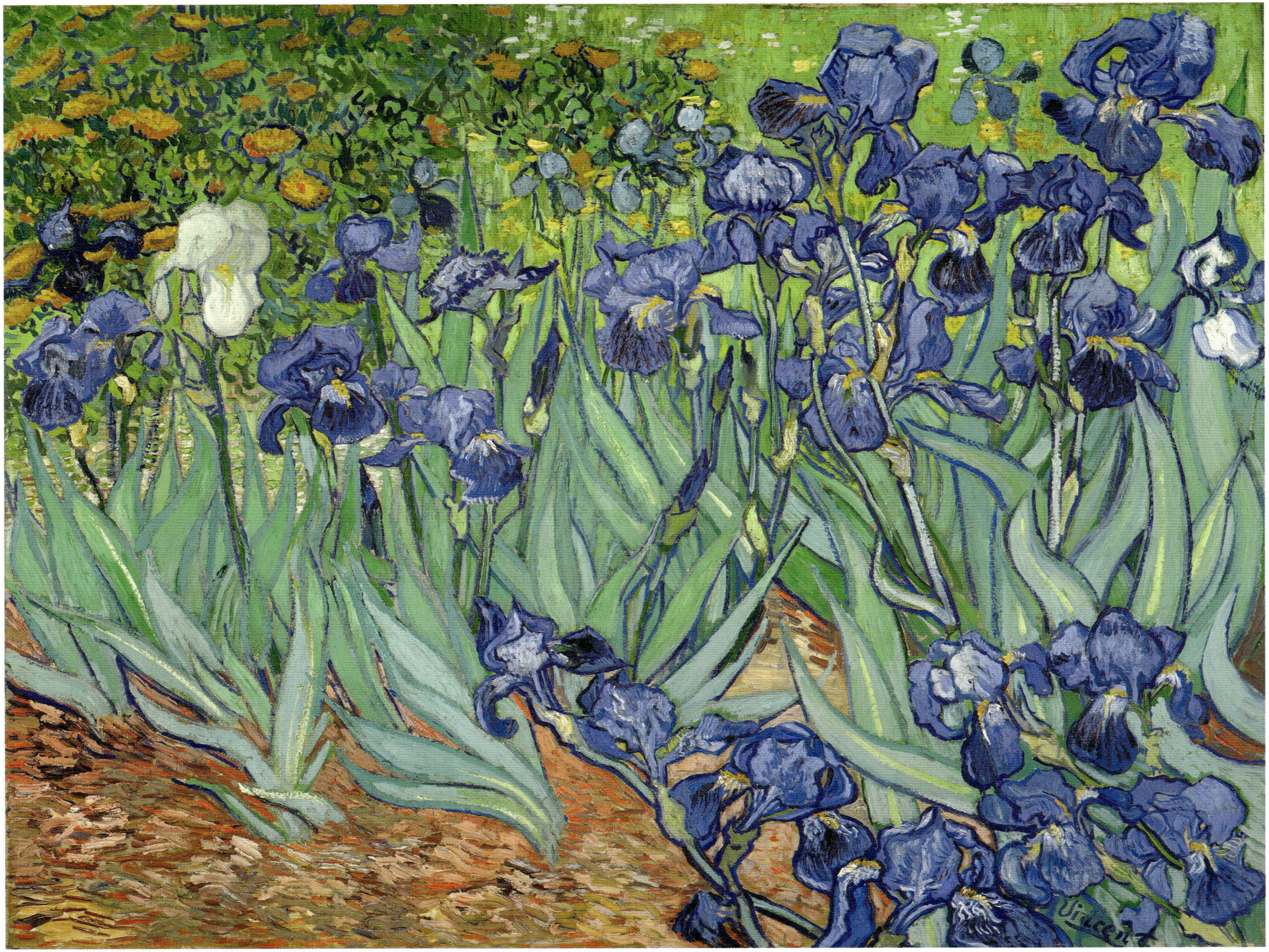

Vincent van Gogh, *Irises*, 1889 (J. Paul Getty Museum, Los Angeles)

JOHN CAUMAN

van Gogh
IN 50 WORKS

PAVILION

CONTENTS

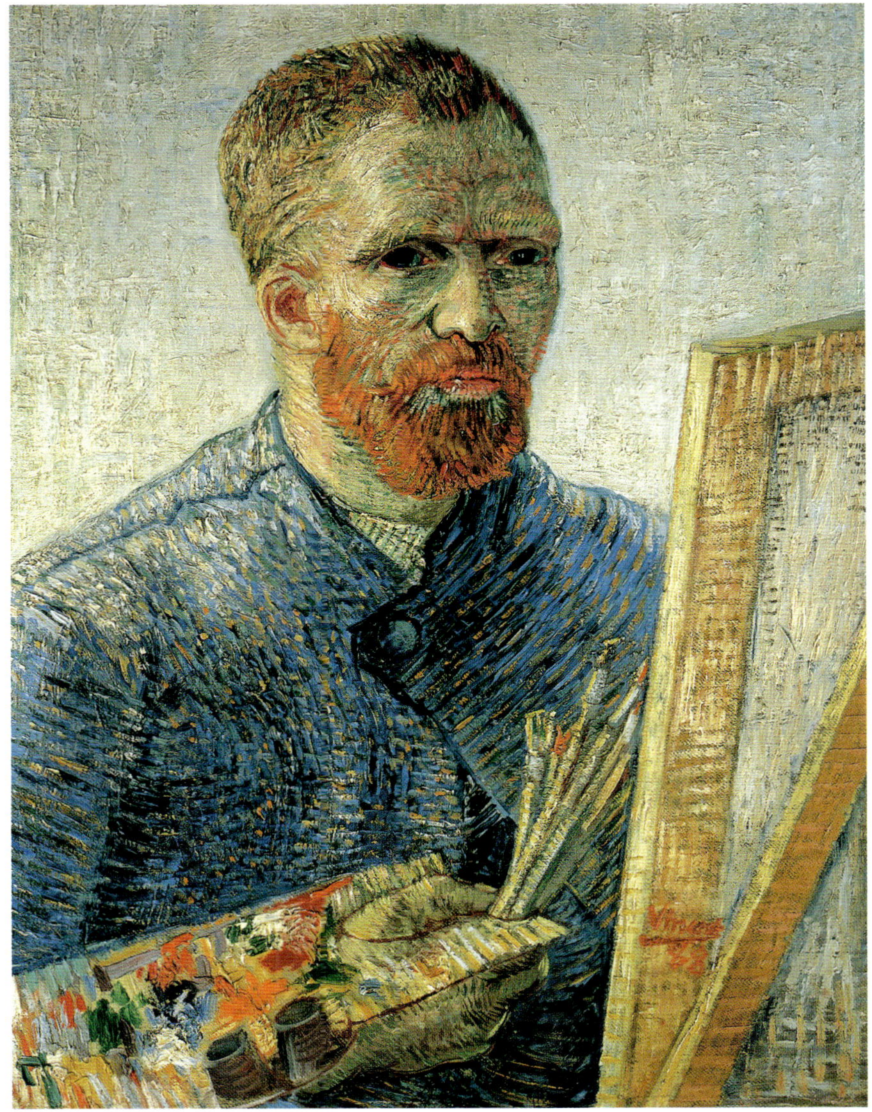

Vincent van Gogh, *Self-Portrait as a Painter*, 1888
(Van Gogh Museum, Amsterdam)

> In a picture I want to say something comforting, as music is comforting. I want to paint men and women with that something of the eternal which the halo used to symbolize, and which we seek to convey by the actual radiance and vibration of our coloring.
>
> Vincent van Gogh to Theo van Gogh, Arles, 3 September 1888[1]

Vincent van Gogh was born on 30 March 1853 in Zundert, a rural Dutch town in the southern province of Brabant, near the Belgian border. The first of the six surviving children of Anna and Theodorus van Gogh, he entered the world a year to the day after the couple suffered the loss of a stillborn baby, also named Vincent.

Vincent was the beneficiary of a family legacy of art and the ministry. Anna, née Carbentus, was a nature-lover and amateur artist who filled notebooks with drawings of plants and flowers; Theodorus was a pastor of the Dutch Reformed Church, a Protestant faith in the predominantly Catholic town of Zundert. Vincent's grandfather had also been a minister, and three of his uncles were art dealers; his uncle Vincent, known as Cent, was a partner in Goupil & Cie, a leading French art dealership. Among his siblings Vincent was closest to his brother Theo, four years his junior, who would join Uncle Cent's business and provide Vincent with moral and financial support throughout his life. Vincent and Theo's voluminous lifelong correspondence – following Vincent's death at the age of 37, Theo survived him by only six months – has provided posterity with detailed accounts of Vincent's art and life, thoughts and feelings.

In 1869, when Vincent was 16, he went to work for Goupil, where he was employed for the next seven years, first at their offices in The Hague and later in London and Paris. The art education he acquired in the process was rooted in conventional naturalistic painting, rather than in the avant-garde. He compiled scrapbooks of reproductions for his own reference, displaying a taste for realist depictions of landscape and peasant life, as found in seventeenth-century Dutch and nineteenth-century French painting. He acquired proficiency in the English and French languages, and educated himself in art history, and in English and French literature.

During his years at Goupil, Vincent gradually became disenchanted with the art business. When he was working at the branch in The Hague, he was an enthusiastic employee, well-regarded by his superiors. At the London branch, however, he proved to be awkward at dealing with customers. In London and, increasingly, in Paris, following his transfer there, Vincent immersed himself in reading the Bible, to the detriment of his gallery work. Finally, in March 1876, he was dismissed from Goupil.

From 1876 to 1880, Vincent spent an itinerant few years. Following brief positions teaching at English boarding schools and working at a Dutch bookshop, he attempted a career in the ministry. After failing his examination in theological studies in Amsterdam, he moved to the Borinage region of Belgium, where for six months he worked as a lay minister to oppressed coal-mine workers. Finally, in August 1880, at Theo's suggestion, Vincent decided to become an artist.[2]

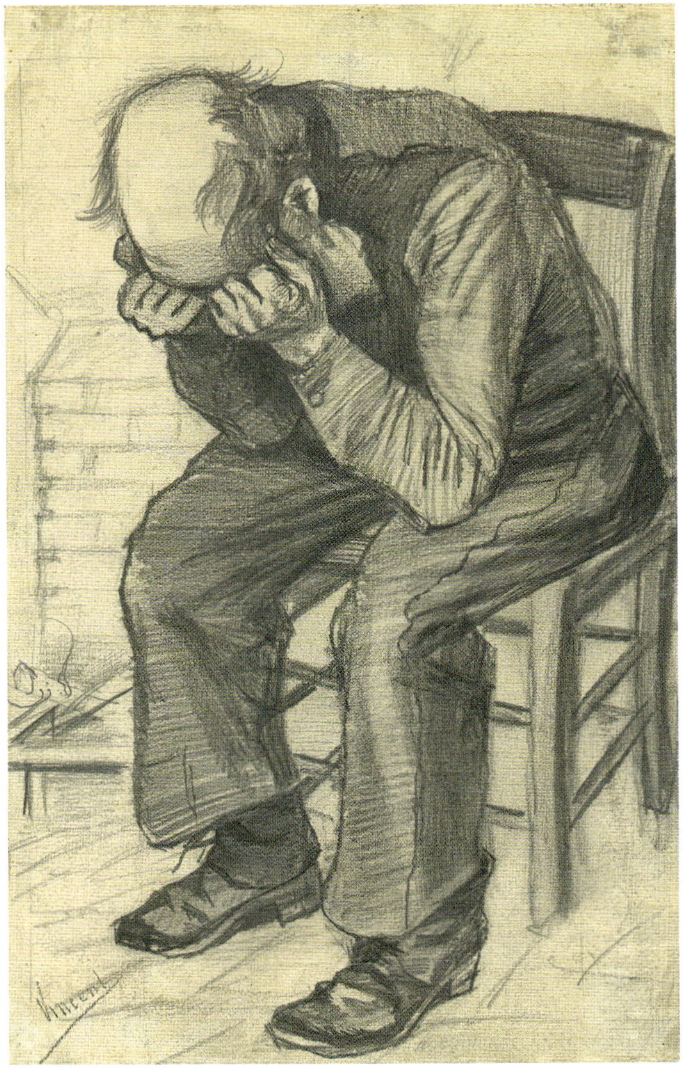

Vincent van Gogh, *Worn Out*, 1882
Pencil on paper | 50.4 × 31.6cm (19⅝ × 12¼in),
Van Gogh Museum, Amsterdam

Vincent had a natural gift for drawing; his first efforts in that direction were made without the benefit of an instructor. Then in November 1881 he moved to The Hague, where, under the tutelage of Anton Mauve, a cousin by marriage on his mother's side of the family, he created his first paintings – still lifes rendered in a predominantly dark palette. Mauve was a leading member of the 'Hague School', Dutch counterparts of the Barbizon School of France, who were realist painters of peasants and rural landscapes. While in The Hague, Vincent made a series of figure drawings of the poor and elderly, including *Worn Out* (November 1882), which depicts a seated, sorrowful resident of the Dutch Reformed Almshouse for Men and Women in The Hague (see left).

Vincent's arrival in The Hague had been preceded by an unhappy attempt at love with a recently widowed cousin, Cornelia 'Kee' Vos Stricker, his senior by seven years. He had encountered Kee while visiting his parents at the parsonage in the town of Etten the previous summer. He professed his love to her; she firmly rejected his advances. He then followed Kee to Amsterdam, where she was staying with her parents; he demanded to see her, but was unable to do so. These unfortunate events seem to have precipitated his first serious bout of mental illness.

In The Hague, in January 1882, Vincent met Clasina Maria 'Sien' Hoornik, with whom he had a domestic partnership for the duration of his stay in the city. It was the only such relationship of his life. Sien, an artist's model and prostitute, had a small child and was pregnant with a second. She gave up prostitution for a time when she was living with Vincent, but this situation could not be sustained as she and her offspring were dependent for their support on Vincent's allowance from Theo, which was insufficient to support them all. Their relationship, which had caused a falling-out between Anton Mauve and Vincent, ended when Vincent departed The Hague for the rural province of Drenthe in September 1883.

The bleak peat moorlands of Drenthe and its economically deprived population were a source of inspiration to Vincent. He tried without success to convince Theo to leave Goupil and join him to pursue his own career as an artist, but a fractious exchange of letters with Theo that affected his monthly payments brought a swifter end to Vincent's time in Drenthe than he had planned. Less than three months after his arrival, in December 1883, he rejoined his parents, who had recently moved to the Brabant town of Nuenen. Despite his often tense relationship with them – particularly his father – they cleared a room that had been used as a laundry to provide a studio, installing a stove and window. His alienation from the family, and what it represented, is evident in a letter from Vincent to Theo, now working for Goupil in Paris. The letter gives an indication of why Vincent signed his artworks with his given name, and never with his surname:

> In my opinion Father is forever lapsing into *narrow*-mindedness instead of being bigger, more liberal, broader and more humane. … I do not beg for your mediation … but I ask you point-blank how we stand – are you a 'Van Gogh' too? … In character I am rather different from the various members of the family, and essentially I am *not* a 'Van Gogh'.[3]

In Nuenen Vincent embarked upon a series of paintings of local peasants and weavers, rendered in a muted palette and painterly brushstroke characteristic of the Dutch tradition. In letters to Theo, he expressed admiration for Delacroix, Millet and Daumier, among others, while conveying his lack of familiarity with the more recent developments in French painting:

> When I hear you mention so many new names, it's not always easy for me to understand because I have seen absolutely *nothing* of them. And from what you told me about 'impressionism' … it's not quite clear to me what it really is.[4]

In February 1884, Vincent's mother Anna broke her thighbone while stepping from a train. To cheer her up during her recovery, Vincent made a painting of the exterior of his father's church and presented it to her as a gift; at this early stage in his life as a painter, he regarded art-making as an instrument of healing, of others as well as of himself. He then resumed painting the people of the environs of Nuenen, as well as of the Brabant landscape, and in May 1884 he found a larger studio, which he rented from a Catholic sexton and his wife; he would later move out of the family home and live in the studio. In his figure studies, his interest lay in portraying the lives of the rural workers, for example *The Potato Eaters* (see p. 37), which he would long regard as a signature work, and *A Peasant Woman Digging* (see p. 39), in which the stooped pose of the subject typical of those working on the land recalls Millet's painting *The Gleaners* (see opposite).

In March 1885 Vincent's father, the Rev. Theodorus van Gogh, died suddenly from a stroke or heart attack. In the autumn of that year, in tribute to him, Vincent reworked the painting of the church at Nuenen that he had given to his mother a year earlier, transforming a winter scene into an autumnal one (see p. 35). The only figure in the original painting was a solitary worker carrying a spade at the centre foreground, but now Vincent added a congregation in the foreground and middle ground and transformed the solitary worker into a mourner. The painting remained in his mother's collection until her death.

In late November Vincent departed for the Belgian port city of Antwerp, where he lived for the next three months. It was his first experience of a metropolis, and it was there that he first began to collect the Japanese prints that were to exert a strong influence on his art. He explored the museums and became familiar with the paintings of Peter Paul Rubens, whose compositions of voluptuous female figures were so much richer in colour than those of the Dutch masters. He also enrolled in the Koninklijke Academie voor Schone Kunsten (Royal Academy of Fine Arts). A fellow student described the impression that he made:

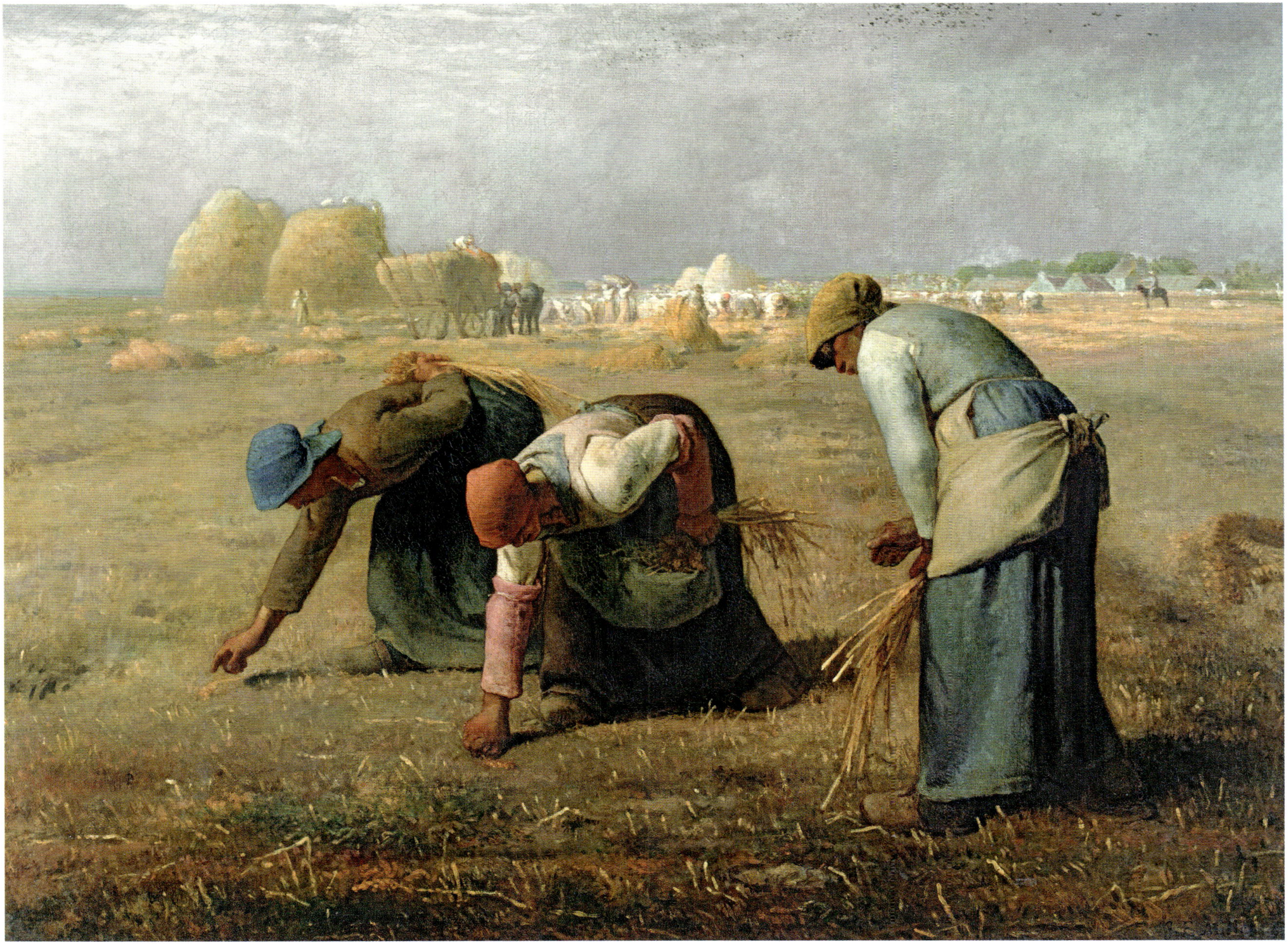

Jean-François Millet, *The Gleaners*, 1857
Oil on canvas | 83.8 × 111.8cm (33 × 44in), Musée d'Orsay, Paris

> Van Gogh arrived one morning, dressed in the sort of blue smock worn by Flemish livestock merchants … In place of a palette, he used a board torn from a crate … [He] began painting feverishly … [laying] on his impasto so thickly that his colors literally dripped from the canvas …

In drawing classes he worked from plaster casts; as a new student, he was not permitted to work from a live model, though he did so at private drawing clubs. When a class was assigned to copy a cast of the Venus de Milo, Vincent's version 'strongly accentuated the width of her hips … The beautiful Greek goddess had become a robust Flemish matron'. The instructor 'tore Van Gogh's sheet of paper with the furious strokes of his crayon, correcting his drawing while reminding him of the immutable canons of art. Then the young Dutchman … flew into a violent rage and shouted at the horrified professor: "You clearly don't know what a young woman is like, *God damn it!* A woman must have hips, buttocks, a pelvis in which she can carry a baby!"'[5]

Theo encouraged his brother to continue his studies in Paris, where he would have contact with recent tendencies in art and could produce more marketable works. Nonetheless, he was unprepared for Vincent's sudden arrival from Antwerp in late February 1886. When Vincent arrived at the Paris train station, he sent Theo a note via a porter: 'Don't be cross with me that I've come all of a sudden. I've thought about it so much … Will be at the Louvre from midday, or earlier if you like.'[6]

Theo had lived in Paris for seven years and was now director of a small gallery in Montmartre owned by Bousson, Valadon & Cie, successors to Goupil & Cie. Vincent joined him in his flat in the Rue Laval at the foot of *la butte* Montmartre (a *butte* is a steep hill with a flat top). In June they moved to larger quarters on the Rue Lépic on top of the hill, with a panoramic view of the city and with three remaining windmills, which reminded the brothers of their native Holland.

The atelier of the academic painter Fernand Cormon was at the foot of *la butte*, on the Boulevard de Clichy. Here Vincent continued his art studies, working from live models and antique casts. In Cormon's studio Vincent came to know young artists who would become his friends and colleagues, including Émile Bernard, Louis Anquetin, John Russell and Henri de Toulouse-Lautrec. The two years that he lived in Paris were a transformational period in Vincent's life as an artist, during which he assimilated the latest tendencies in French art into his work. He attended the eighth and final Impressionist exhibition, held in May–June 1886, which included work by Edgar Degas, Berthe Morisot and Mary Cassatt, as well as paintings in the Impressionist style by Paul Gauguin, executed under the influence of his mentor Camille Pissarro. The exhibition marked the debut of Georges Seurat's *A Sunday Afternoon on the Island of La Grande Jatte* (see opposite), a visual manifesto of a new style that would be designated 'Neo-Impressionism' by the critic Félix Fénéon (and would also be known as Pointillism or Divisionism); in August the painting was reshown at the unjuried Salon des Indépendants.

Neo-Impressionism was a method of rendering the Impressionist style in a more systematic, quasi-scientific manner in which the image is broken up into nearly uniform dots of pure colour which are mixed in the viewer's eye, rather

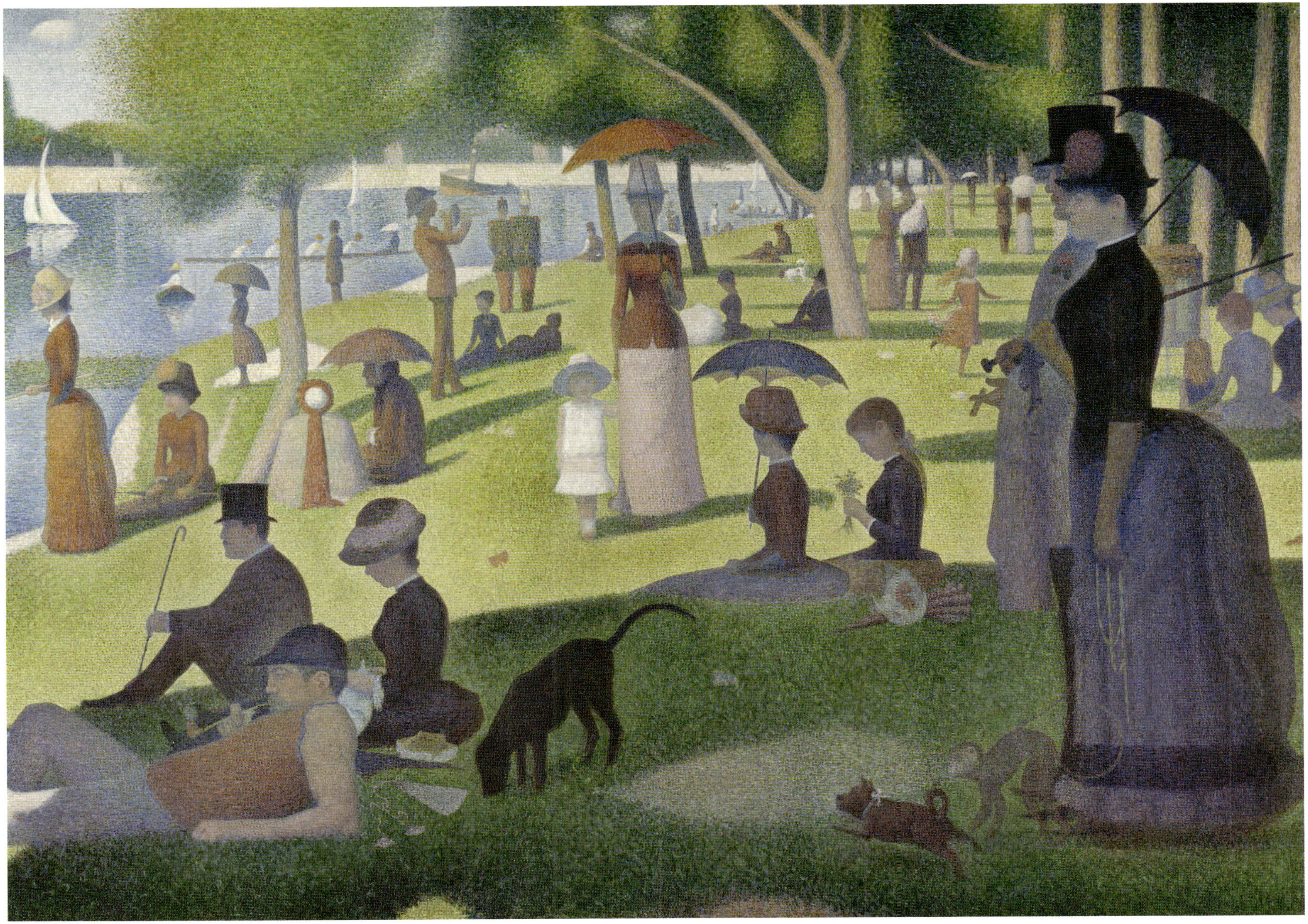

Georges Seurat, *A Sunday Afternoon on the Island of La Grande Jatte*, 1884–6
Oil on canvas | 207.5 × 308.1cm (81¾ × 121¼in), Art Institute of Chicago

than on the canvas, with the goal of achieving greater luminosity. Seurat had won converts to this new style, including Paul Signac, four years his junior, and the veteran painter Camille Pissarro, both of whom showed Neo-Impressionist paintings at the exhibition.

Although Vincent was by nature an intuitive rather than a systematic artist, both Neo-Impressionism and Impressionism affected the work he did in his Paris years and beyond. This influence is evident in *The Interior of a Restaurant* (see p. 41), which was probably painted in Asnières, a suburb northwest of Paris where Vincent often painted landscapes and occasionally encountered Signac.

The transformation of Vincent's style during his Paris years is particularly evident when comparing two of his landscapes of *la butte* Montmartre – the first painted in spring 1886 (see opposite), soon after his arrival, and the second painted a little more than a year later, in summer 1887. The first is rendered in the realist manner of the Hague School, with solid forms, modelling in light and shade and muted colour. The second (see p. 45), with its dots and brushstrokes of brilliant, luminous paint, reveals the atmospheric luminosity of late nineteenth-century French painting.

Vincent's interest in Japanese woodblock prints, known as ukiyo-e, which had begun when he was living in Antwerp, increased in Paris; he and Theo collected them, as had such artists as Manet, Monet and Degas. Like his predecessors, Vincent admired their cropped compositions, bold outlines, flattened perspective, decorative patterning and areas of intense colour. He made copies in oil paint, now in the Van Gogh Museum, Amsterdam, of three prints: one of a courtesan by Keisai Eisen (1790–1848), and two of landscapes by Utagawa Hiroshige (1797–1858). In each case he decorated the space around the image with a frame of Japanese characters or motifs borrowed from other ukiyo-e prints; see *Bridge in the Rain (after Hiroshige)*, p.14. For Vincent, the term 'Japanese' was synonymous with the characteristics of the advanced modern art of his time.

Vincent was a frequent visitor to the Montmartre art supply shop and picture gallery of Julien 'Père' Tanguy. He greatly admired Tanguy, who was both a political radical and a supporter of avant-garde artists. When Vincent painted his portrait (see p. 47) he depicted him against a background of ukiyo-e prints, even though they were not actually displayed at Tanguy's shop; Vincent used this background to punctuate characteristics he wished to bring out in his sitter.

Another spot in Montmartre frequented by 'artists of the *petit boulevard*' (as Vincent referred to the younger generation of avant-garde artists in Paris) was the Café du Tambourin. Vincent painted a portrait of the proprietress, Agostina Segatori, seated in the café drinking beer, at a time when the ukiyo-e print collection of Vincent and Theo was displayed on the café's walls. Vincent used Edgar Degas' *In a Café (Absinthe)* of 1875–6 (see p.15) as a prototype for this portrait.

Over the course of his two years in Paris, Vincent grew rapidly as an artist and for the first time in his life became part of an artistic community, albeit on its periphery. Yet urban life was not his natural habitat, and by the winter of 1888 he was feeling stressed, eager to travel southward, to the light of the Midi. His final painting in Paris was a self-portrait (see p. 49), the last of some two dozen he had made while in the city.

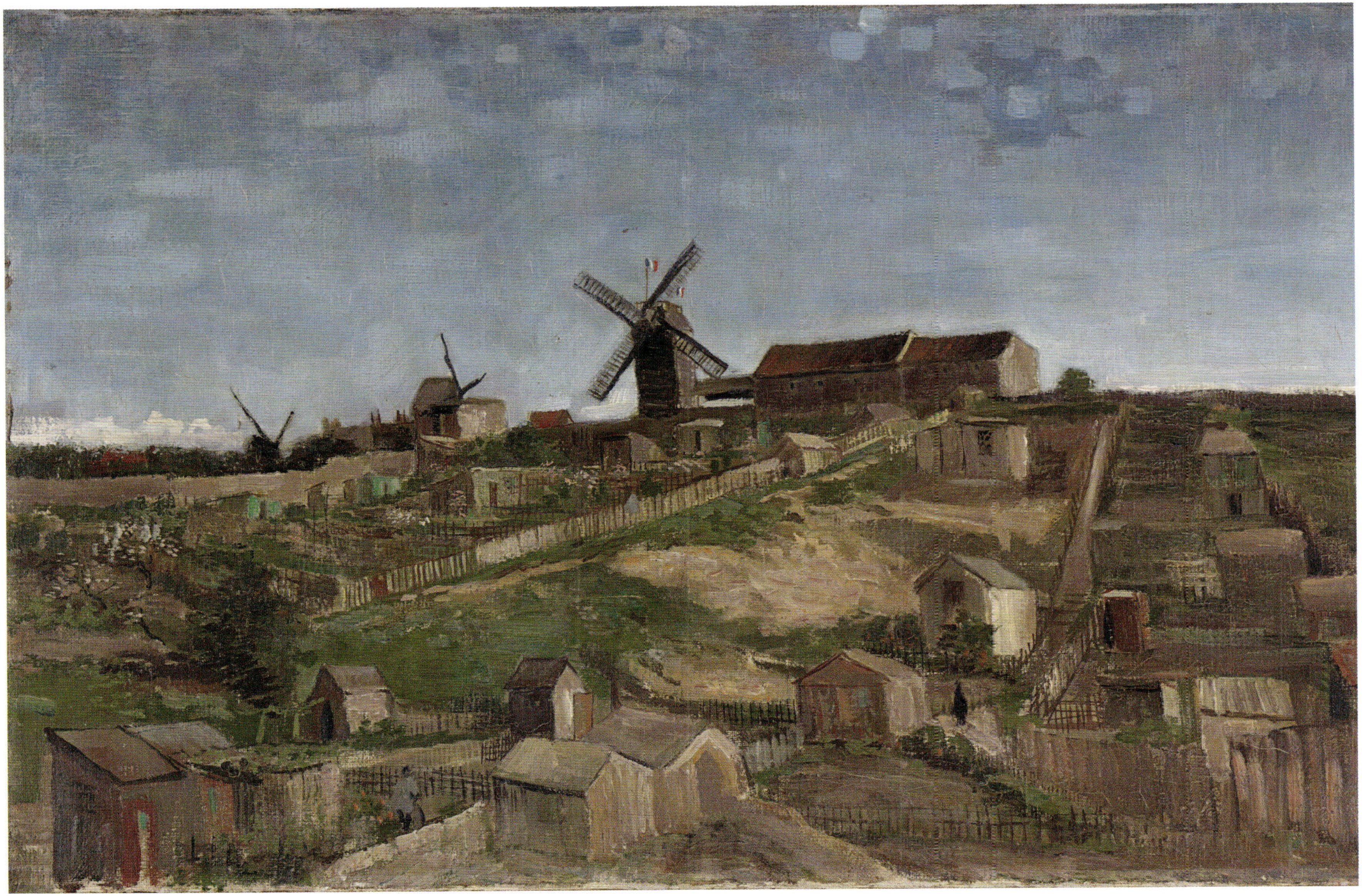

Vincent van Gogh, *La Butte Montmartre*, 1886
Oil on canvas | 36 × 61cm (14⅛ × 24in), Kröller-Müller Museum, Otterlo

On 19 February 1888 Vincent took the train from Paris to the town of Arles in Provence, along the river Rhône. He arrived the next day, a journey of some sixteen hours, and would remain in the town for the next fifteen months. Having sought the warmth and sunlight of the Midi, he arrived during an unusually cold February. He took a room at the Hôtel-Restaurant Carrel on rue Cavalarie, and wrote to Theo the following morning: 'I'll begin by telling you that there's about two feet [60cm] of snow everywhere …' Looking on the bright side, he added, 'I have seen some splendid red stretches of soil planted with vines, with a background of mountains of the most delicate lilac. And the landscapes in the snow, with the summits white against a sky as luminous as the snow, were just like the winter landscapes that the Japanese have painted.'[7]

Due to the strength of the mistral (see glossary), it was several weeks before he could work outdoors. Eventually, in mid-March, the mild weather returned. Exploring the countryside, Vincent discovered a drawbridge along a canal which evoked for him the landscapes of both his native Netherlands and Hiroshige woodcuts, and there he painted *The Langlois Bridge at Arles with Women Washing* (see p. 51). This work would launch a prolific period in his life as an artist, when he would paint a series of spring landscapes and seascapes in the mediums of oil on canvas, watercolour on paper and drawings on paper rendered with a reed pen.

On 1 May Vincent sent a letter to Theo, accompanied by a sketch of a house on Place Lamartine, Arles:

> Today I rented the right-hand wing of this building, which contains 4 rooms, or more precisely, two, with two little rooms. It's painted yellow outside, whitewashed inside … What I'd like to do would be to furnish a room, the one on the first floor, to be able to sleep there … I could live at the new studio with someone else, and I'd very much like to. Perhaps Gauguin will come to the south.[8]

The following week, after a dispute with the *patron* of the Hôtel-Restaurant Carrel over his bill, Vincent found new living quarters at the Café de la Gare on Place Lamartine, run by Joseph Ginoux and his wife Marie. In

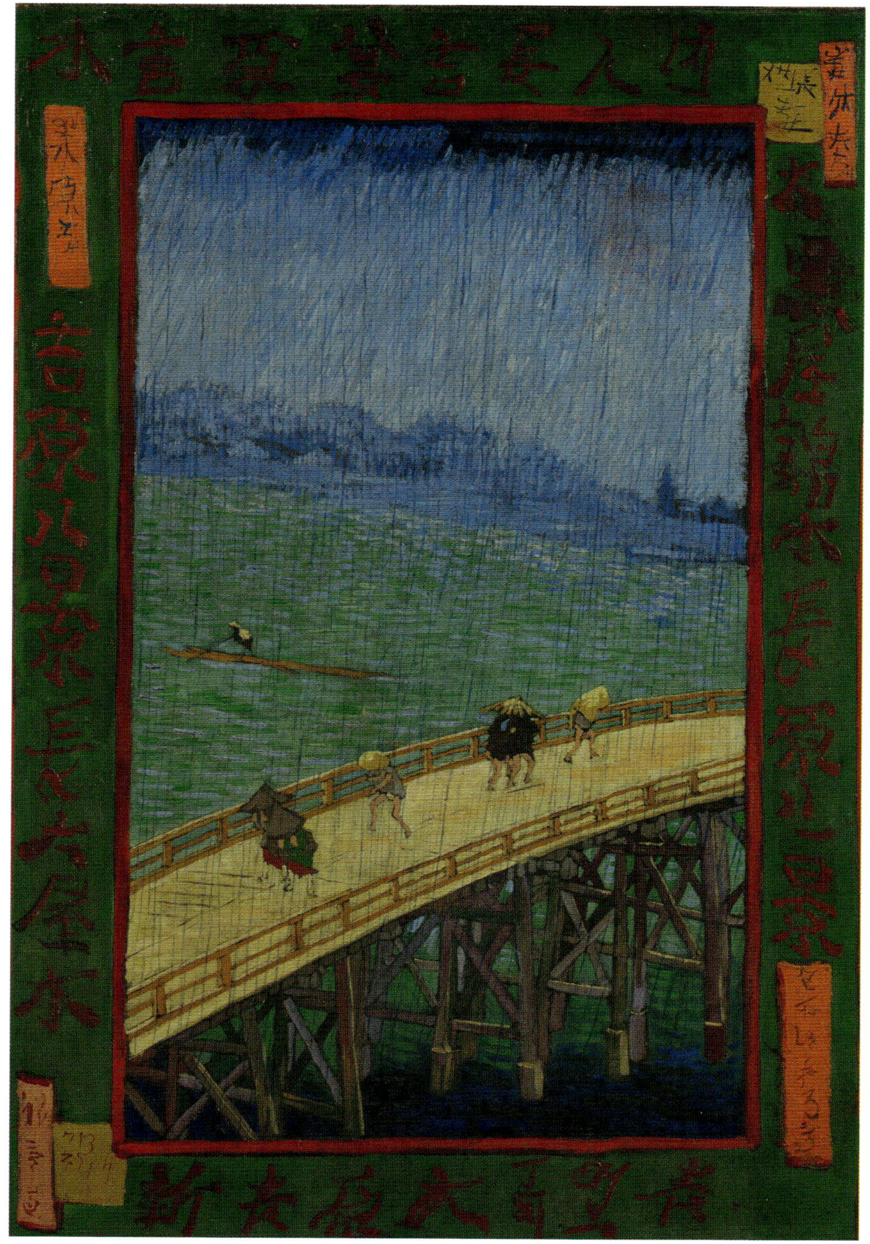

Vincent van Gogh, *Bridge in the Rain (after Hiroshige)*, 1887
Oil on canvas | 73.3 × 53.8cm (28¾ × 21¼in), Van Gogh Museum, Amsterdam

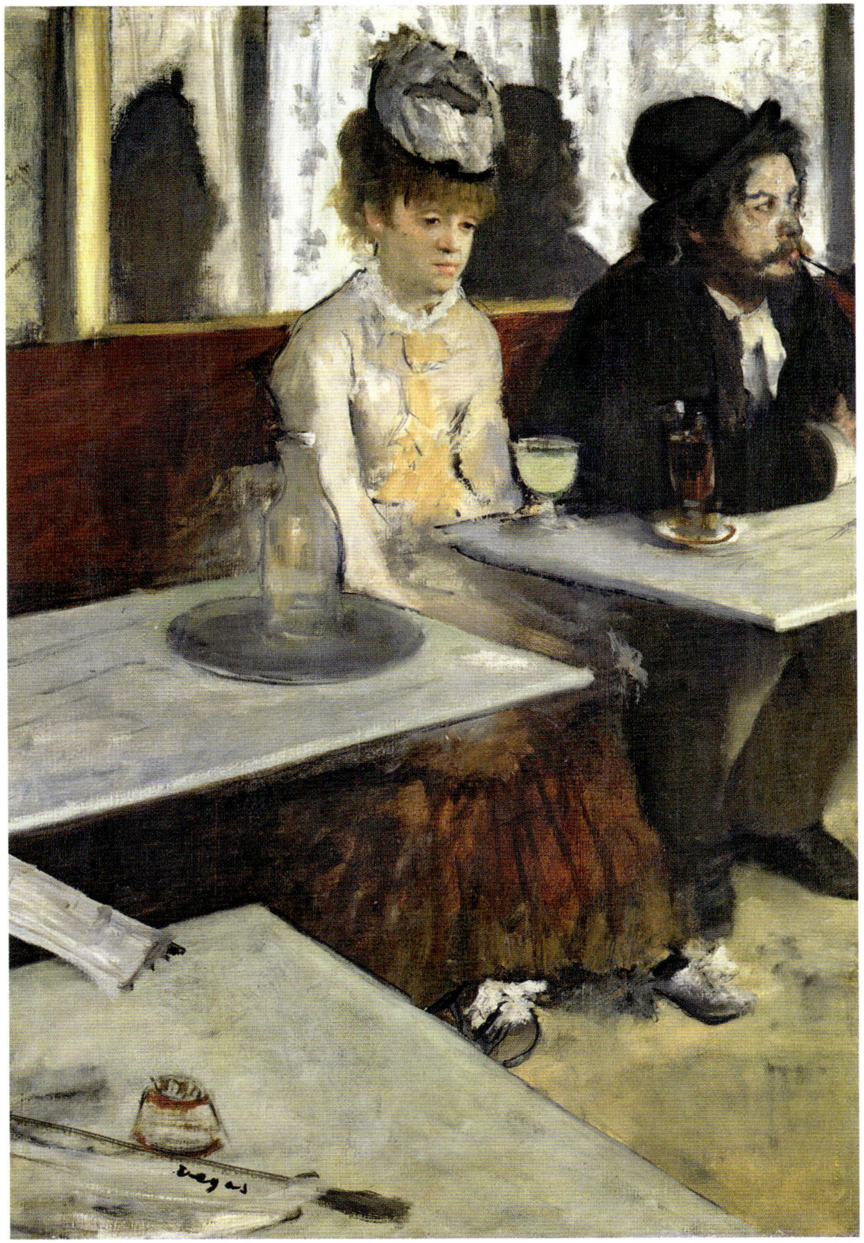

Edgar Degas, *In a Café (Absinthe)*, 1876
Oil on canvas | 92 × 68.5cm (36⅕ × 27in), Musée d'Orsay, Paris

months to follow, Vincent, while living in an upstairs room at the Café de la Gare, would increasingly focus on furnishing and decorating the Yellow House on Place Lamartine. He would come to see it as the headquarters of a future artists' colony in the south, much as Pont-Aven, Brittany, was the headquarters for a group of artists in the north, among them Émile Bernard and Paul Gauguin.

On 30 May he left the town for a five-day sojourn in the coastal fishing village of Saintes-Maries-de-la-Mer, where he composed a series of drawings and paintings of the beach, the sea and the town. This was his first view of the Mediterranean, and his exhilaration is evident in *Seascape at Saintes-Maries* (see p. 55), a depiction of sailing boats at sea, painted with a new-found freedom. It was done *in situ* without preliminary sketches, inspired in its approach by Eugène Delacroix's *Christ Asleep during the Tempest* (see p. 16).

Upon his return to Arles, Vincent produced a calligraphic adaptation in the form of a drawing on paper with a reed pen (see p. 59), a dynamic composition rendered with a spontaneity that surpasses that of the painting. A drawing and painting of fishing boats on the beach at Saintes-Maries reverses this process. The drawing (see p. 16) was made *in situ*, with instructions written on each boat and mast regarding the colours of the final painting. Executed upon Vincent's return to Arles, the painting retains the word '*Amitié*' inscribed on the central boat, which implies that the group of boats symbolizes the friendship of a future community of artists in Arles.

June was harvest time in Provence, which provided a theme for the next stage in Vincent's art, prompted by an exhibition of Monet's paintings of Antibes that were filled with the light of the south. The exhibition was held at Theo's gallery and drew an admiring review from the critic Gustave Geffroy, who also wrote to Theo with a view to acquiring some of Vincent's work. Vincent promptly cancelled a proposed return to Saint-Maries and headed instead for the plain of La Crau, which lies between the river Rhône and the Alpilles mountains. There, wheatfields lay golden beneath brilliant sunlight, and Vincent completed nearly a dozen paintings in the

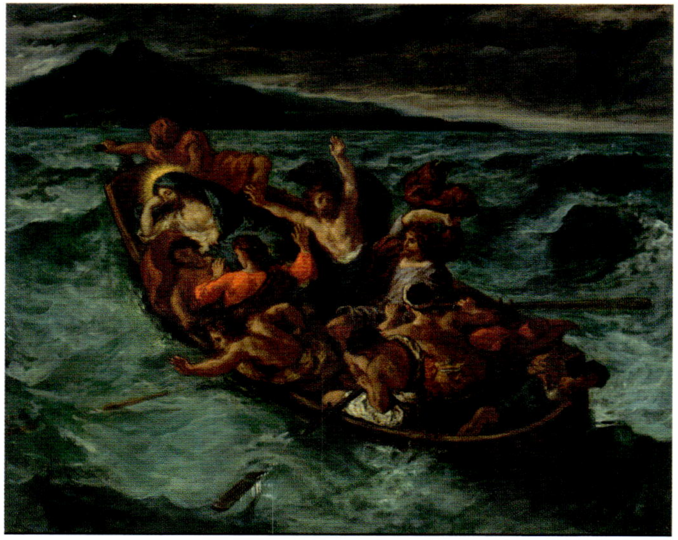

Eugène Delacroix, *Christ Asleep during the Tempest*, c.1853
Oil on canvas | 50.8 × 61cm (20 × 24in), The Metropolitan Museum of Art, New York

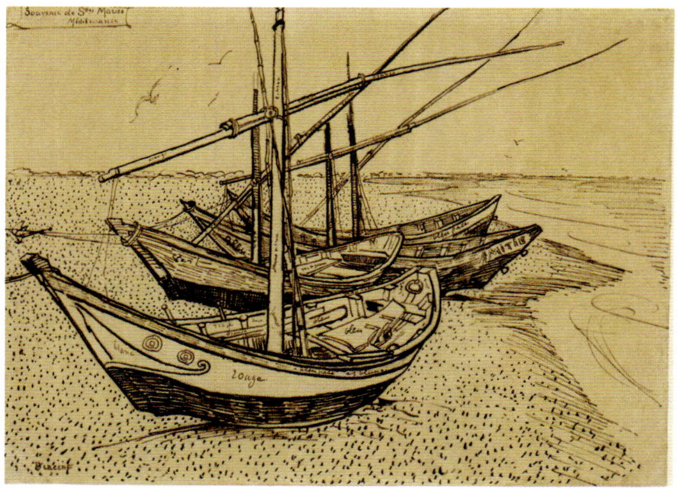

Vincent van Gogh, *Fishing Boats on the Beach at Saintes-Maries*, 1888
Reed pen | 39.5 × 53.5cm (15½ × 21in), Private collection

course of a fortnight. *The Harvest* (see p. 61), a panoramic landscape on a large scale, has a composition influenced by Dutch seventeenth-century landscape painting, here transformed via the painterly spontaneity and luminous colour of the *petit boulevard*.

While making sketches of the harvest, Vincent painted *The Sower* (see p. 65), a landscape of a setting sun over a wheatfield, incorporating a figure derived from Jean-François Millet (see opposite). Vincent admired Millet for his identification with rural workers, but for the luminous colour of the composition, derived from oppositions of yellow and violet, he was inspired by another of his heroes, Delacroix. In a letter to Theo he wrote of the latter's *Christ Asleep During the Tempest* (see left) in reference to this painting, noting that it 'speaks a symbolic language through colour itself.'[9]

Back in Arles and eager to use his studio at the Yellow House, Vincent encountered a problem that would often plague him: a difficulty in finding models for figure studies. Peasants whose portraits he wished to paint had no inclination to pause while he sketched them. Then, in the middle of June, a Zouave – a soldier indigenous to North Africa – arrived unbidden in his studio. Not only was he willing to pose in the distinctive uniform of his French army regiment (see *The Seated Zouave*, p. 71), he liked to draw, too, giving the artist and his model a shared interest that developed into sketching trips to the countryside together.

In July, there came another model – a Provençale girl in her early teens. The title *La Mousmé* comes from a character in a novel he had recently read, *Madame Chrysanthème* by Pierre Loti, which helped to shape the Japan of his imagination. Then, the next month, he returned to a familiar theme. Unlike his earlier painting *The Potato Eaters* or Millet's *Man with a Hoe* (see p. 18) that depicted caricatures, *Portrait of Patience Escalier,* p. 73, captured a rural worker with the dignity and sympathy that typified Vincent's portraits in Nuenen. With these portraits, Vincent was moving away from the Impressionist-influenced paintings of his Paris period: 'Instead of trying to render exactly what I have before my eyes, I use colour more arbitrarily in order to express myself forcefully,' he wrote to Theo.[10]

In August, when the summer heat in Arles was excessive, Vincent painted still lifes as an alternative to working outdoors. In his still life of *Oleanders* (see p. 69), an oleander plant emerges from a glazed jug resting on a table, set against a pale-green background. Sharing the table with the jug of oleanders is Emile Zola's novel *La Joie de vivre*, a life-affirming

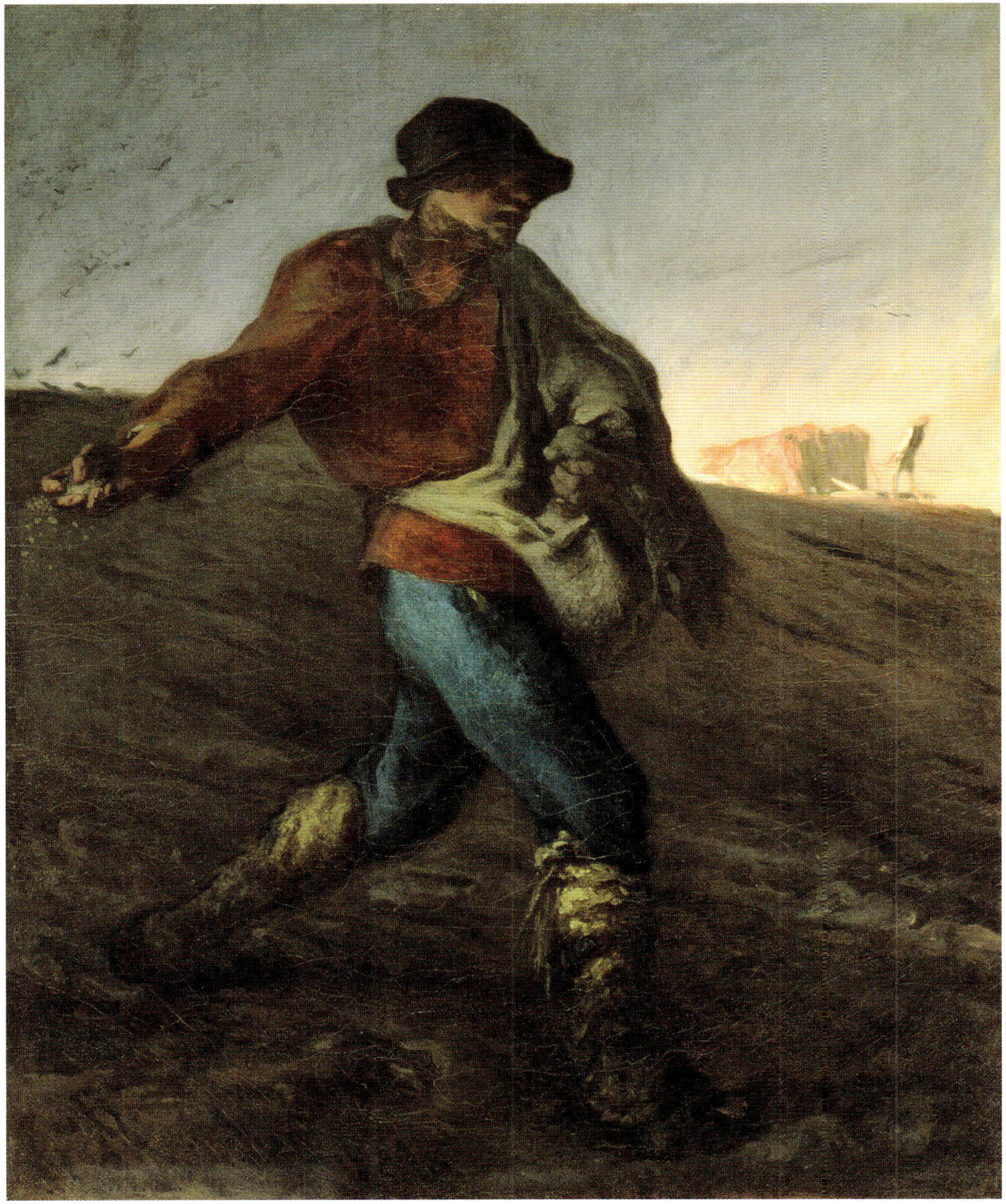

Jean-François Millet, *The Sower*, 1850
Oil on canvas | 101.6 × 82.6cm (40 × 32½in), Museum of Fine Arts, Boston

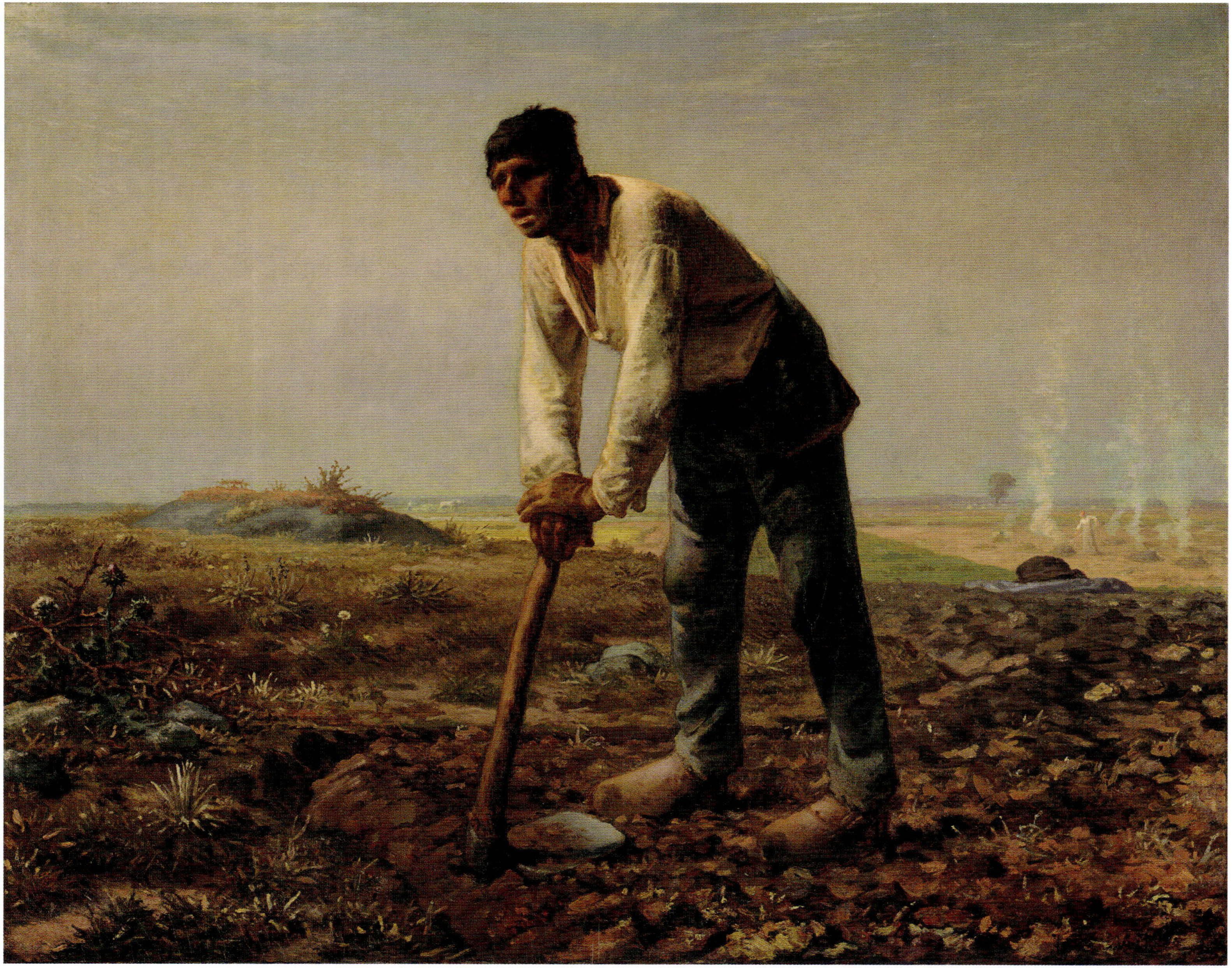

Jean-François Millet, *Man with a Hoe*, 1860–2
Oil on canvas | 81.9 × 100.3cm (32¼ × 39½in), J. Paul Getty Museum, Los Angeles

work which was one of Vincent's favourites. He had previously included the book in *Still Life with Bible* (1885, Van Gogh Museum, Amsterdam), painted in Nuenen as a tribute to his then recently deceased father.

In the last week of August Vincent created still lifes of sunflowers, with the purpose of decorating the Yellow House, to create effects 'like those of stained-glass windows in Gothic churches.'[11] In the painting illustrated on p. 75, the yellows of the composition, and the flowers themselves, are tributes to the sun of the Midi. By placing his signature at the centre of the Provençal vase, Vincent implied his identification with the flowers.

In early September, while still living at the Café de la Gare, Vincent painted *The Night Café* (see p. 77), one of his most ambitious and memorable works. The café remained open all night, populated by people on the margins of society. He reported to Theo: 'to the great delight of the lodging-house keeper … the prowling night-visitors and myself, for 3 nights I stayed up to paint, going to bed during the day. It often seems to me that the night is much more alive and richly coloured than the day.'[12] Employing exaggerated perspectival devices and intense contrasts of complementary colours, the artist conveys a vividly dystopian vision of the scene.

As a benign counterpart to *The Night Café*, Vincent painted, nearly contemporaneously, *Café Terrace at Night* (see p. 79). An exterior rather than interior scene, it depicts not the Café de la Gare on Place Lamartine but the terrace of a café and a cobblestone street on Place du Forum. In this painting, the night sky of Provence makes its first appearance in Vincent's work; in *Starry Night over the Rhône* (see p. 81) he gave it his full attention and painted a sparkling firmament, its shimmering reflections in the water, and silhouettes of Romanesque churches on the horizon.

Pursuing his goal of establishing an artist's colony in Arles, Vincent encouraged an exchange of self-portraits among his artist friends, a practice in which Japanese artists were known to take part. After receiving self-portraits from Gauguin and Bernard, in mid-September he painted *Self-Portrait Dedicated to Paul Gauguin* (see p. 83) and sent it to Gauguin in Brittany. In keeping with his trope of Provence as the new Japan, he presents himself in the guise of a Buddhist monk, emphasizing his spiritual demeanour and the Asiatic features of his face.

In mid-September, following the death of their Uncle Cent, Theo was able to provide funds for furnishing the Yellow House, and Vincent spent his first night there; he himself had inherited nothing, and his uncle had even made his disapproval of his penniless artist nephew very clear in his will. Vincent set up an adjoining guest room, in the hope that Gauguin would soon join him. Vincent composed a painting of the house and street (see p. 85) in celestial colours of yellow and blue and in early October wrote to Gauguin:

> Even while working I never cease to think about this enterprise of setting up a studio with yourself and me as permanent residents, but which we'd both wish to make into a shelter and a refuge for our pals at moments when they find themselves at an impasse in their struggle … Now I'd like to see you taking a very large share in this belief that we'll be relatively successful in founding something lasting.[13]

In mid-October, Vincent painted *Bedroom in Arles* (see p. 87), his sanctuary in the Yellow House, employing the exaggerated perspectival devices of *The Night Café* but to opposite effect. He sent a sketch and description to Gauguin, thanking him for promising to come to Arles 'as early as the twentieth'.[15] Gauguin finally arrived in Arles on 23 October, looking more robust than Vincent had expected from seeing his portrait. 'As you learned from my wire,' Vincent wrote to Theo, 'Gauguin has arrived in good health. … I have every confidence that we shall do loads of things with him. He will probably produce a great deal here.'[15]

Gauguin's stay in Arles lasted nine weeks, from his arrival in late October to his abrupt departure on 26 December. On 10 November Vincent wrote to Theo: 'We are having wind and rain here, and I am very glad not to be alone. … Gauguin … is very interesting as a friend, I must tell you that he knows how to cook perfectly.'[16] Vincent gave visual expression to their partnership in the Yellow House in the form of two pendant works, *Van Gogh's Chair* (see p. 89) and *Gauguin's Chair* (see opposite), which, while technically belonging to the genre of still life, are in effect symbolic portraits of the absent sitters – the first relatively coarse, the second more refined.

During Gauguin's stay in Arles the two artists shared a model: Mme Marie Ginoux, proprietress of the Café de la Gare. Both of them painted her portrait with the title *L'Arlésienne*. Gauguin also included a portrait of her in his version of *Night Café in Arles*, while Vincent painted two versions of *L'Arlésienne* (the second of which is illustrated on p. 93), both of which reveal the influence of Gauguin and his fellow Pont-Aven painters.

Vincent also made a series of portraits of the Roulin family – Joseph Roulin, his wife Augustine, their sons Camille and Armand, and their infant daughter Marcelle. Joseph, 13 years Vincent's senior, was a good and loyal friend, and between July 1888 and April 1889, Vincent painted six portraits of him. In December 1888 he painted a portrait of Augustine and Marcelle (see p. 91) while *La Berceuse* ('the lullaby') is a portrait of Augustine Roulin (see p. 99), of which Vincent painted five versions between December 1888 and February 1889. The period during which the portraits of the Roulins were composed was a stressful time for Vincent. In mid-November he had signalled to Theo that he was beginning to appreciate Gauguin's ideas: 'Gauguin, in spite of himself and in spite of me, has proved to me a little that it was time for me to vary things a bit – I'm beginning to compose from memory.'[17]

As December rolled by, however, Vincent became increasingly manic in his behaviour. In Gauguin's memoir *Avant et Après*, written 15 years after the events, he recalled:

> During the latter part of my stay, Vincent became excessively brusque and noisy, then silent. Several nights I surprised Vincent, who, having risen, was standing over my bed … Invariably, it sufficed for me to say to him, very gravely, 'What's the matter, Vincent?' for him to go back to bed without a word and fall into a deep sleep.
>
> I came upon the idea of doing his portrait while he painted the still life that he so loved – some sunflowers [*Vincent van Gogh Painting Sunflowers*, 1888, Van Gogh Museum, Amsterdam]. And, the portrait finished, he said to me, 'It's me all right, but me gone mad.'

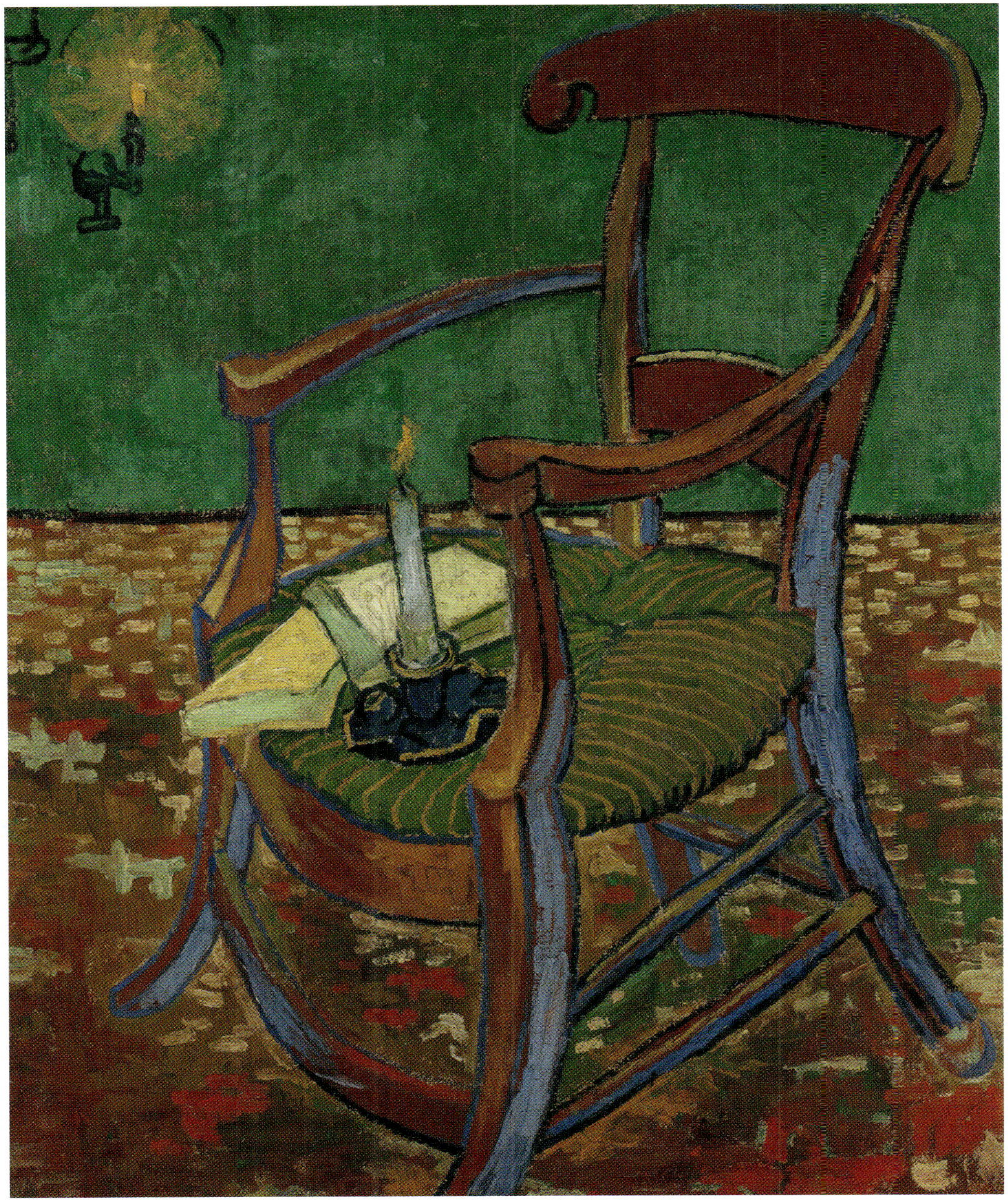

Vincent van Gogh, *Gauguin's Chair*, 1888
Oil on canvas | 90.5 × 72.7cm (35⅞ × 28⅔in), Van Gogh Museum, Amsterdam

> That same evening we went to the café: he took a light absinthe.
>
> Suddenly he threw the glass and its contents at my head.'[18]

In her 'Memoir of Vincent van Gogh by His Sister in Law', Johanna van Gogh-Bonger recounted:

> The situation became more and more strained. In … December Theo received from Gauguin the following letter: '… I must go back to Paris. Vincent and I simply cannot live together in peace because of incompatibility of temper.' … The quarrel was made up … But it was only the calm before the storm.[19]

'The storm' finally broke on the evening of 23 December. Gauguin later recalled:

> 'I felt the need to go out alone and take in the air, scented with flowering laurels … I heard behind me a familiar short footstep, rapid and irregular. I turned just at the moment when Vincent rushed towards me … My look at that moment must have been powerful indeed, for he stopped, and lowering his head, took off running in the direction of the house.'[20]

There remains an open question of whether Vincent had 'an open razor in his hand' when he confronted Gauguin that night on the Place Lamartine.[21] That was Gauguin's recollection when he penned his memoir; yet when he described the event to Émile Bernard just six days after it occurred, he made no mention of a razor.[22]

Gauguin spent the night in a local hotel. Returning to the Yellow House next morning, he was met at the door by the local commissioner of police, who escorted him to Vincent's bedroom. 'In the bed, Vincent lay completely enveloped in the sheets … he appeared lifeless,' Gauguin later recalled. 'I touched the body, whose warmth surely announced life … Almost in a whisper, I said to the commissioner of police: "Be so kind, sir, as to awaken the man with great care, and, if he asks for me, tell him that I have left for Paris."'[23]

In its issue of 30 December 1888, *Forum Républicain*, the local newspaper in Arles, reported the following:

> Last Sunday, at 11:30 at night, one Vincent Vangogh [sic], painter and native of Holland, presented himself at the maison de tolérance [legal brothel] no. 1, asked for one Rachel, and gave her … his ear, saying, 'Guard this object carefully.' Then he disappeared. Informed of this act, which could only have been that of a poor, deranged person, the police went the next morning to his house, and found him lying in his bed, giving almost no sign of life.
>
> The unfortunate man was immediately admitted to the asylum.[24]

Scholars have arrived at differing conclusions regarding how much of his ear Vincent had severed; suffice it to say, he cut off a substantial portion of his left ear. On 24 December he was admitted to the Hôtel Dieu, the hospital in Arles, under the care of Dr Félix Rey. Gauguin summoned Theo to Arles, but the two returned to Paris on 26 December. While Vincent was hospitalized, a frequent visitor was Joseph Roulin, who kept Theo apprised of his progress. Although Vincent's condition was initially diagnosed as critical, by 7 January he was well enough to return to the Yellow House, accompanied by Joseph Roulin.

Vincent soon began to paint again. *Self-Portrait with Bandaged Ear* (see p. 95) conveys optimism; he depicts himself dressed for winter, in front of a ukiyo-e print of geishas and a crane before Mount Fuji, a suggestion of his early hopes for Arles as a 'New Japan'. As his wound healed, he continued as an out-patient of the Arles hospital, and was visited at the Yellow House by his physician Dr Félix Rey, who brought other doctors with him to look at his pictures. Joseph Roulin was another frequent visitor. 'Roulin has been splendid to me, and I dare say that he will remain a lasting friend,' Vincent informed Theo.[25] Unfortunately, on 21 January Roulin left Arles for a new position in Marseilles. In February Vincent experienced another delusional attack, and he was again taken to the hospital.

Peach Trees in Blossom (see p. 101), painted in April, was among the last works that Vincent created in Arles. For this landscape he returned to La Crau, site of *The Harvest* (see p. 61), painted in June the previous year when he was full of hope for a 'New Japan' and for a community of artists in the south. On 8 May he left Arles for Saint-Rémy de Provence, about 19km (12 miles) to the northeast, where he was admitted as a voluntary patient at the Saint-Paul de Mausole psychiatric asylum.

A former monastery, built in the twelfth and thirteenth centuries, the asylum is surrounded by vineyards, olive groves and wheat fields, and is bordered to the south by the Alpilles mountain range. Presiding over the asylum was Dr Théophile Peyron, formerly of the French Navy. Dr Peyron was, as Julian Bell observes, 'not so much enlightened as laissez-faire. There was no concerted program to address the mental problems of the thirty-odd male and female inmates and provisioning was on the cheap – recycled bean stews were their principal fare.'[26]

Vincent had a bedroom and an adjoining studio, from the barred windows of which he could view the Provençal landscape. He was permitted to paint in the hospital grounds, and, on occasion, accompanied by an orderly, in the surrounding fields. Soon after his arrival he was drawn to the hospital garden, where he made a virtue out of necessity by painting a landscape of *Irises* (see p. 103) from such a low vantage point that there is no horizon. Painted in May, *Irises* was created during a period of relative calm in Vincent's emotional life. In June, by contrast, he painted a pair of canvases – *The Starry Night* and *The Olive Trees* (pp. 105 and 107) – using rapid, turbulent brushstrokes that indicated his growing agitation.

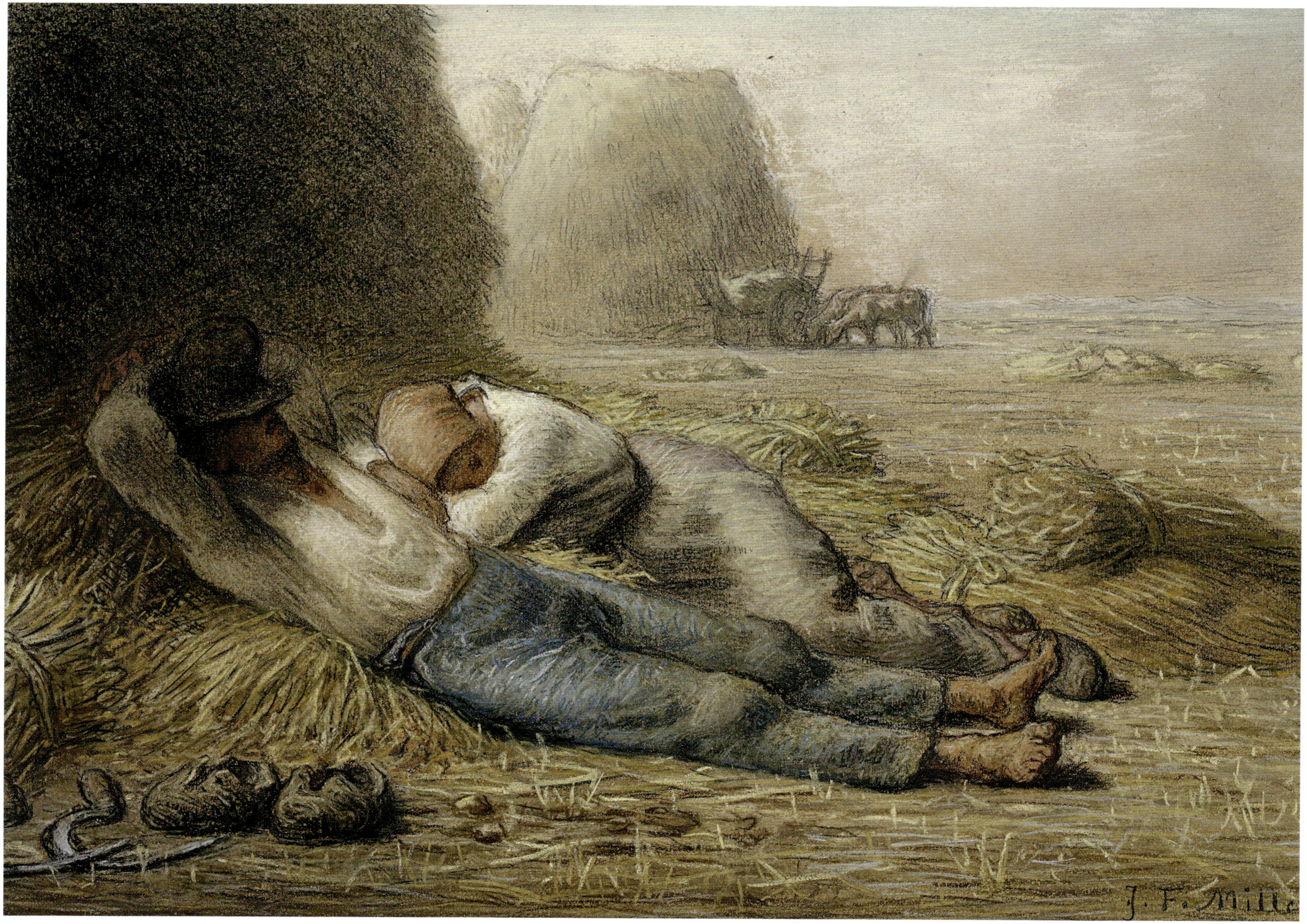

Jean-François Millet, *Noonday Rest*, 1866
Pastel and black conté crayon on buff wove paper | 29.2 × 41.9cm (11½ × 16½in),
Museum of Fine Arts, Boston

In August he wrote to Theo with bad news:

> I am terribly distressed because the attacks have come back … *My mind has been absolutely wandering*, as in Arles . . . and presumably the attacks will come back again in the future; it is *abominable*. For four days I have been unable to eat because of a swollen throat.[27]

According to Dr Peyron's notes in the asylum register, Vincent had eaten paint and drunk turpentine, accounting for his swollen throat and for his being barred from the studio.[28]

By September Vincent was back at work, painting a *répétition* of a landscape he had created in June, *A Wheatfield with Cypresses* (see p. 109). The painting combines a classical, nearly symmetrical composition with turbulent clouds and the spiralling verticals of the trees. In *Self-Portrait* (see p. 111), also painted in September, Vincent depicts himself against a background of pale green, white and blue swirling patterns that resemble those in the sky in *The Starry Night*. Nevertheless, his facial expression is purposeful and the painting conveys his determination to carry out disciplined work as a painter during periods of lucidity.

In part, due to Vincent's limited opportunities to paint the human figure while he was an inmate at the asylum, he did a series of paintings based on works by various artists whom he admired. *Noon: Rest from Work (after Millet)*, which depicts a couple napping after a morning's labour, was based on a set of engravings after pastel drawings by Millet that showed the working day of peasants in the fields (see opposite). The composition combines three of Vincent's favourite genres: landscape, figure composition and still life. The field, the sky, the stacks of grain and the couple's garments are rendered in the swirling brushstrokes that characterized so many of Vincent's Saint-Rémy paintings.

While Vincent was still recovering from his major attack in August, he was reluctant to leave the hospital and instead painted three interior scenes. *Corridor in the Asylum* (see p. 115) is a work on paper depicting the ground-floor passageway of the building, a former monastery. The architecture, a series of diminishing Romanesque arches, suggests a labyrinth from which escape is impossible; the fleeing figure in the background suggests the hopelessness of such an effort. On 23 December 1889, precisely a year after he had mutilated his ear, Vincent suffered yet another attack. A week later he wrote to Theo: 'Odd that I had been working perfectly calmly on some canvases that you will soon see, and that suddenly, without any reason, the aberration seized me again.'[29]

In January 1890, the first issue of the French literary review *Mercure de France* appeared, featuring '*Les Isolés: Vincent van Gogh*' ('The Isolated Ones') by the Symbolist poet and critic G. Albert Aurier. Much of the article is in the form of a dense prose-poem which seeks to present an equivalent of Vincent's art. Aurier praises 'the strange, intense and feverish work of Vincent van Gogh, that compatriot and not unworthy descendant of the old Dutch masters.'[30] It was the only critical study of Vincent's work to appear in his lifetime. Theo sent a copy of the article to Vincent at the Saint-Rémy asylum. Vincent, flattered (although taken aback at being designated as an 'isolated one'), wrote to Aurier in gratitude.

On 19 January Vincent went to Arles, where he visited his former landlady, Marie Ginoux. Two days after his return, he suffered another breakdown, which lasted a week. On 31 January Theo wrote to Vincent:

> Dr Peyron writes to me that you have again been seized by an attack of your illness. … I'm infinitely sorry … It's the only cloud in our happiness, for … Jo … has brought into the world a fine boy who cries a lot but who seems to be in good health.

The child, Theo added, would be named Vincent, after his uncle and godfather.[31]

Soon Vincent was at work on a painting that celebrated the birth of his nephew and namesake – an almond tree, the first blossoming of the season (see *Almond Blossom*, p. 117). For this work, Vincent returned to the style of his early paintings in Provence, 'the Japan of the south'. A prototype can be found in the blossoming branches of a ukiyo-e print by Utagawa Kunisada (see opposite).

Yet on 22 February, when Vincent made an excursion to Arles, he suffered another major attack. The following day Dr Peyron sent two men with a carriage to bring him back to the asylum, where it took him two months to recover.

Vincent was increasingly dissatisfied with life in Saint-Rémy, and desirous of returning to the north, but he needed the consent of Dr Peyron for his release. On 26 March Theo made the acquaintance of Dr Paul Gachet, a physician with experience in working with psychiatric patients. Gachet had a practice in Auvers-sur-Oise, a north-western suburb of Paris, and was also an art collector who had known many artists, among them Courbet, Manet, Pissarro, Renoir and Cézanne. On 29 March Theo wrote to Vincent: 'I met Dr Gachet, that physician Pissarro mentioned to me … As soon as you come here we are going to see him; he comes to Paris several times a week for his consultations.'[32]

On 29 April, Vincent wrote to Theo, describing his distress and asking him to send some of his old figure studies for him to copy. *At Eternity's Gate* (see p. 119) personifies Vincent's emotional state. Its prototype was *Worn Out,* a drawing that he had made in The Hague in 1882 (see p. 7). Given Vincent's mournful condition, it is evident why he chose to recreate this image, yet its title suggests the hope of redemption.

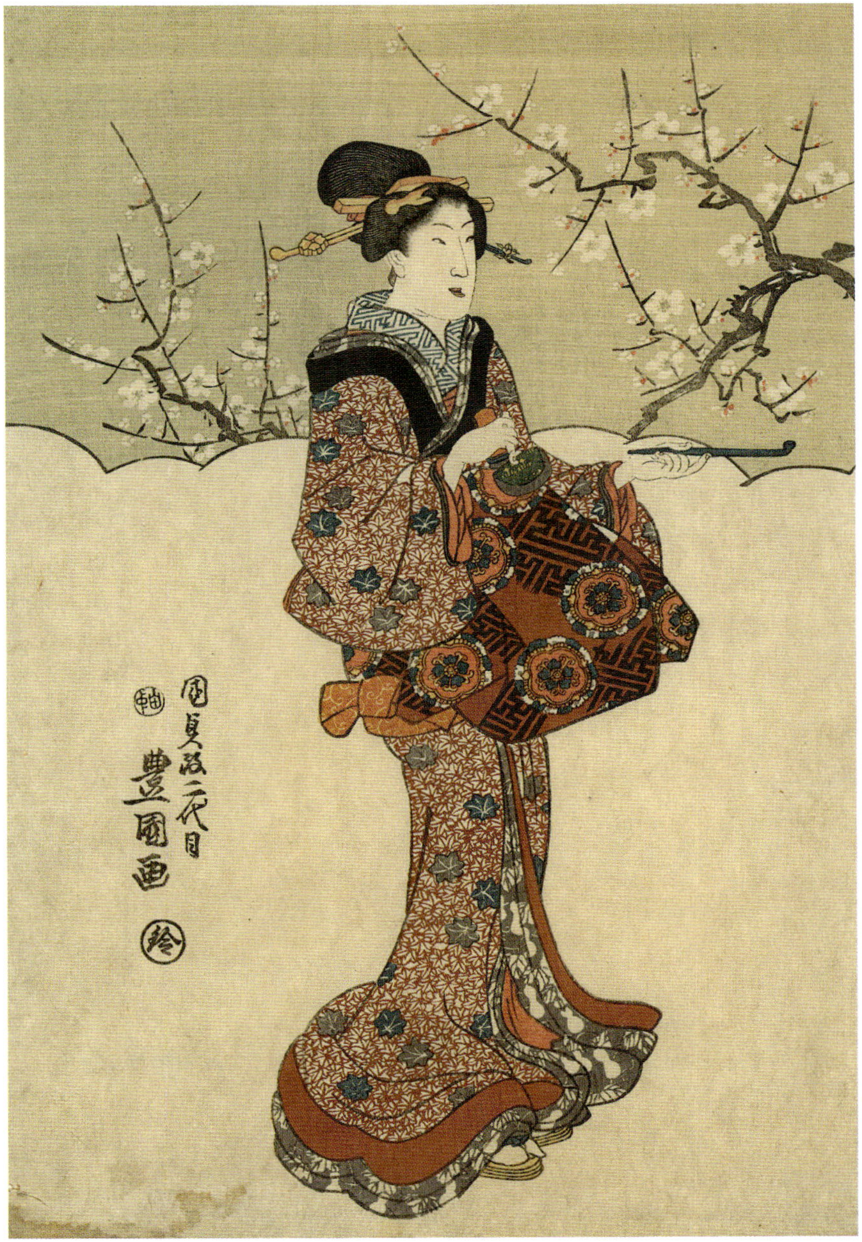

Utagawa Kunisada, *Portrait of a Woman*, left wing of triptych *Three Beauties*, 1844–5
Colour woodcut on Japan paper | 38 × 26cm (15 × 10¼in), Van Gogh Museum, Amsterdam

Long Grass with Butterflies (see p. 121) was one of the last canvases Vincent painted in Saint-Rémy. Here he revisited the asylum garden, one of the first subjects he had painted upon his arrival (see *Irises*, p. 103), and made a work that embodies the paradox of his life as an artist and patient, free yet restricted.

On 13 May 1890 Dr Peyron officially released him from the asylum. In the register of voluntarily interned patients, Peyron enumerated and described the psychotic episodes that Vincent had endured during his stay; in the column headed 'Observations' he wrote 'Cured.'[33]

On 17 May Vincent arrived at the Gare de Lyon in Paris. He was joined at the station by Theo, who brought him to the young family's Montmartre flat. The walls were covered with Vincent's pictures, among them *Almond Blossom* (see p. 117), *The Potato Eaters* (see p.37), *The Harvest* (see p. 61), and *Starry Night over the Rhône* (see p. 81). Here, Vincent met Theo's wife Johanna and their infant son Vincent for the first time. Johanna later recalled: 'I had expected a sick man, but here was a healthy, broad-shouldered man, with a healthy color, a smile on his face, and a very resolute appearance … "He seems perfectly well; he looks much stronger than Theo", was my first thought.' Theo brought Vincent to see the little boy in his cradle. 'Silently the two brothers looked at the quietly sleeping baby – both had tears in their eyes.'[34]

Vincent spent three days in Paris, in the course of which he saw artist friends (not specified in Johanna's recollection) and visited Père Tanguy's shop. Then, armed with Theo's letter of introduction to Dr Paul Gachet, he departed for Auvers-sur-Oise, 32km (20 miles) northwest of Paris.

Arriving on 20 May, Vincent immediately reported to Theo and Jo: 'Auvers is really beautiful … I've seen Dr Gachet, who gave me the impression of being rather eccentric.' Vincent was impressed that Gachet had 'fine' paintings by Cézanne and Pissarro.[35] The doctor recommended an inn, but Vincent, finding it too expensive, instead rented an attic room at the Auberge de Ravoux on the Place de la Mairie.

Vincent painted Gachet's portrait, in two versions; the doctor so liked the first version that Vincent painted a second (see p. 123) and presented it to him as a gift. Gachet had admired Vincent's *Self-Portrait* from Saint-Rémy (see p. 111) and Vincent set to bring some of its qualities to his portrait of the doctor; Vincent found him to be a sympathetic spirit, and imparted a melancholy feeling to his countenance and pose. The art historian John Rewald characterized Gachet as:

> A fascinating and eccentric person indeed. A rabid republican … a Darwinist, a free-thinker and socialist who had been connected with the world of letters and arts since his youth. He had … frequented the various cafés in Paris where Manet and his friends used to gather.[36]

Not only did Gachet offer supportive company, Auvers evoked in Vincent fond memories of his native Netherlands, and he did a series of paintings of the town. The church, an early Gothic building with adjoining Romanesque chapels, brought back memories of the Old Church Tower of Nuenen. Vincent painted the church in the naturalistic manner of seventeenth-century Dutch painting, but with the brilliant colour and loose brushstrokes of the artists of the *pétit boulevard* (see p. 140).

Stairway at Auvers (see p. 127) portrays the Rue de la Sansonne, close to Vincent's lodgings on the Place de la Mairie. The houses with their thatched roofs and also the garb of the figures reminded Vincent of the Netherlands; it is perhaps not surprising that the sinuous lines of the composition convey not the emotional turbulence of Saint-Rémy landscapes such as *The Starry Night* (see p. 105), but a gentle, picturesque view of the village and its inhabitants.

On 6 July Vincent took the train to Paris and saw Theo, Jo and little Vincent for the last time. It was not a visit that brought him any solace. Jo and Theo were very worried about their baby, who was ill and cried constantly, and Theo, blaming lack of money for some of their troubles, was resentful about his low salary and had told his employers that he would leave if they did not increase it; he planned instead an insecure life as an art dealer, with some financing from his brother-in-law Andries Bonger. It had become clear that Theo's prime concern was looking after his own family, with the fear that his own health was failing.

There was another disappointment, too: Vincent had nursed a hope that Theo and his little family would join him in Auvers, where they could benefit from fresh air and a healthier life. Now Theo was planning to move down to the ground floor of his apartment building, where he would share a garden with Andries and his wife. A bitter quarrel broke out, and Vincent departed in haste for Auvers, from where he wrote to Theo describing himself as 'a burden'.

Not only did Vincent fear another attack of mental illness, he was now anxious about Theo's future financial support and suffered increased feelings of isolation that were expressed in two paintings of vast fields of wheat with no signs of the comforting warmth of human habitation; in *Wheatfield with Crows* (see p. 129), an ominous flock of crows swarms toward the picture plane beneath a swirling sky.

Vincent's final painting in his landscape series of the town of Auvers was *Farms near Auvers* (see p. 131). Still unfinished at his time of death, it was probably the penultimate painting of his life.[37] Like *Wheatfield with Crows*, it is rendered in a double-square rectilinear format, but in this painting there is no ominous atmosphere; instead, it is as if the artist were presenting a salutary vision of country life as shelter from a storm he fears is approaching.

On 23 July Vincent sent a final letter to Theo which begins: 'Perhaps I'd rather write to you about a lot of things, but … the desire to do so has completely left me, and then I feel it is useless.' He enclosed four sketches, including one of thatched cottages and two of wheatfields.[38] Theo wrote to Jo, then in Holland: 'There was a letter from Vincent which … I find incomprehensible. … When will a happy time come for him? He's so thoroughly good and helped me so much to keep going.'[39]

Tree Roots (see p. 133), Vincent's final painting, is unfinished. According to Andries Bonger, he was working on it the morning before his death. It is a view of the earth, with little or no horizon. Depicting gnarled roots, trunks, branches and leaves growing from chalky soil, it is rendered, like *Wheatfield with Crows* and *Farms near Auvers*, in a double-squared, horizontal frieze format. With its unfinished quality and all-over composition, it verges on pure abstraction. Given that the artist would take his own life later than day, the painting raises the inevitable question: is it a premonition of his own death? Could the green serpentine forms, swooping in from the left, suggest a fatal menace?[40]

On the evening of 27 July 1890, Vincent, who had been painting in the Auvers countryside, placed his easel against a haystack and shot himself in the chest with a revolver. He managed to walk back to his attic room at the Auberge Ravoux without disclosing to anyone what had happened. He was eventually found by innkeeper Arthur Ravoux, who summoned Dr Gachet and a local practitioner. It was decided that the bullet should not be removed and Dr Gachet contacted Theo, who arrived the next day. Vincent died on 29 July at 1.30 a.m.[41]

Theo, who had long been frail of health, died only six months later, on 25 July 1891; Albert Aurier, author of the only critical study of Vincent's work to appear in his lifetime, died of typhoid fever in 1892. Vincent's standing today as a pioneer Post-Impressionist and forerunner of two great movements of twentieth-century art, Fauvism and Expressionism, is due in large part to the heroic efforts of Theo's widow, Johanna van Gogh-Bonger, and the generosity of her son Vincent. Following Theo's death, Jo inherited about 200 of Vincent's works and maintained the collection, while strategically selling a few pieces. She assiduously edited Vincent and Theo's correspondence, and wrote a memoir of her brother-

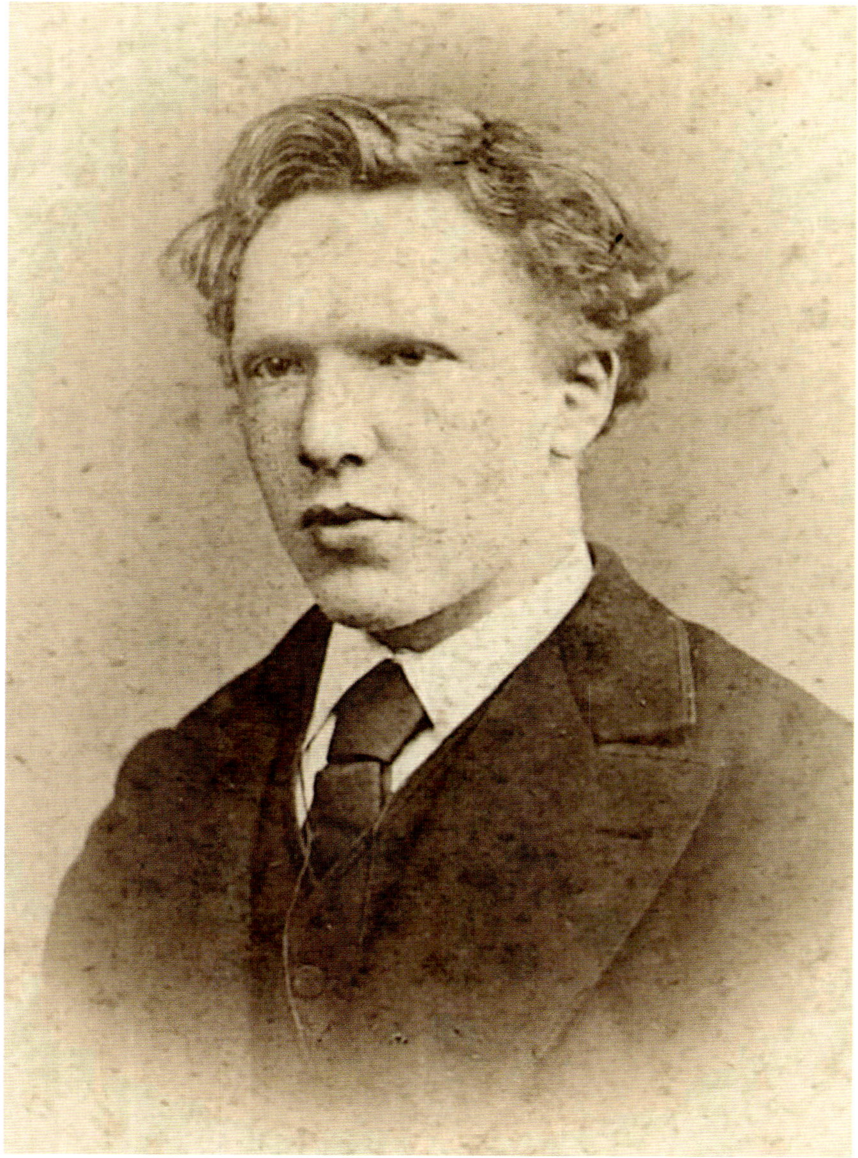

Vincent van Gogh, aged 19, 1872

in-law.[42] Upon her death in 1925, her art collection was inherited by her son, who in 1962 transferred the collection to the Vincent van Gogh Foundation; in 1973 the Van Gogh Museum, Amsterdam, opened its doors.

In Paris, Émile Bernard organized a small exhibition of Vincent's paintings in 1892 and 'Père' Tanguy continued to show Vincent's work at his shop until his death in 1894. Ambroise Vollard held a Van Gogh exhibition at his Paris gallery in 1895 and in 1896–7. In 1901 there was a major Van Gogh retrospective of 73 works at the Bernheim-Jeune Gallery in Paris; a second major retrospective was held at the 1905 Salon des Indépendants. At these exhibitions Matisse and his Fauve colleagues Derain and Vlaminck became aware of Vincent's work.

The term 'Post-Impressionism' was coined by the British critic Roger Fry on the occasion of a major international exhibition of modern art, 'Manet and the Post-Impressionists', held at the Grafton Galleries, London, in 1910, which included 17 paintings by Van Gogh. In 1912, the Sonderbund Exhibition in Cologne included 108 paintings and 16 drawings by Van Gogh; one-third of them were lent by German collectors, and most of the remaining works were lent by Jo van Gogh-Bonger. The Armory Show, held in New York in 1913 (and subsequently travelled to Chicago and Boston), included 17 paintings by Van Gogh.

After World War I, large-scale exhibitions of Vincent's work sprang up in many places, usually with the assistance of Jo van Gogh-Bonger. Large solo exhibitions were held at the Leicester Gallery, London, in 1923 and 1926. In 1929, the newly founded Museum of Modern Art in New York opened with an exhibition of the four 'old masters' of Post-Impressionism: Cézanne, Seurat, Gauguin, and Van Gogh. In 1935–6 Alfred Barr, the founding director of the museum, held a Van Gogh retrospective, accompanied by a scholarly catalogue.[43]

Any artist who paints in an expressive style owes a debt to Van Gogh, from the German and Austrian Expressionists and the Norwegian Symbolist

Edvard Munch to artists of the twentieth and twenty-first centuries. To cite just one example, in 1908 Henri Matisse created a major composition, *Harmony in Red*, an interior juxtaposed with a picture window overlooking a park. Featuring a maidservant who clears a table after a meal, it presents images of dynamic organic growth: the blooming trees and flowers of the park, the fruit-and-flower still life of the table, and the flowerpot-and-arabesque patterning of the wallpaper and tablecloth. Matisse was inspired by Vincent's use of arabesque and floral patterns in the background of *La Berceuse* (see p. 99). Matisse's maidservant, like Mme Roulin, the postman's wife, is surrounded by floral and arabesque patterns which seem to emanate from her, embodying fertility and growth.

A major legacy of Vincent to modernist painting is the all-over composition, found in such paintings as *Irises* (see p. 103), *Long Grass with Butterflies* (see p. 121), *Almond Blossom* (see p. 117) and *Tree Roots* (see p. 133). In these works, to varying degrees, figure and ground merge, and there is no one place for the viewer's eye to rest. In this regard Vincent is a forerunner of Abstract Expressionist painters such as Jackson Pollock.

When Vincent van Gogh committed suicide in July 1890 he was only 37 years old. He put years of a tortured existence to an end but left behind more than 2,000 works of art, nearly 900 of which were oil paintings – a fact that becomes all the more remarkable when we realize that most of these works were made within a ten-year period. In the latter years of his life, his creative efforts offered the only release from inner demons that hovered overhead like crows over a wheatfield. As with the fates of other great artists who die before their time, we can only imagine what would have happened had he lived a long and productive life. By examining the creative efforts of artists who sought inspiration from his example we can catch a glimpse of what might have been. That process continues to this day and will assuredly continue well into the future, the ultimate indication of an artist's enduring legacy.

THE PAINTINGS

1884-5

CONGREGATION LEAVING THE REFORMED CHURCH IN NUENEN

Van Gogh Museum, Amsterdam

Oil on canvas | 41 × 32cm (16⅛ × 12⅝in)

After a period spent in the rural province of Drenthe, in late 1883 Vincent returned to live with his parents, who at the time were occupants of the rectory in the town of Nuenen. Shortly afterwards, in February 1884, Vincent's mother broke her thighbone while stepping from a train. Vincent wrote to Theo, now working for their Uncle Cent's firm of Goupil & Cie in Paris: 'Taking her difficult situation into consideration, I am glad to say Mother's spirits are very even and bright. And she is amused by trifles. The other day I painted for her the little church with the hedge and the trees (like this).'[1]

Vincent's letter included a pen-and-ink sketch of his painting of 'the little church' – the Dutch Reformed Church where his father addressed the congregation on Sundays. It is a small structure, built in the early nineteenth century in the Gothic Revival style. In the sketch, there is no group of churchgoers, only a single silhouetted labourer, standing in the foreground.

In March 1885, at the age of 63, Vincent's father Theodorus died suddenly, of a stroke or heart attack. In autumn of that year Vincent reworked the painting, adding the congregation in the middle ground and foreground, including a woman in mourning at the foreground centre, where the labourer had previously been located. Studies involving X-rays and raking (oblique, bright) light have revealed that at the time the figures were added, the painting had changed considerably. The dark, wintry scene had become autumnal. The brighter colours and looser brushstrokes of the trees, hedges and footpath reflect not only seasonal changes but an evolution in Vincent's style during the nearly two-year period between the original picture and its revisions.[2]

Vincent's gift to his mother, originally intended to aid her healing from a physical injury, had become a tribute to a husband and father, and would serve to facilitate a different kind of healing.

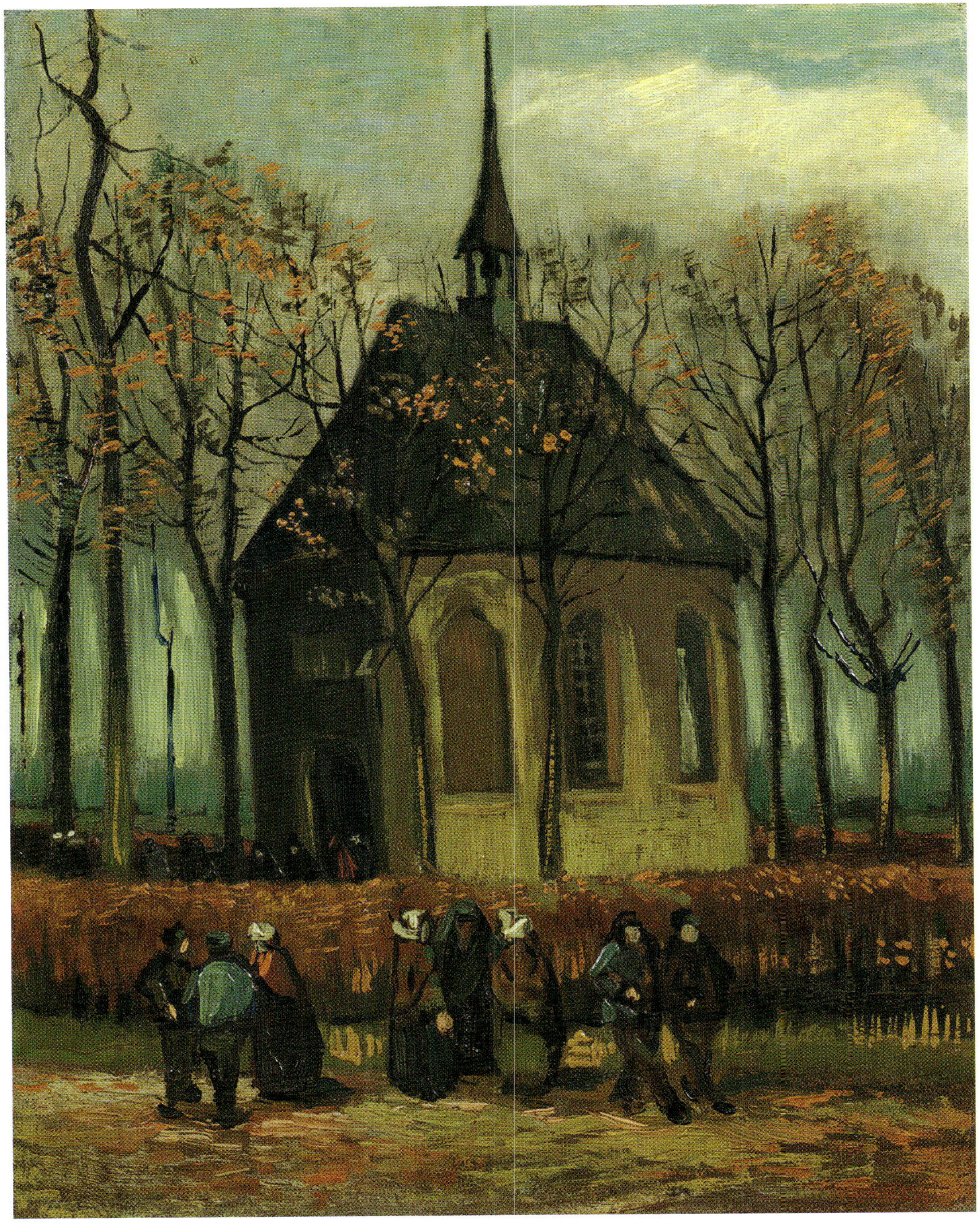

April
1885

THE POTATO EATERS

Van Gogh Museum, Amsterdam

Oil on canvas | 81.5 × 114.5cm (32⅓ × 44⁹⁄₁₀in)

In Nuenen, Vincent produced a series of studies of weavers and peasants, culminating in *The Potato Eaters*, his first major composition. Rendered in dark tonalities of green, blue and brown, and illuminated by a single lantern, a peasant family is seated for their evening meal. The use of chiaroscuro and the sacramental character of the event hark back to seventeenth-century Dutch painting. Notwithstanding the homeliness of their features, the participants emanate a touching dignity, all the more so in the artist's refusal to idealize them. He sought to convey his empathy with poor and oppressed people, an impulse that was manifest in his previous vocation as a lay minister.

Vincent expressed these intentions in a letter to his brother Theo: 'These folk … have tilled the earth themselves with these hands they are putting in the dish … they have thus honestly *earned* their food.' He added: 'One would be wrong to give a peasant painting a certain conventional smoothness. If a peasant painting smells of bacon, smoke, potato steam – fine.'[3]

The figures, the walls, the ceiling, the table and the repast are painted in earth tones that reinforce the potato eaters' close relationship to nature. It appears to be a cold winter evening – the clock shows the hour of seven and it is already dark outside. The family's shelter seems to provide little comfort from the cold exterior; the two male figures wear coats and hats, and the women are bundled up; one woman pours hot coffee as steam rises from the potatoes. Vincent originally painted the figures in more conventional flesh tones, but they appeared to be too light for the composition. 'I quickly repainted them,' he reported to Theo, 'and the colour they're painted now is something like the colour of a really dusty potato, unpeeled of course.' He drew inspiration from the mid-century Barbizon painter Jean-François Millet, known for his realist agricultural scenes: 'While I was doing it I thought again about what has so rightly been said of Millet's peasants – "His peasants seem to have been painted with the soil they sow."'[4]

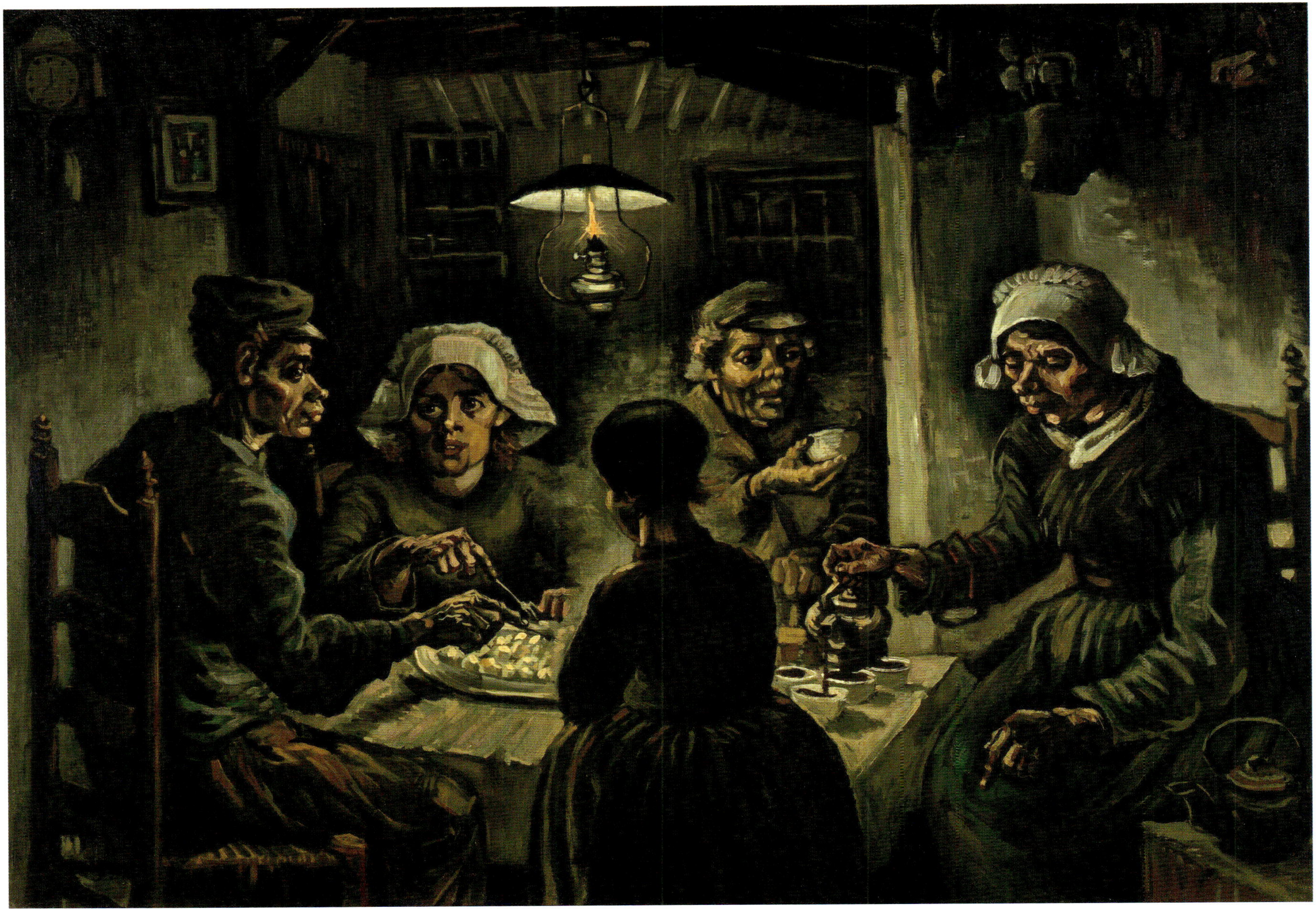

August
1885

A PEASANT WOMAN DIGGING

Barber Institute of Fine Arts, Birmingham

Oil on canvas | 42 × 32cm (16½ × 12⅝in)

After arriving in Nuenen Vincent initially lived and worked in his parents' home, but in May 1884 he rented a studio in town and following the death of his father in March 1885 he moved there. Seizing opportunities for subjects in Nuenen's environs, he drew and painted an extensive series of portraits and figure compositions of weavers and peasants as well as the landscape. Vincent identified with rural workers; he respected their humanity and dignity.

'When will the figure not be superfluous?' Vincent wrote to Theo in July 1885. 'When the digger digs, when the peasant is a peasant and the peasant woman, a peasant woman.' These subjects, Vincent believed, had an authenticity that more exotic subjects lacked: 'Those who paint rural life or the life of the people . . . may wear better in the long run than the painters of the exotic harems and Cardinals' receptions, painted in Paris.'[5]

A Peasant Woman Digging of August 1885 presents a monumental single female figure labouring in a field. She is not individualized, nor is she idealized. She is stooped, so we cannot read her features. Despite the muted palette, luminosity is effectively conveyed on the clouded horizon at the upper left, in the field behind the figure, on the earth in the foreground, and in the sunlit highlights of the woman's back, neck and hands.

Vincent was an admirer of the Barbizon painter Jean-François Millet (1814–75) for his realistic and respectful depictions of peasants in the countryside. Millet's *The Gleaners* (see p. 9) is a figure-and-landscape composition of three women belonging to the poorest class of rural workers; the act of gleaning is collecting leftover crops from farmers' fields. The pose of Vincent's peasant woman echoes that of the two leftward gleaners in Millet's composition. Yet Millet's graceful, smoothly rendered and colouristically syncopated figures seem idealized in comparison with Vincent's ungainly digger.

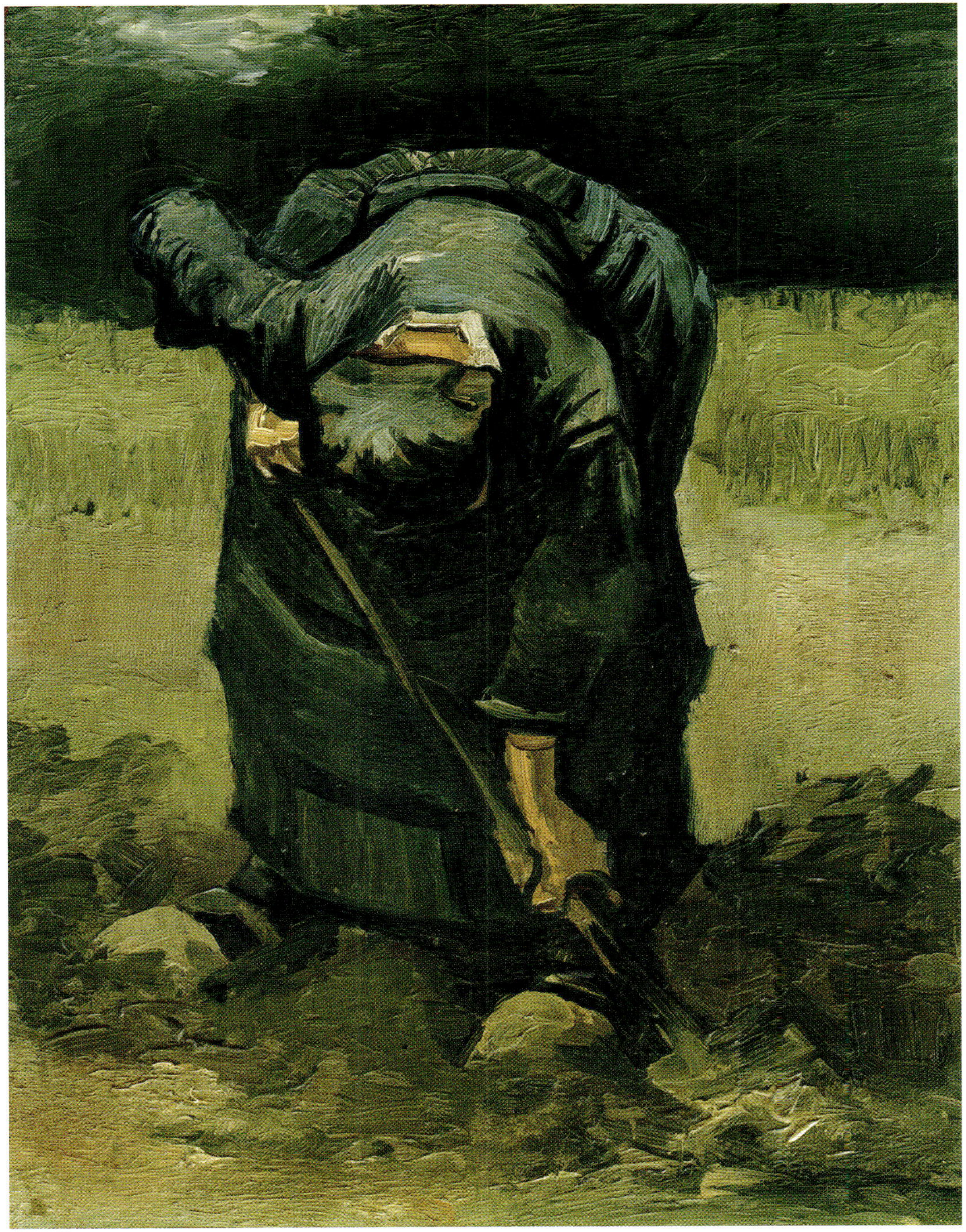

Late June
– Early July
1887

THE INTERIOR OF A RESTAURANT

Kröller-Müller Museum, Otterlo

Oil on canvas | 45.5 × 56.5cm (18⅛ × 22½in)

In March 1886 Vincent arrived in Paris. In May and June of that year, the eighth (and last) Impressionist Exhibition was held, marking the debut of Georges Seurat's *A Sunday Afternoon on the Island of La Grande Jatte* (see p. 11). Its style – in which the image is systematically broken up into dots of pure colour which are mixed in the viewer's eye, rather than on the canvas – was designated 'Neo-Impressionism' by the critic Félix Fénéon. Through Theo, Vincent met Camille Pissarro – veteran Impressionist and recent convert to Neo-Impressionism – as well as Seurat himself; and at Père Tanguy's shop (see p. 46), he encountered the painter Paul Signac, dedicated proselytizer of the new style.

Vincent's working method was by nature intuitive rather than systematic, but he was attracted to Neo-Impressionism – also known as Divisionism or Pointillism – and executed several works loosely based on its precepts; these were mostly landscapes painted at Asnières, a northwestern suburb of Paris. Signac later recalled that he and Vincent would occasionally meet in Asnières for lunch and walk back to Paris together: 'Van Gogh, dressed in a blue workman's blouse, had painted little dots of colors on his sleeves. Sticking close to me, he shouted and gesticulated, brandishing his large, freshly covered canvas, and with it he polychromed himself as well as passers-by.'[6]

The Interior of a Restaurant is an outlier in Vincent's oeuvre in that Pointillist techniques are applied to an interior, rather than to a landscape. The restaurant is not recognizable as one of those frequented by Vincent and Theo in Montmartre and its likely location is Asnières. The work's Pointillist touch is particularly effective in the presentation of the walls and floor of the light-filled room, with the use of complementary colours of red/green and yellow/violet. The setting is effervescent, bright and elegant – the tables set, the wine glasses turned upside down, a vase of flowers on each table. Hanging on the wall is a top hat, an homage to the top-hatted gentlemen of Seurat's *Grande Jatte*. The Pointillist technique is not consistently applied, however, and the perspective, while exaggerated, is relatively traditional, as is the solid rendering of the tables and chairs.

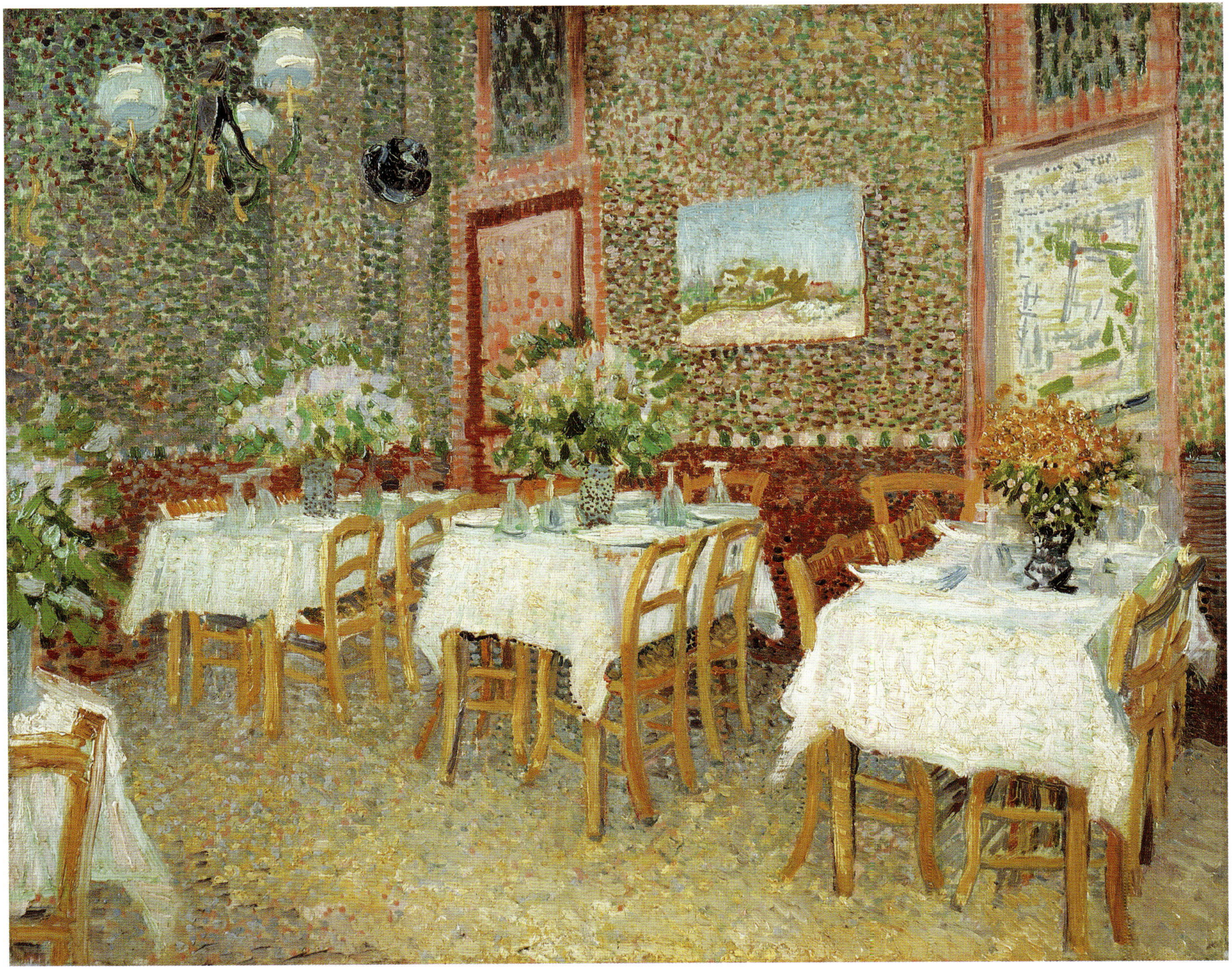

Spring
1887

AGOSTINA SEGATORI SITTING IN THE CAFÉ DU TAMBOURIN

Van Gogh Museum, Amsterdam

Oil on canvas | 55.5 × 46.5cm (22 × 18½in)

Agostina Segatori, known as 'La Segatori', a former artist's model for Corot and Gérôme among others, was proprietress of the Café du Tambourin on the boulevard de Clichy, a short distance from Vincent and Theo's residence in Montmartre. The cabaret-restaurant was frequented by artists and writers. Vincent and his colleagues exhibited paintings there, and on occasion exchanged artworks for meals. At the time this portrait was created, in spring 1887, the café's walls displayed Japanese prints from Vincent and Theo's collection.

The theme of a woman sitting in a café, drinking, was a favoured subject of the French Impressionists; perhaps the best-known example was Edgar Degas' *In a Café (Absinthe)* (see p.15). By contrast with Degas' sitter, with her sorrowful, vacant stare, La Segatori's demeanour is pensive yet engaged with her surroundings, her eyes fully open. Attired, in bohemian fashion, in a red feathered headdress, decorated jacket and non-matching skirt, she rests her folded arms on the table, a lit cigarette in her hand. The full glass rests on two saucers, indicating that this is her second beer. The table and the two stools on either side of her are designed to resemble tambourines, emblematic of the restaurant for which she is the muse. A folded Japanese parasol rests on the left-hand stool and a ukiyo-e print is visible on the wall, linking La Segatori to Japonism and hence to Vincent's vision of modern art. The work is painted in loose brushstrokes of broken colour, evoking light and atmosphere. In scarcely more than a year since his arrival in Paris, Vincent has assimilated Impressionist techniques into his personal style.

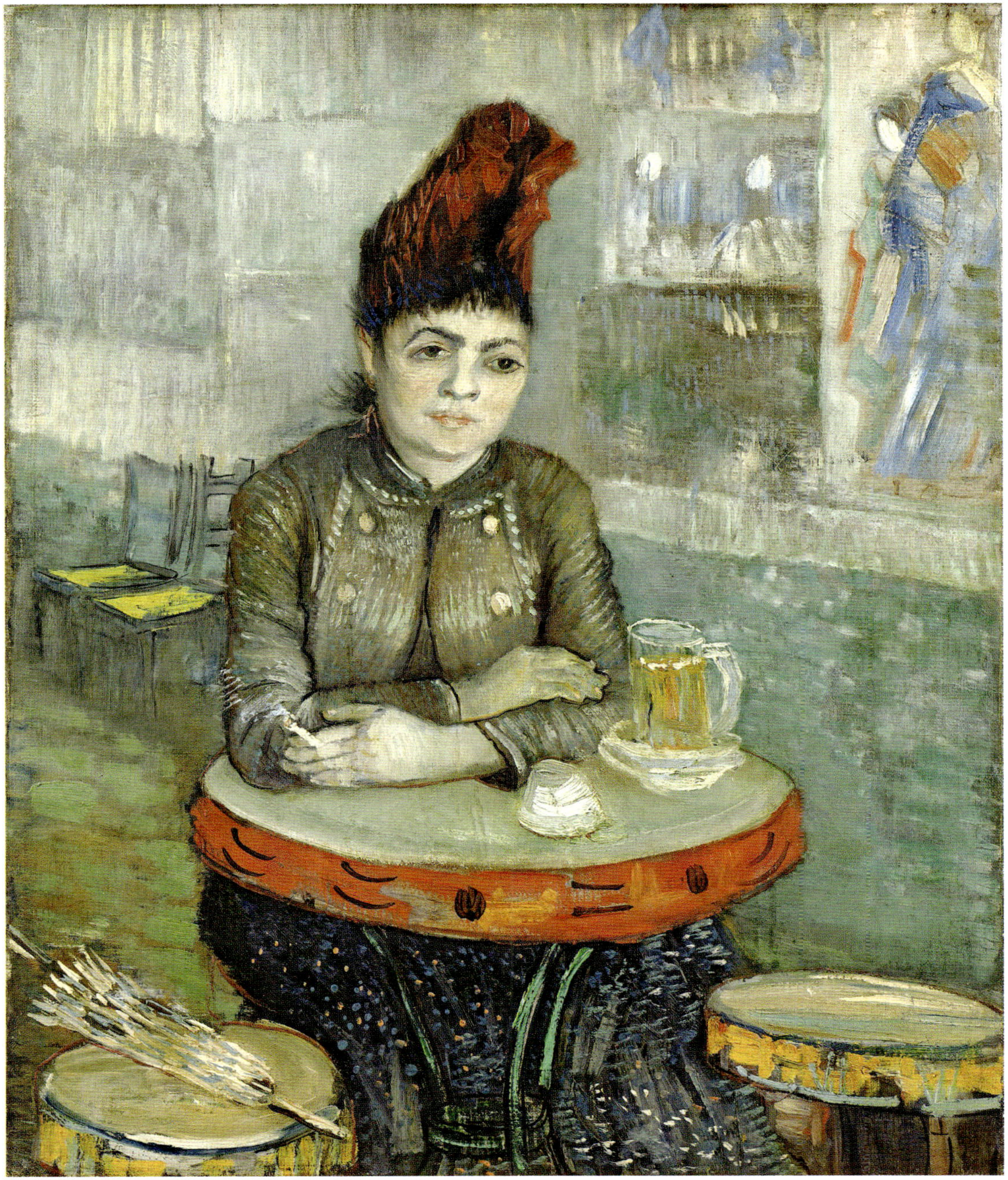

July
1887

VEGETABLE GARDENS IN MONTMARTRE: LA BUTTE MONTMARTRE

Stedelijk Museum, Amsterdam

Oil on canvas | 96 × 120cm (37¾ × 47¼in)

When Vincent arrived in Paris he moved in with his brother Theo in Montmartre. Located in the northwestern part of the city, Montmartre is a *butte*, or steep hill with a flat top. It is a quarter known for its lively cafés, restaurants and nightlife and its population of artists and writers. When Vincent arrived there, Montmartre had three remaining windmills, reminders of his native Netherlands, and was bordered by countryside, enabling him to paint rural scenes while living in the city.

Vegetable Gardens in Montmartre: *La Butte Montmartre* is the largest painting in all of Van Gogh's work. In July 1887 he wrote to Theo that he was 'working on a big one', and added, 'I know that these big long canvases are difficult to sell, but later on people will see that there is open air in them and good humor.'[7] Depicting the north slope of the butte, it was painted *en plein air*, without preliminary sketches. The luxuriance of the vegetation indicates full summer. Vincent has set up his easel far back from the scene, so that the large triangle of road at the right occupies one quarter of the pictorial surface, leading the viewer's eye to the blades of the windmill that dominate the horizon. The artist has freely adapted Impressionist and Neo-Impressionist brushstrokes to suit his own needs, composing the architecture, fences and trees with dots and strokes, and the sky with a softer and more atmospheric application of paint.

As a measure of the extraordinary evolution of Vincent's style during his stay in Paris, it is instructive to compare this work to the artist's *La Butte Montmartre* of just over a year earlier. Painted in April–May 1886 (see p. 13), the earlier picture depicts the same view, albeit at a closer perspective. It is painted in the realist manner of The Hague school, in accordance with the teachings of Vincent's Dutch teacher, Anton Mauve, and features the solidity of form and modelling in light and shade associated with the mid-century Barbizon painters. In the course of one year, Vincent had transformed himself into an avant-garde painter.

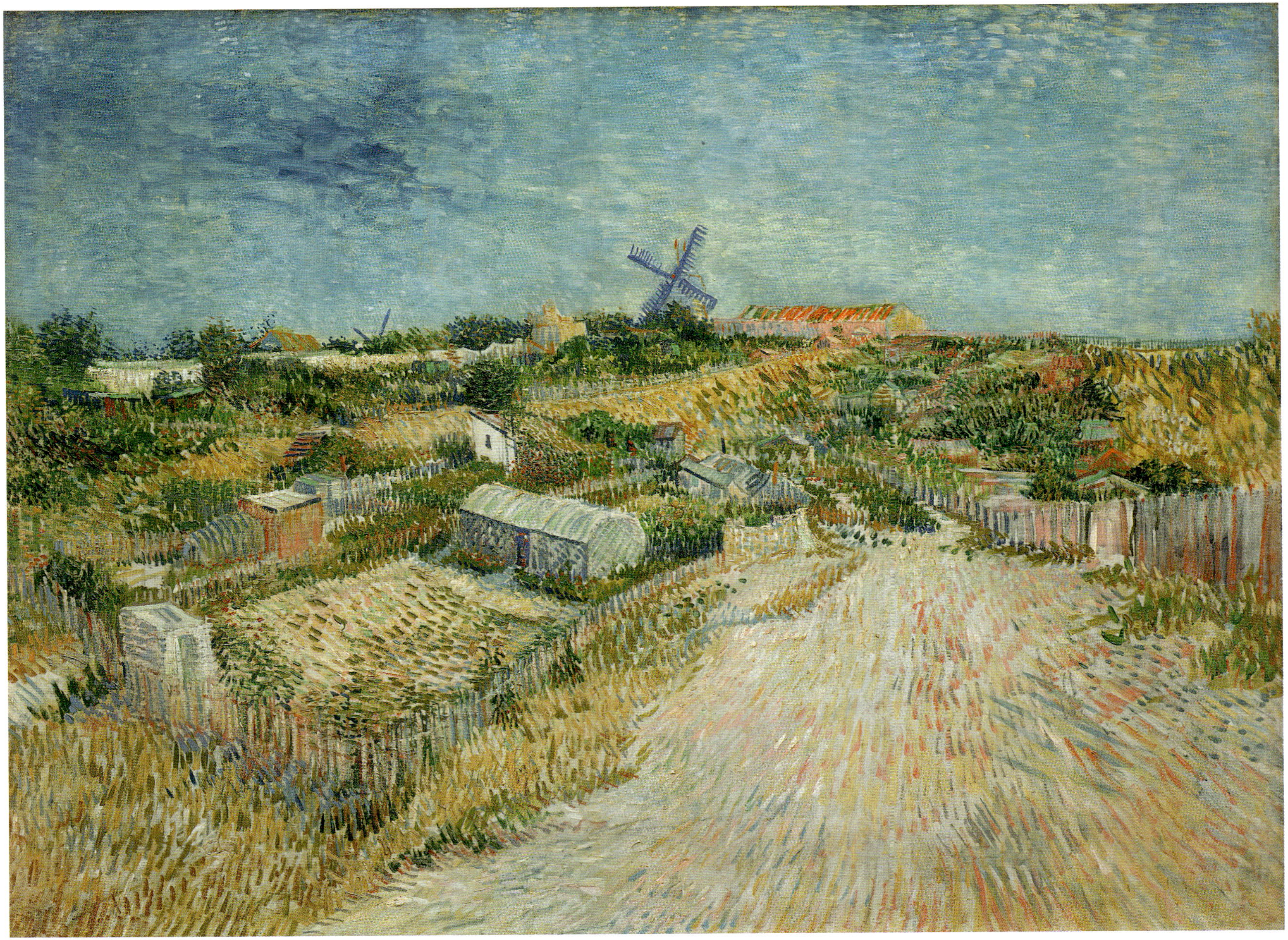

April
1887

PÈRE TANGUY

Musée Rodin, Paris

Oil on canvas | 65 × 51cm (25³⁄₅ × 20in)

Julien Tanguy (1825–94), affectionately known as 'Père' Tanguy, owned an art-supply shop and adjoining picture gallery on the rue Clauzel in the Montmartre district of Paris, not far from Vincent and Theo's residence on the rue Lépic. Tanguy, a political radical and veteran of the Paris Commune of 1871, often accepted paintings in exchange for pigments. His clients included Impressionist and Post-Impressionist painters, among them Monet, Pissarro, Renoir, Toulouse-Lautrec, Seurat, Signac, Gauguin, Cézanne, and Vincent van Gogh. The painter Émile Bernard later recalled that soon after meeting Tanguy in 1886, Vincent became 'the most frequent visitor in the shop. He practically lived there … He had immediately taken a liking to this good working-class man who looked so favorably on all the innovations and who wore his heart on his sleeve … It didn't take long for them to become fast friends.'[8]

This painting, the third and largest of Vincent's three portraits of Tanguy, is the second that presents him before a background of Japanese prints. He is seated frontally and symmetrically, his hands serenely folded before him, a pose often found in Japanese statues of the Buddha. In a visual pun, his stability and gentle strength are accentuated by the image of Mt Fuji, which appears to rise from his wide-brimmed, upwardly turned hat.

Vincent had begun collecting Japanese prints while still in Antwerp; his collection grew rapidly after his arrival in Paris, as did the collection of his brother Theo. The flattened perspective and brilliant, unmodelled colour that he found in the works of such artists as Utagawa Hiroshige (1797–1858) and Keisai Eisen (1790–1848) embodied for Vincent, in condensed form, the innovations of modern painters in Paris. Tanguy is not believed to have posed in front of the wall of prints in the picture – they are depicted in larger scale than his figure, and he did not display Japanese works in his shop. The background images comprise works in Vincent's collection, including a Hiroshige landscape at right, and below it, an Eisen courtesan figure. Both figure and background are painted with the visible brushstrokes and adjacent complementary colours that Vincent had recently discovered in the works of his Neo-Impressionist colleagues Pissarro, Seurat and Signac. The expressiveness of the brushstrokes, particularly apparent in the sitter's jacket and trousers, is particular to Van Gogh.

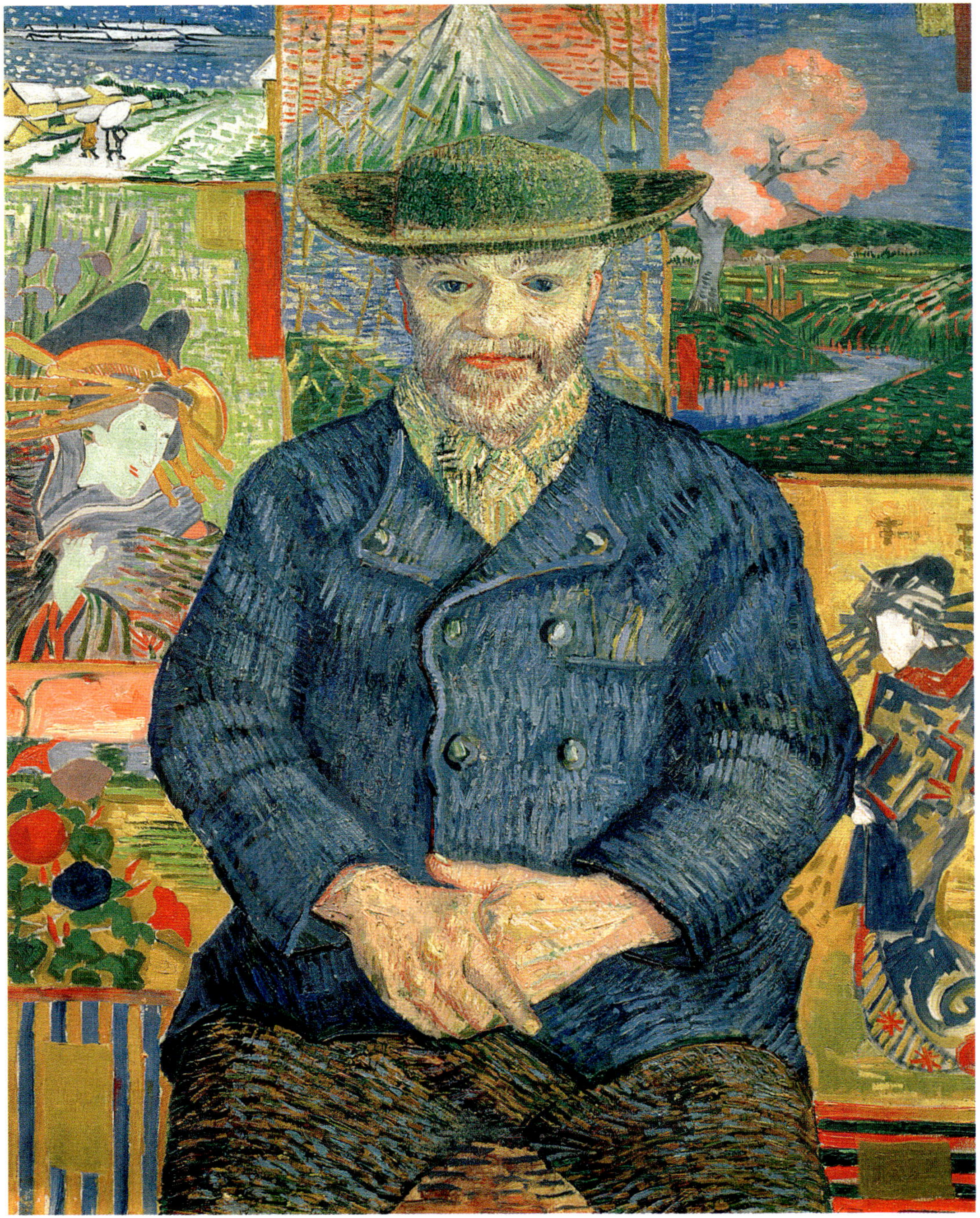

February
1888

SELF-PORTRAIT AS A PAINTER

Van Gogh Museum, Amsterdam

Oil on canvas | 65 × 50.5cm (25⅝ × 20⅛in)

In February 1888, shortly before his departure from Paris for Arles in the south of France, Vincent painted *Self-Portrait as a Painter.* He had long been an admirer of Rembrandt's *Portrait of the Artist at his Easel* (1660) at the Louvre. The Dutch master's self-portrait clearly served as a prototype for Vincent: in both works, the artist is posed before his easel, holding his brushes; his direct gaze meets that of the viewer; the face bears a melancholy expression.

In all likelihood, Vincent's self-portrait was already underway when he attended the Louvre's *One Hundred and Four Portraits of Painters,* which opened on 14 February, five days before his departure. In addition to Rembrandt, the exhibition included self-portraits by Poussin, David, Delacroix and Courbet, among others, reinforcing Vincent's awareness of his lineage in the Western pictorial tradition.

In other respects, Vincent's self-portrait is a thoroughly modern work. The palette that he holds in his hand shows painterly smears of all the colours in the spectrum. These colours are mixed neither on the palette nor on the canvas. The composition is made up of complementaries of blue and orange, red and green. Vincent is dressed in a blue linen jacket, highlighted with brushstrokes of orange. The face, beard and hair are defined by brushstrokes of red and green. The canvas at the easel and its wood frame are depicted by cross-hatchings of orange, green and white, and the background is composed of scumbled and impastoed brushstrokes of grey-green and white.

Vincent has not attempted to disguise the anxiety he was undergoing in his final days in Paris; it is evident in his troubled facial expression, and is emphasized by the green highlights of the face. The following summer, with the painting in Theo's hands, Vincent would recreate the work for his sister Wil with a 'painting in words': 'A pinkish-gray face with green eyes, ash-colored hair, wrinkles in forehead and around the mouth, stiff, wooden, a very red beard, considerably neglected and mournful, but the lips are full … You will say that this resembles somewhat … the face of – Death …'[9]

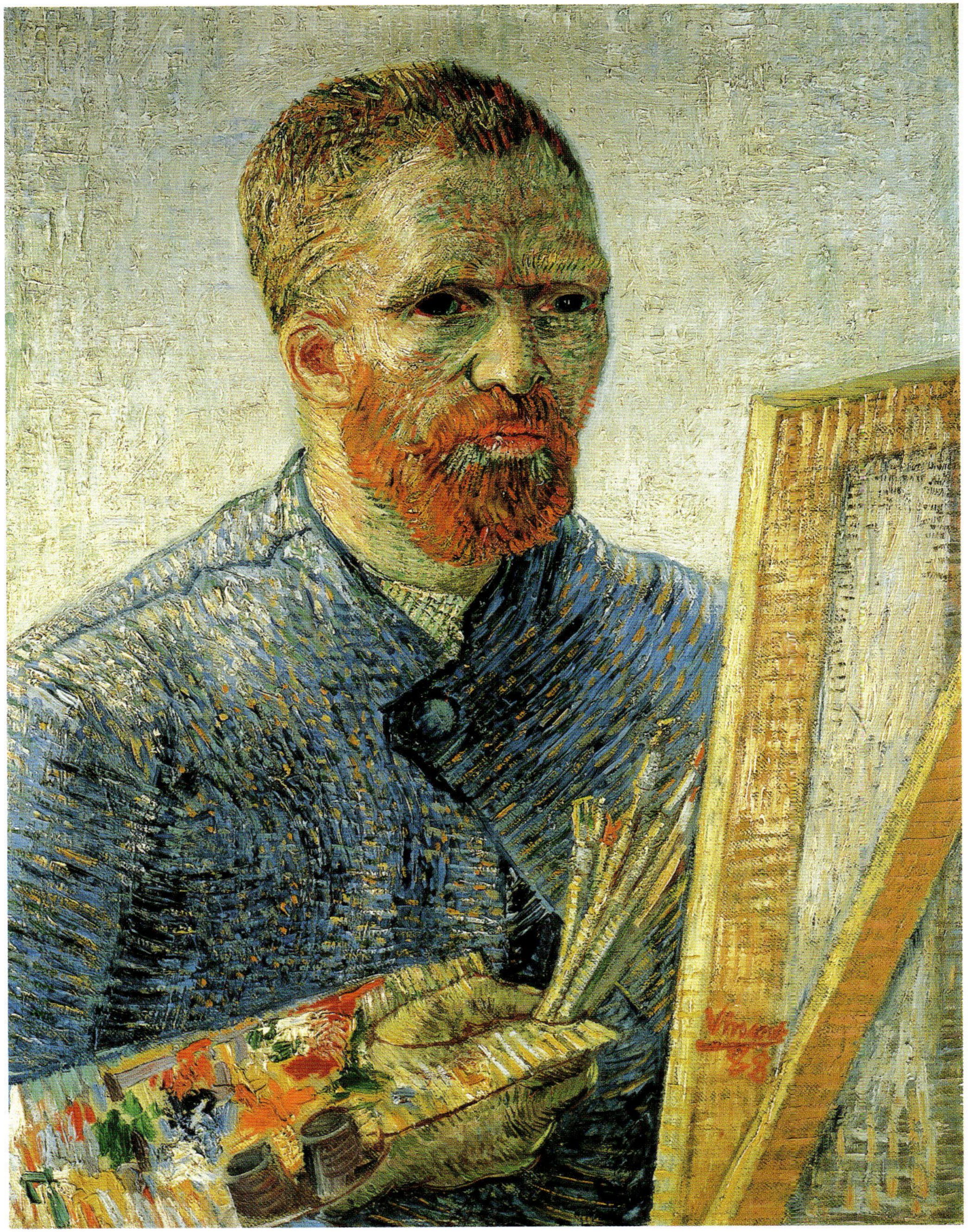

Mid-March
1888

THE LANGLOIS BRIDGE AT ARLES WITH WOMEN WASHING

Kröller-Müller Museum, Otterlo

Oil on canvas | 54 × 65cm (21¼ × 25⅝in)

In February 1888 Vincent arrived in Arles. In mid-March, the weather cleared. As he explored the countryside, he was exhilarated to discover that it evoked for him the Japan of his imagination. On one of his perambulations he encountered a sight familiar to him from his native Netherlands: a drawbridge. Built by a Dutch engineer, it spanned the canal linking Arles to Port-de-Bouc to the south. (The bridge is no longer standing; in 1935 it was replaced by a concrete structure, which was destroyed by the Germans in the Second World War.)

'This part of the world seems to me as beautiful as Japan,' Vincent wrote to Émile Bernard. 'The stretches of water make patches of a beautiful emerald and a rich blue in the landscapes, as we see it in the Japanese prints.' In his letter Vincent included a sketch of couples on the shore, with the bridge in the background. 'I have another study', he added, 'of the same drawbridge with a group of washerwomen.'[10]

In contrast to the loose, painterly brushwork of Vincent's Paris paintings, *The Langlois Bridge at Arles with Women Washing* is rendered with hard edges and clear spatial demarcations. The wooden drawbridge is depicted in brilliant yellow with orange and blue shadows; the brick structure below, in contrasting blue and yellow, orange and green, is shadowed in blue; and both are set against a clear blue sky, with the blue water below, more textured and variegated, and highlighted in reds, yellows and whites. On the orange-and-green banks of the river are the rhythmic forms of peasant women, in brightly coloured caps and garments, washing clothes, while riders in a horse and carriage traverse the bridge above. In overall effect, with its sharp edges and vivid colour contrasts, the painting is reminiscent of – albeit in clear, sunny weather – *Bridge in the Rain* (see p. 14), Vincent's copy of a Hiroshige woodcut, painted in Paris the previous year.

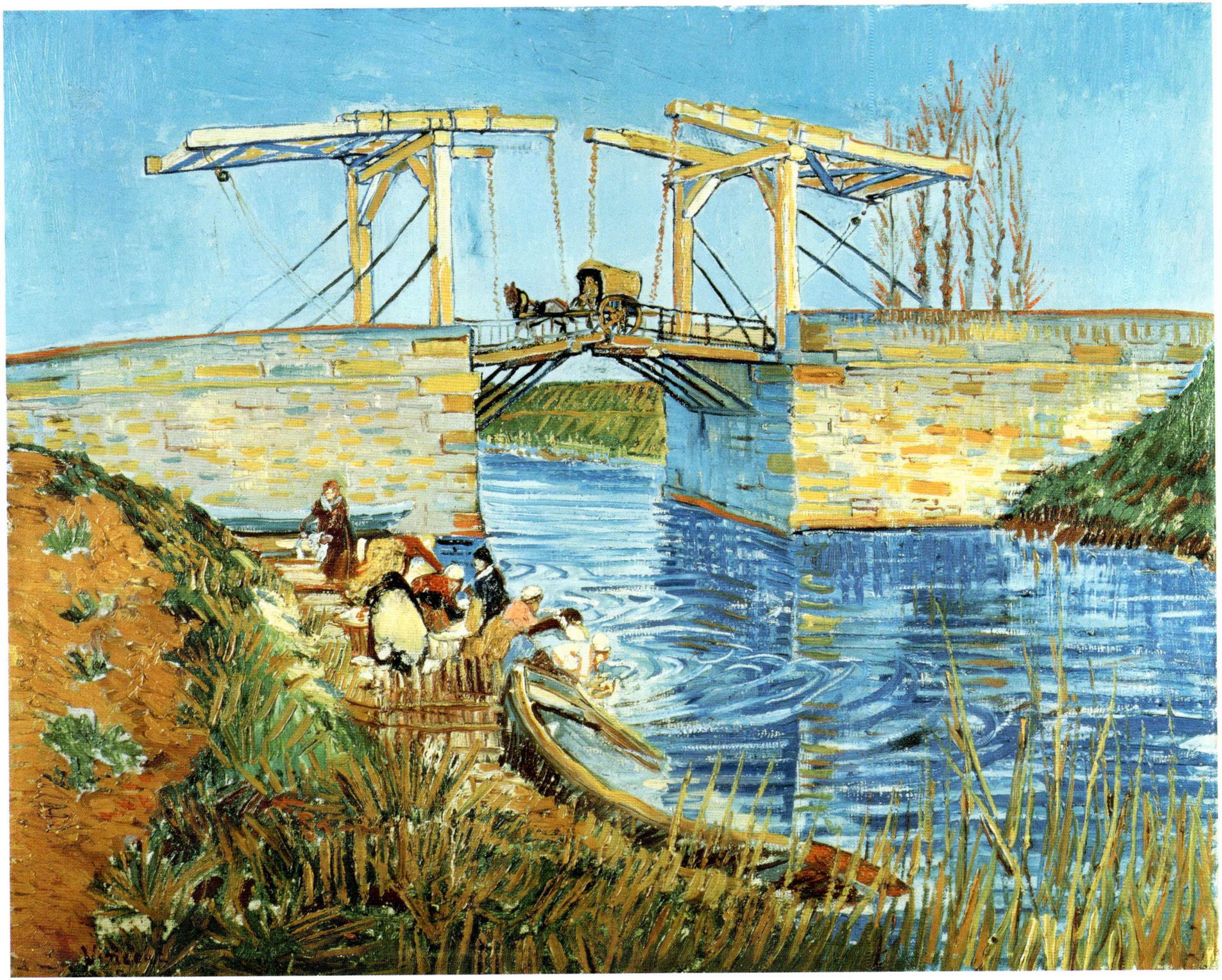

THE LANGLOIS BRIDGE AT ARLES WITH WOMEN WASHING

May

1888

STILL LIFE: BLUE ENAMEL COFFEEPOT, EARTHENWARE AND FRUIT

Goulandris Foundation, Liechtenstein

Oil on canvas | 65 × 81cm (25⅝ × 31⅞in)

In May 1888 Vincent painted *Still Life: Blue Enamel Coffeepot, Earthenware and Fruit*, a work which held great importance for him. He described it in detail in letters to Theo and to the painter Émile Bernard, in both cases accompanied by sketches; the one Bernard received was embellished with detailed annotations indicating the colours, 'a variation of blues, livened up by a series of yellows that go as far as orange'.[11]

In June Vincent completed a major landscape painting, *The Harvest* (see p. 61), which, he reported to Theo, 'absolutely kills all the rest; there's only a still life with coffee-pots and cups and plates in blue and yellow that can stand beside it'.[12] For this still life, Vincent depicts the objects on his table with extraordinary clarity and precision. By contrast, the textured yet atmospheric background is portrayed with a universalizing generality, in tones of yellow which, from left to right, evolve from warm to cool and back to warm again, and the tablecloth is rendered in loose, painterly brushstrokes of light blue, cobalt and white. The colouristic intensity of the still-life objects is enhanced by the juxtaposition of complementaries, for example the placement of the lemons against the violet coffee pot and of the oranges at the left and the saucer at the right on the blue tablecloth. In the case of the jug and cup on the right, the complementary colours are emblazoned in the designs that decorate the objects. This majolica jug, like the chequered milk pitcher on the opposite side of the coffee pot, seems to carry on a visual dialogue with the cup and saucer adjacent to it.

The objects on Vincent's table, grouped together with care, the tiered coffee pot and triad of lemons at the centre, take on a ritualistic significance. They are to consecrate the Yellow House, headquarters of a future artist's colony of the south.

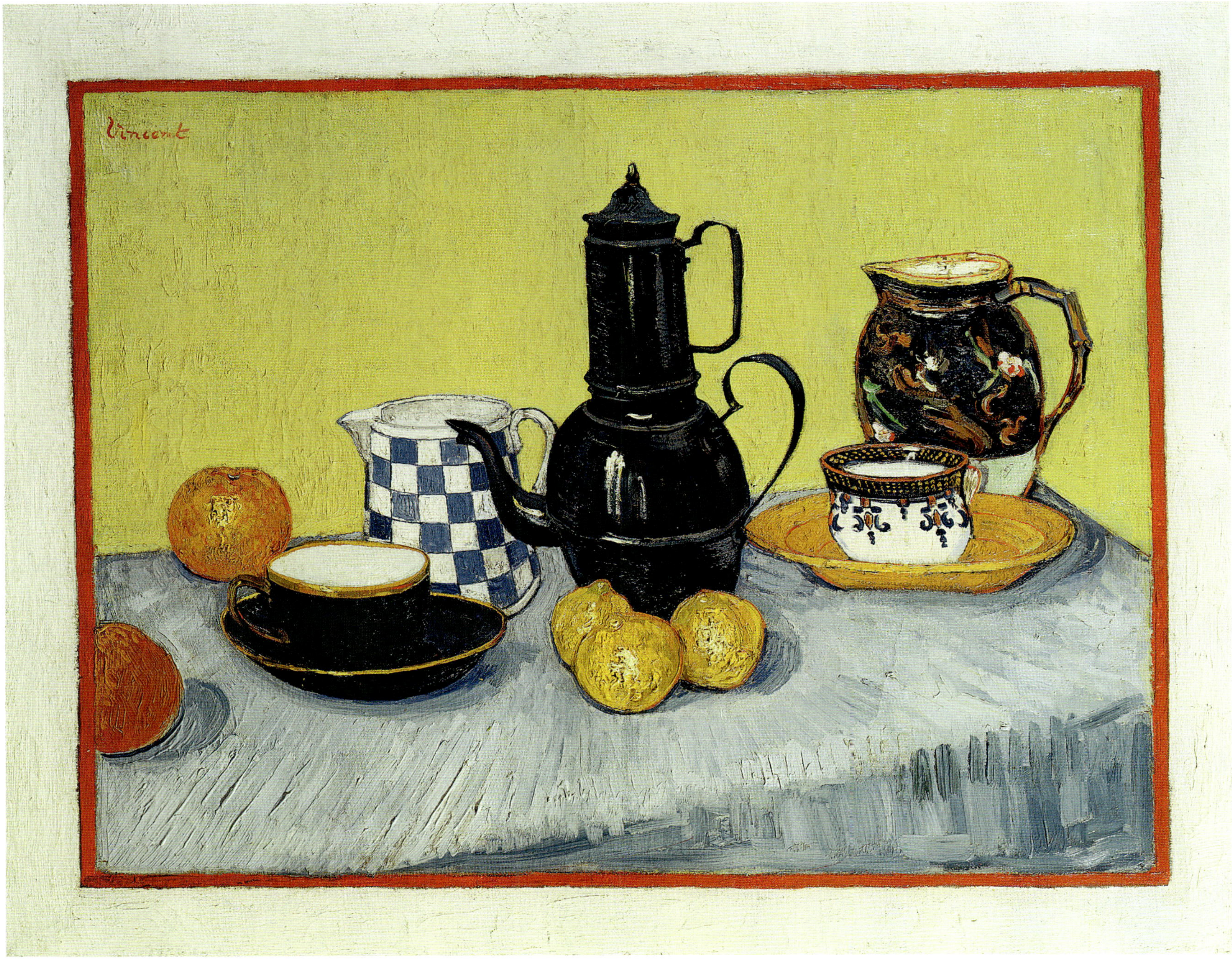
Vincent

June

1888

SEASCAPE AT SAINTES-MARIES

Pushkin Museum, Moscow

Oil on canvas | 44 × 53cm (17⅜ × 20⅞in)

In summer 1882, after he and Theo had walked along sand dunes near The Hague, Vincent wrote to his brother, 'What we saw together . . . sand – sea – sky – is something I certainly hope to express one day.'[13] That hope would be realized six years later, when in May he left Arles for a visit to the coastal village of Saintes-Maries. 'The Mediterranean has the colors of mackerel, changable I mean', he informed Theo. 'You don't always know if it is green or violet, you can't even say it's blue, because the next moment the changing light has taken on a tinge of pink or gray.'[14]

In the course of his five-day stay in Saintes-Maries, Vincent produced nine drawings and three paintings, including two seascapes, the smaller of which is shown here. With its high horizon, the painting depicts sailing boats only in its upper third; much of the pictorial surface is devoted to the sea itself, in nearly abstract swirls of paint in a range of colours – blue, green, violet, orange and white. The boats are likewise rendered in a loose, painterly manner, in white, red, orange, green, blue and black.

The colouristic freedom, spontaneity of brushstroke and high horizon of the seascape all suggest the influence of *Christ Asleep during the Tempest* by the French Romantic painter Eugène Delacroix (see p. 16). Vincent would describe this painting admiringly to Theo as a 'blue and green sketch with touches of purple and red and a little lemon yellow for the halo, the aureole', which 'speaks a symbolic language through colour itself'.[15]

Seascape at Saintes-Maries displays a new spontaneity, achieved in part because Vincent dispensed with his perspective frame (a wooden frame with threads stretched across it in a grid, for aid in depicting nature in three dimensions), and also because he painted it at the site, with neither preparatory drawings nor revisions in the studio.

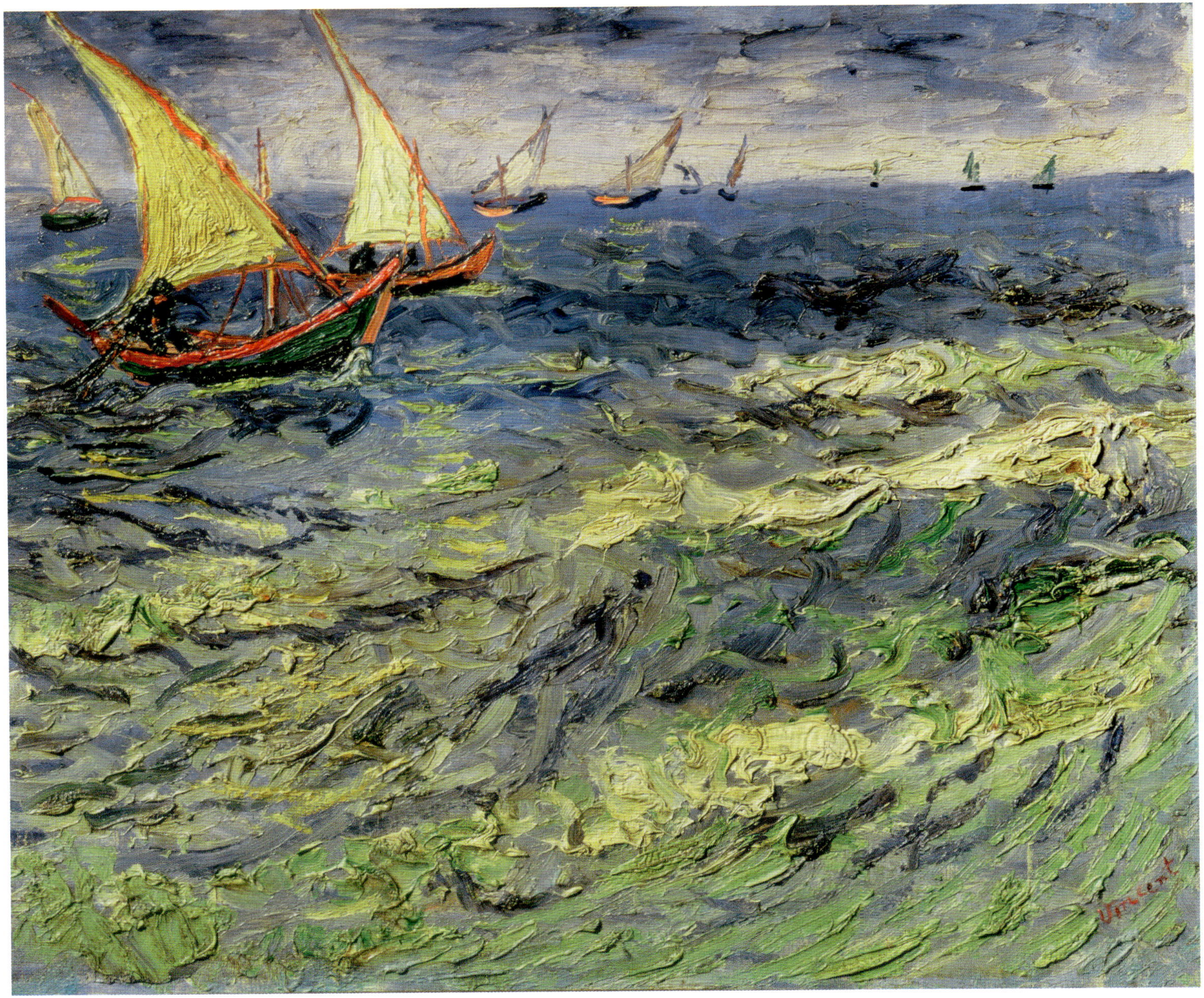
Vincent

June
1888

FISHING BOATS ON THE BEACH AT SAINTES-MARIES

Van Gogh Museum, Amsterdam

Oil on canvas | 65 × 81.5cm (25⅝ × 31⅞in)

Not long after his return to Arles, Vincent informed Theo, 'I'm sending you … some drawings of Saintes-Maries. I did the drawing of the boats as I was leaving, very early in the morning, and I'm working on the painting … with more sea and sky on the right.'[16] 'At last I have seen the Mediterranean,' he declared to Émile Bernard.[17] He described the scene: 'On the perfectly flat, sandy beach little green, red, blue boats, so pretty in shape and color that they made one think of flowers.'[18]

The drawing on p. 16, inscribed at upper left 'Souvenir de Stes Maries Mediterannée', is also inscribed with instructions on the colours on each boat and its mast – instructions to which the artist faithfully adheres in the final painting. The boats are arranged in a syncopated rhythm along the shore. The third boat has the word 'amitié' on its bow, an inscription retained in the final painting – a harbinger of the friendship of a future community of artists envisioned by Vincent, with the cluster of boats embodying such a community.[19]

As Vincent indicated to Theo, the vista of the painting expands that of the drawing, with an addition of 'more sea and sky on the right'. The two parts of the painting – beach and sea – differ somewhat in style. On the beach, the boats and their masts, with their sharp black outlines, linear patterns and brilliant, unmodelled colour, reveal the influence of Japanese woodcuts. 'I am going to put the black and the white, just as the color merchant sells them to us, boldly on my palette,' Vincent explained to Émile Bernard. 'I am speaking of the simplification of color in the Japanese manner.'[20] By contrast, the sea, the foamy waves and the four sailboats at sea are depicted in a painterly, more Impressionist manner, as are the beach itself and the scumbled sky, which unify left and right in the composition. The boats at sea have been loosely adapted from a painting done *en plein air* by the artist: *Seascape at Saintes-Maries* (see p. 55).

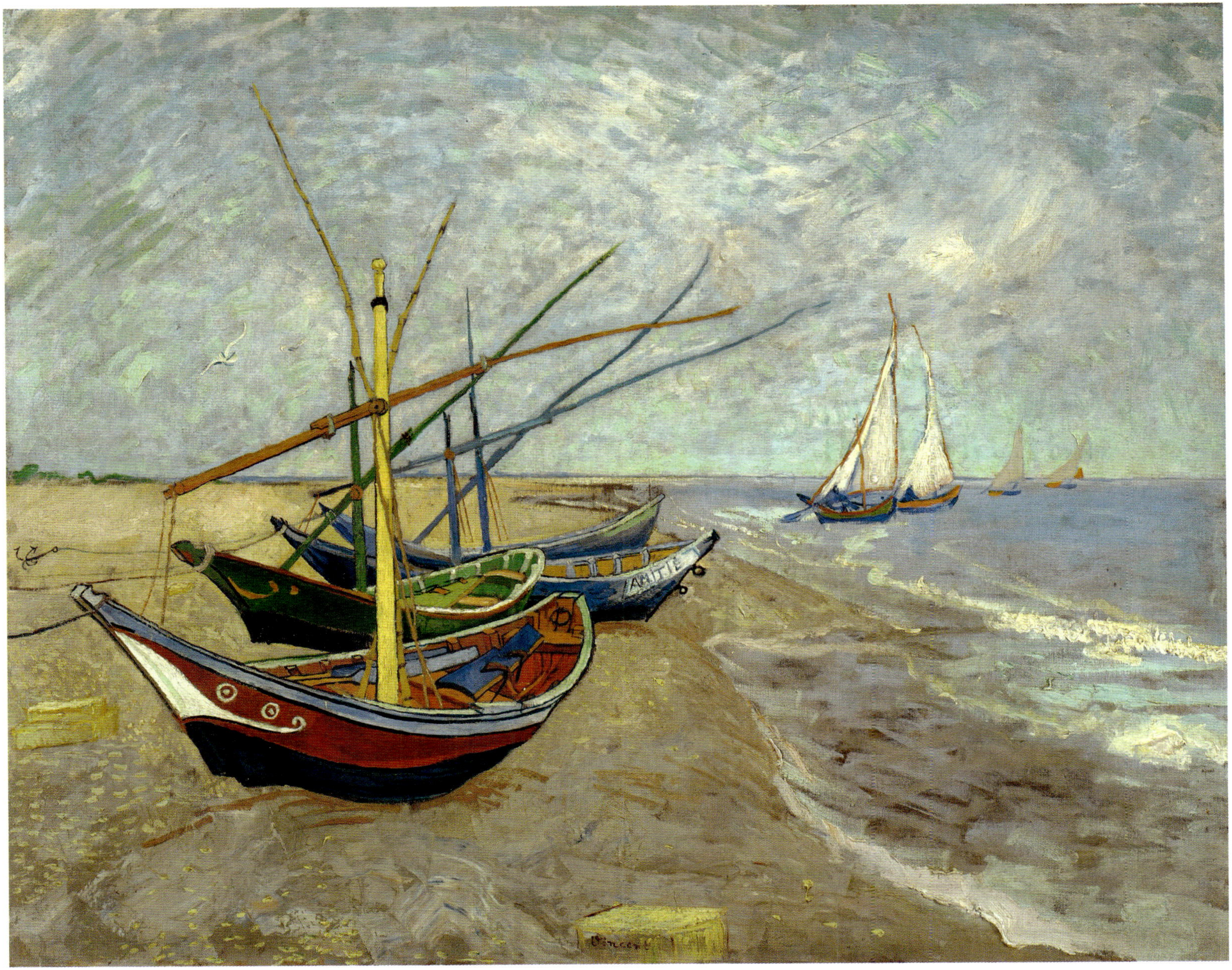

June
1888

BOATS AT SEA, SAINTES-MARIES-DE-LA-MER

Staatliche Museum, Berlin

Reed pen and ink over graphite on woven paper | 24 × 32cm (9½ × 12½in)

'Now that I have seen the sea here, I am absolutely convinced of the importance of staying in the Midi,' Vincent wrote to his brother Theo, soon upon his return to Arles from Saintes-Maries. 'I wish you could spend some time here, you'd … see things with an eye more Japanese … The Japanese draw quickly, very quickly, like a lightning flash.'[21]

While the oil painting *Seascape at Saintes-Maries* (see p. 55) was hanging to dry on his studio wall at the Yellow House, Vincent made this copy – really a calligraphic adaptation – in reed pen and ink, which he sent to Émile Bernard. (Two additional drawn adaptations were made; one was sent to the Australian painter John Russell, another to Theo.)

Each boat is commandeered by a single sailor; unlike the painting, the drawing renders two of the sailors with some visibility. The drawing was accompanied by a letter to Bernard, which read in part: 'The material difficulties of the painter's life make collaboration, the uniting of painters, desirable … we are at present sailing the high seas in our wretched little boats, all alone on the great waves of our time.'[22] Accordingly, these individually commandeered boats, like the *Fishing Boats on the Beach at Saintes-Maries* (see p. 57) affirm Vincent's yearning for a community of artists.

The drawing is executed with a bamboo reed pen, an instrument that renders images with greater spontaneity than the quill pens Vincent had employed before arriving in the Midi. The reed pen, with its knife-cut tip, quickly runs out of ink; thus it necessitates rapid execution, and the images that result show affinities with those of ukiyo-e Japanese paintings and woodblock prints. Each element of the seascape has its own linear identity: the serpentine and floral waves of the sea in the foreground, the more tempered ripples of the sea in the midground and background; the precisely rendered sails and hulls of the fishing boats; and the horizontal bands of the sky, more dense at left, more atmospheric at right. The composition that results is one of vibrancy, dynamism and vitality.

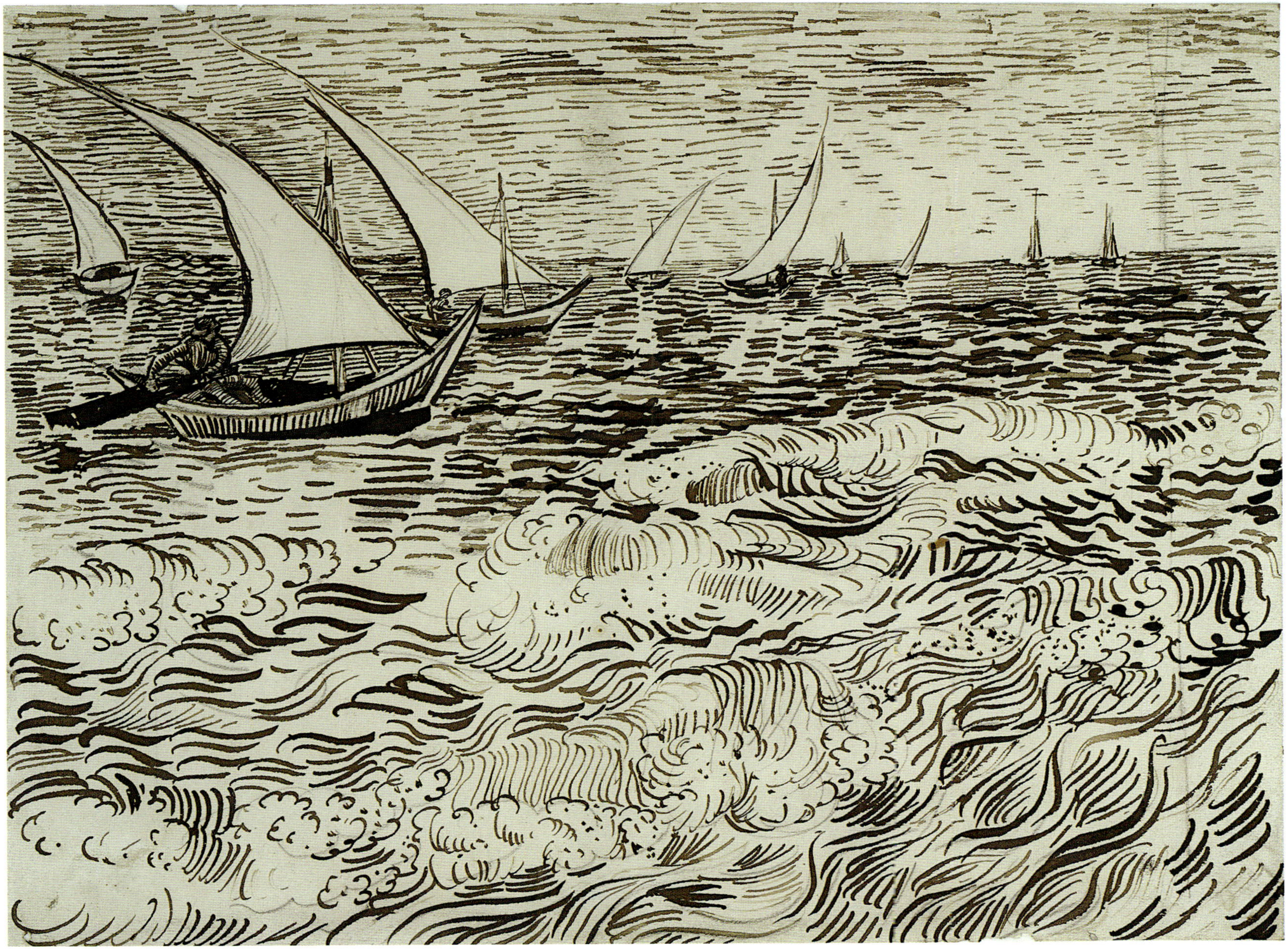

Mid-June
1888

THE HARVEST

Van Gogh Museum, Amsterdam

Oil on canvas | 72.5 × 92cm (28¾ × 36¼in)

When Vincent returned to Arles from Saintes-Maries-de-la-Mer in mid-June 1888, it was harvest time in Provence – a seasonal occurrence that provided him with the theme of the next phase of his art. A major work in the series was *The Harvest,* a panoramic landscape painting depicting a field on the plain of La Crau, 5km (3 miles) northeast of Arles. 'I am working on a new subject,' Vincent informed Theo. 'Fields green and yellow as far as the eye can reach. I have already drawn it twice, and I am starting it again as a painting.'[23]

Vincent set up his easel on the periphery of the field and worked on it for long hours each day. He felt energized, he informed Theo, by feelings of solidarity with rural workers: 'During the harvest my work was not any easier than what the peasants who were actually harvesting were doing. Far from complaining of it, it is just at these times in artistic life … that I feel almost as happy as I could be in the ideal, in that real life.'[24]

At the centre is a blue wagon, destined to be filled with hay; on the left there is a haystack. Figures in the middle distance gather, transport and stack grain. The landscape is punctuated by a series of reed fences and farmhouses, leading to the Mont de Cordes in the centre background, with the Alpilles behind it, and, on the far left, the Abbey of Montmajour. For Vincent, the prototype for this canvas, with its vastness of scale and its depiction of agricultural production, was Dutch seventeenth-century landscape painting.[25]

The upper third of the picture, however, resembles a landscape by Cézanne, with orange-roofed Provençal farmhouses receding into the distance and the mountain range lining the horizon. 'The countryside near Aix,' Vincent wrote to Theo, 'it's precisely the same as here … Coming home with my canvas, I say to myself: look, I've arrived precisely at *père* Cézanne's tones.'[26]

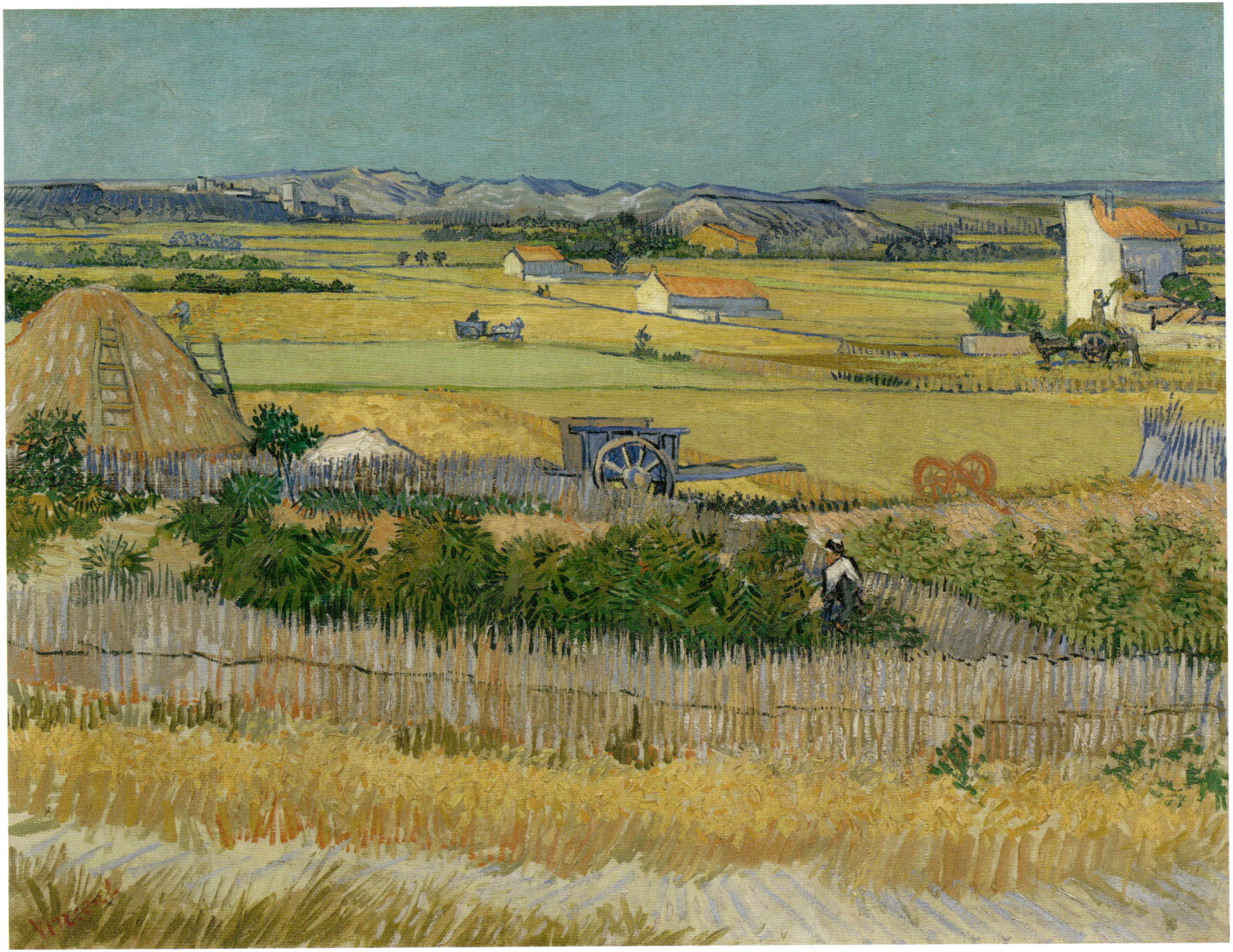

Mid-June
1888

HARVEST LANDSCAPE

Staatliche Museum, Berlin

Reed pen, quill and ink over graphite on woven paper | 24 × 32cm (9½ × 12⅝in)

Vincent's landscape painting *The Harvest* (see p. 61) was accompanied by four drawings of the same subject executed in reed pen, quill and ink. Two of the drawings – later embellished with watercolour – were preliminary sketches, and two were copies after the finished painting. Vincent called the copies '*répétitions*'. The *répétition* shown here was sent to Émile Bernard (a second, more faithful to the original, was sent to John Russell). Vincent wrote to Bernard that he felt exhilarated: 'I'm in better health here than in the north – I even work in the wheatfields at midday, in the full heat of the sun, without any shade whatever, and … I revel in it like a cicada.'[27]

The drawing that Vincent sent Bernard, one-third the size of the painting, was his fourth depiction of the subject, its having been preceded by the painting and two preliminary sketches. The composition is broadly the same, but it has been transformed by altered proportions and a different pictorial language in which line, rather than colour, becomes his means of expression. The foreground is broader, the sky narrower. The cart, the haystack and the figures play less prominent roles; now they may have no more significance than picket fences or blades of grass. The mountains are rendered with vertical strokes of the reed pen, so that they nearly resemble the fences of the foreground. The composition is rendered in calligraphic spontaneity, in loose strokes, squiggles and dots. It is no longer directly based on observations of nature, but is a synthesis of impressions of nature and abstract line and form. As Vincent's painting style evolved, it would acquire more of the spontaneity of his drawings.

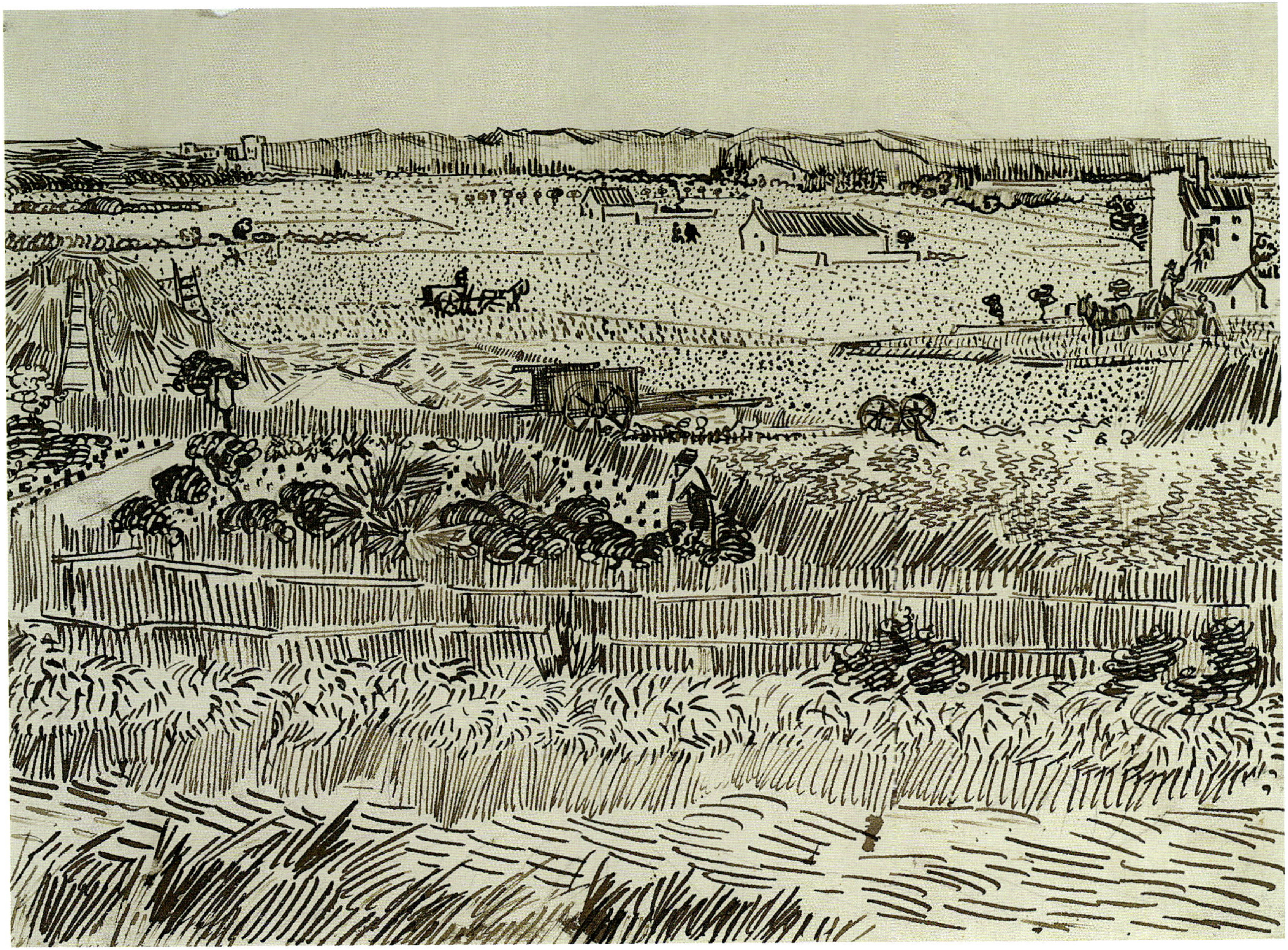

Mid-June
1888

THE SOWER

Kröller-Müller Museum, Otterlo

Oil on canvas | 64 × 80.5cm (25¼ × 31⅞in)

Vincent long admired the Barbizon painter Jean-François Millet (1814–75) as both a role model and a kindred spirit. Millet, himself of peasant stock, created iconic images of rural workers, while affirming their dignity and spirituality. In Nuenen in 1885, Vincent wrote to Theo, 'Millet is *father Millet* – that is, a guide and counselor to the younger painters in all things.'[28]

While sketching landscapes of the harvest at Arles in the summer 1888, Vincent made a study of a wheatfield juxtaposed with the image of a sower inspired by Millet (see p. 17). He wrote excitedly to Theo of his plans for a painting: 'In a ploughed field … of clods of purple earth … a sower in blue and white. On the horizon a field of short, ripe wheat. Above all that a yellow sky with a yellow sun. You can sense from the . . . nomenclature of the tonalities – that *colour* plays a very important role …'[29]

For the colour in this painting, Vincent looked to a different source of inspiration – not Millet, but Delacroix. Citing the latter artist's *Christ Asleep during the Tempest* (see p. 16) he noted: 'Christ's boat … speaks a symbolic language through colour itself. Millet's sower is colourless grey.'[30]

With *The Sower*, Vincent has taken intensity of colour to a new level, based on a powerful opposition of yellow and violet. A thickly impastoed yellow sun in the upper fourth of the canvas radiates energy, signified by pulsating brushstrokes of red, yellow and orange, illuminating the sky and the wheatfield. By contrast, the soil is dominated by arcs and squiggles of blue and violet, a reversal of the usual order of nature. The silhouette of the sower is based rather faithfully on its prototype in Millet's painting. (The combination of the image of a sower – or planter of seeds – with the seasonal anomaly of a wheatfield in harvest may be a Biblical reference to Ecclesiastes III, 2, 'a time to sow and a time to reap'.)

At the foreground centre a triangular yellow path leads the viewer's eye toward a blue house with a red roof on the horizon, adjoined by a pair of trees and balanced by a green-and-blue hill in the upper right. A few birds are perched or flying above the field. It is a spare and simple composition, with the striding sower, the setting sun at his back, reigning supreme above the horizon.

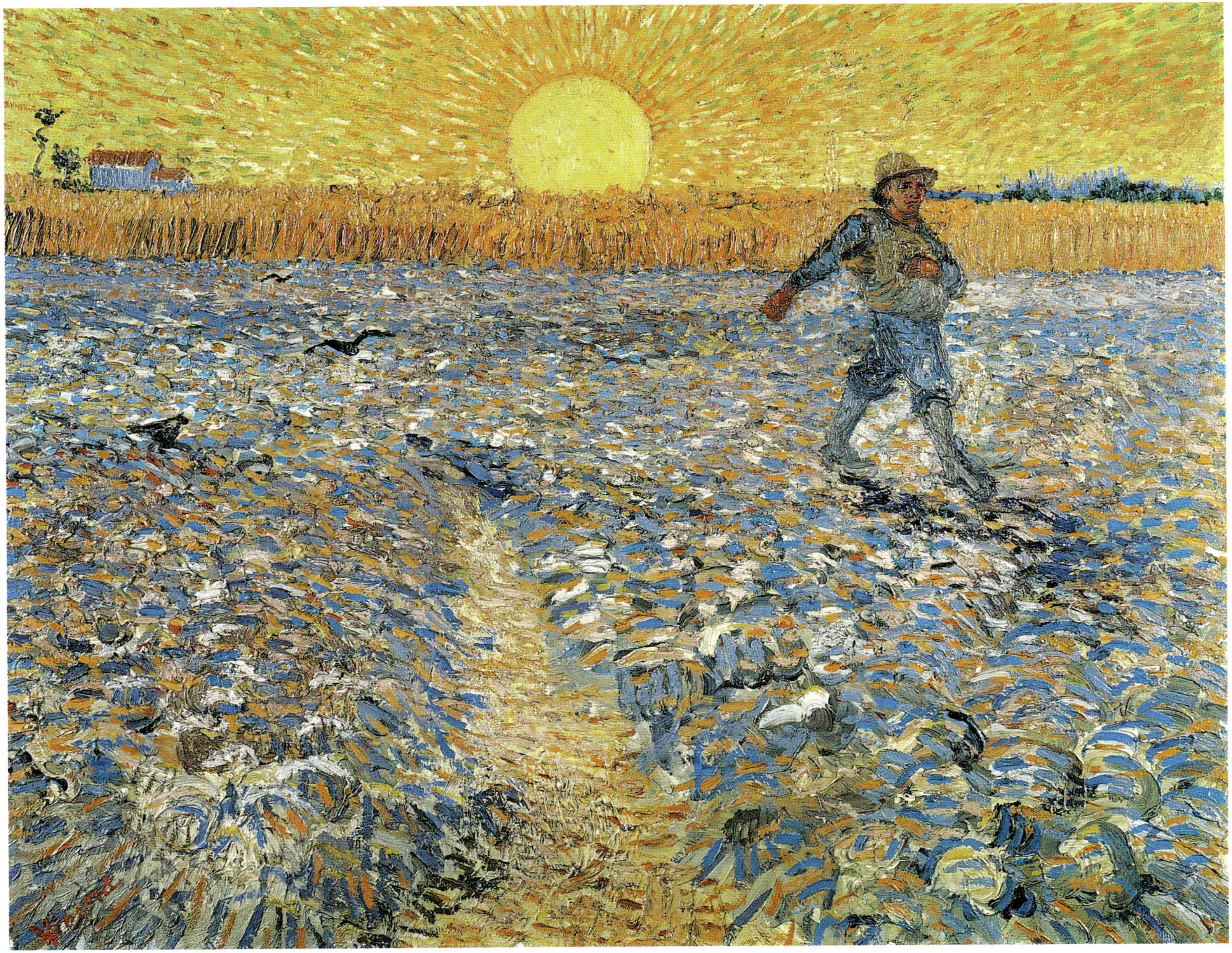

July

1888

LA MOUSMÉ

National Gallery, Washington

Oil on canvas | 73 × 60cm (28⅞ × 23¾in)

'I feel as though I were in Japan,' Vincent wrote to Theo from Arles in the winter of 1888.[31] That summer he had declared to Theo, 'If you know what a "*mousmé*" is (you will know when you have read Loti's *Madame Chrysanthème*), I have just painted one. It took me a whole week … A mousmé is a Japanese girl – Provençale in this case – 12 to 14 years old.'[32]

In his novel *Madame Chrysanthème*, published that same year of 1888, Pierre Loti describes a *mousmé*: 'Over her quaint little head, her round umbrella with its thousand ribs threw a great halo of blue and red, edged with black, and an oleander-tree full of flowers … spread its glory beside her, bathed, like herself, in the sunshine.'[33]

The semi-circular arc of the young woman's skirt, and the sprig of oleander in her hand, echo Loti's description. Despite her impassive demeanour, she seems to emanate a contrapuntal energy of forms and colours, as if signifying an emerging sexuality of which she is only partially aware. The complementary orange spots and blue ground of her skirt are juxtaposed with her bodice, with its arabesques of red and deep violet stripes, the undulating row of orange buttons, and the arcs of the oversize bentwood chair. Like the young woman, the sprig of oleander that she holds is blooming. In contrast to the flat, near abstraction of her skirt, her hands are vividly modelled in complementary pink and green, set against shimmering white, pink and green cuffs. Her face is a tactile presence, in pink, green and white, and is delicately framed by the red ribbon, the hair highlighted in violet, and a white collar shadowed in green. The warmth of her presence is highlighted by the scumbled, cool, pale green background.

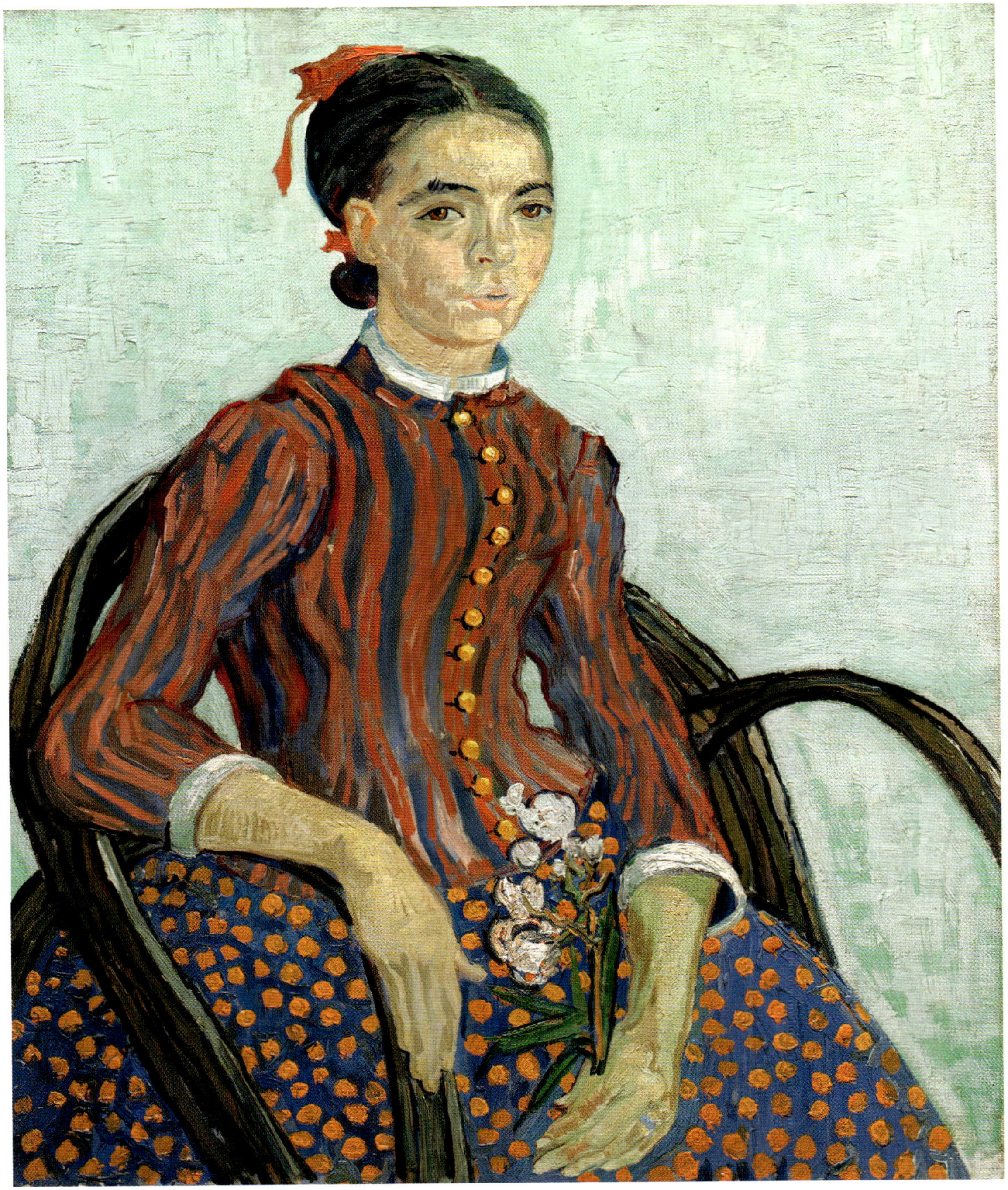

August
1888

OLEANDERS

The Metropolitan Museum of Art, New York

Oil on canvas | 60 × 73cm (23⅝ × 28¾in)

The spring and summer of the year 1888 in Arles was a highly productive period in Vincent's life as an artist. When the summer heat made painting landscapes excessively arduous, still-life painting was an effective alternative. *Oleanders*, created in August, has qualities of landscape transposed into still life. Presented in a horizontal format, it features oleanders with fragrant red-and-pink flowers and splaying green leaves emerging from a glazed multi-coloured jug, which rests on a loosely painted table top of light earth tones and is set against an abstract, pale green background, luminous and warm, like a summer sky.

The dense, massive flowers seem to defy gravity as they spread outward, contrasted in both colour and contour by the spiky branch-like leaves. Dynamic colour interactions enliven the composition: the deep green of the leaves and their lighter green highlights are set against the yellow-green wall and these interactions are echoed by the pair of books on the table, in yellow and two tones of ochre, in addition to the white of the pages which echoes the white highlights of the flowers. The surface of the table, which is rendered in near abstraction, has three horizontal brushstrokes in pale blue at the right, which interact with the pale-blue base of the jug; a forked abstract line that emerges from the centre of the jug's base is reminiscent of a tree's shadow.

Vincent would later write to Theo, 'The oleander – ah, it speaks of love …'[34] The life-affirming qualities of this composition are emphasized by the title of the top book at the table's edge, printed on both cover and spine – Emile Zola's *La Joie de vivre* (*The Joy of Living*). Zola's novel, serialized in *Gil Blas* in 1883 and published in book form in 1884, is a tale of its protagonist's steadfast optimism in the face of overwhelming tragedy.

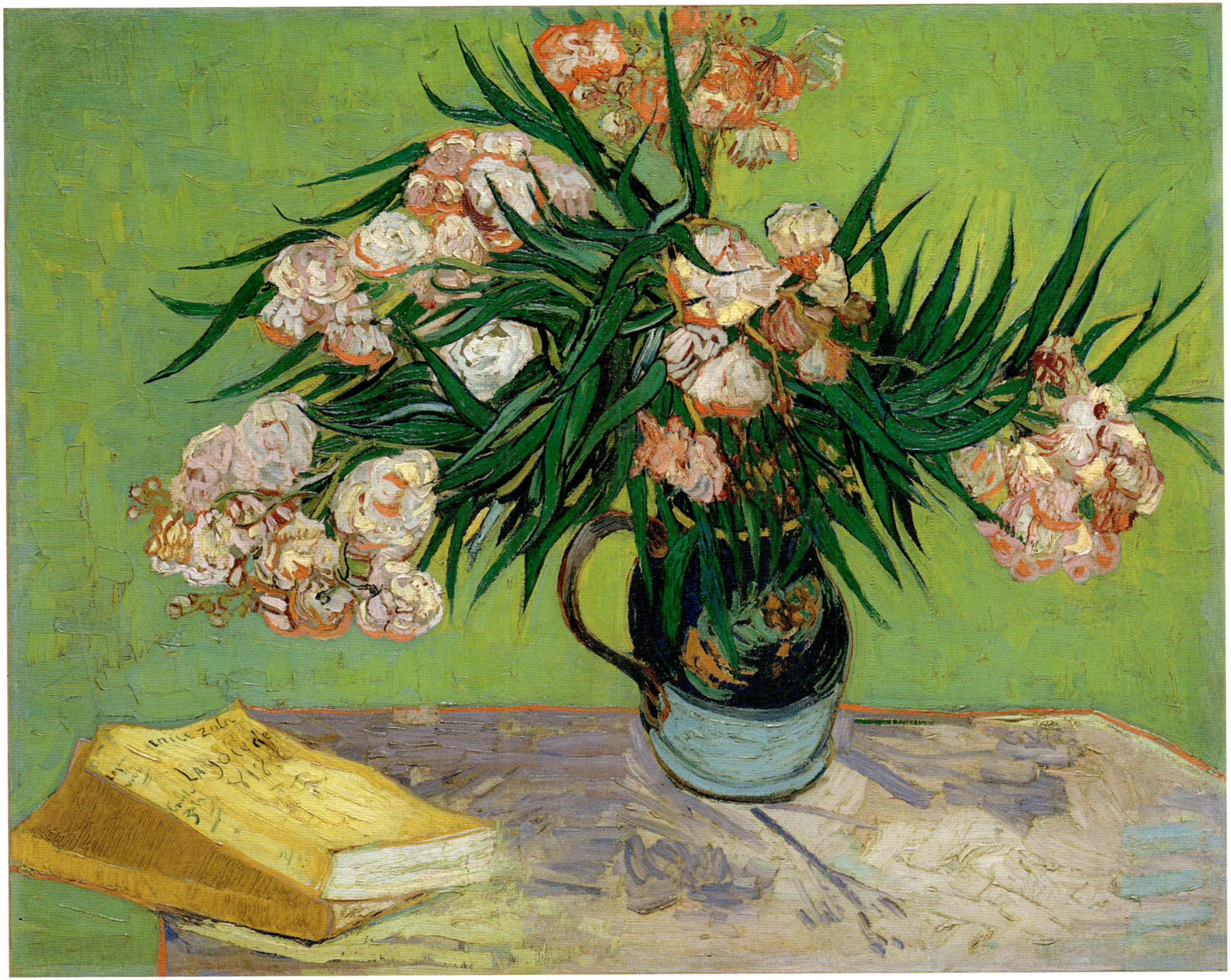

August
1888

THE SEATED ZOUAVE

Private collection, Argentina

Oil on canvas | 81 × 65cm (31⅞ × 25⅝in)

Vincent relished the opportunity to paint portraits, and in fact regarded portraiture as a kind of mission. 'In a picture I want to paint something comforting, as music is comforting,' he told Theo. 'I want to paint men and women with that something of the eternal which the halo used to symbolize, and which we seek to convey by the actual radiance and vibration of our coloring.'[35]

On 21 June 1888 Vincent wrote to his brother, 'I have a model at last – a Zouave – he's a lad with a small face, the neck of a bull, the eye of a tiger, and I started doing one portrait and started again on another.' The first version (now in the Van Gogh Museum, Amsterdam) is bust-length; the second (completed by 8 August) 'will be seated; full length, against a white wall'.[36]

The term 'Zouave' refers to a regiment of the French Army (disbanded in 1962, at the end of the Algerian War) whose original recruits were Berbers, indigenous people of North Africa, and who wore a distinctive uniform of red fez, a blue tunic ornamented in gold, a brightly coloured sash and red flared trousers.

As Meyer Schapiro observes, 'The distinctive division of the picture is not of left and right, but of upper and lower halves.'[37] The upper half is frontal and nearly symmetrical, with the figure presented against a white plaster wall with perpendicular green bands. The face is not idealized but, meeting the viewer's gaze, projects a certain nobility. In the lower half, the knees are spread to an anatomically impossible degree and the tiled floor is viewed from an aerial perspective. As a consequence the Zouave projects both restful calm and a readiness for action. The nobility of the figure is accentuated by the vibrant colour: the complementaries of red fez, trousers and floor tiles and the green of the sash and wall panels – a vibrancy which is enhanced by the white of the wall, the white shoe uppers, and the white brushstrokes representing highlights on the trousers.

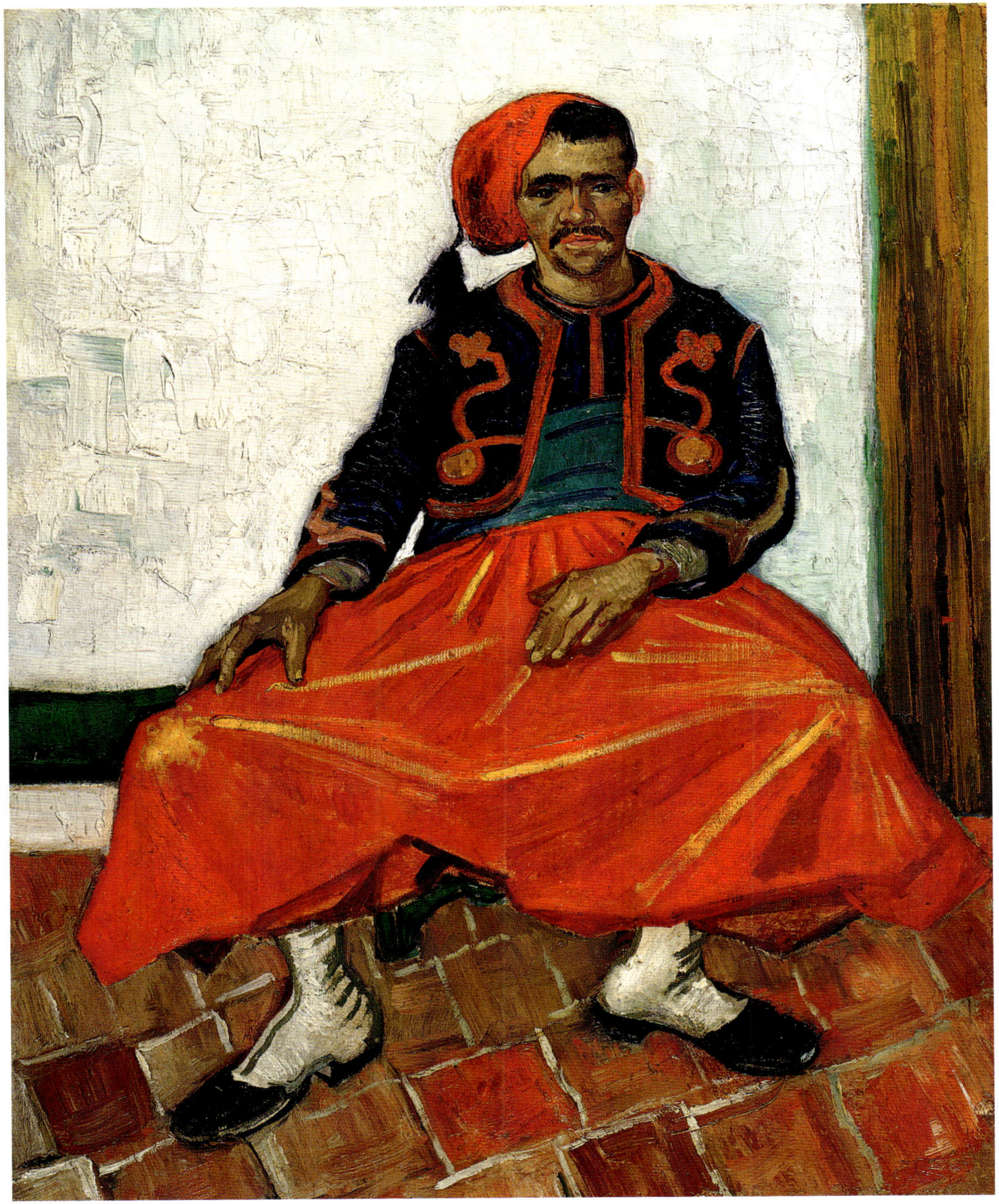

August
1888

PORTRAIT OF PATIENCE ESCALIER

Collection Stavros S. Niarchos

Oil on canvas | 69 × 56cm (27⅛ × 22⅛in)

In Arles, Vincent made a portrait of a peasant, returning to a theme that had preoccupied him in his native Netherlands (see *The Potato Eaters*, 1885, p. 37). He hired an elderly gardener to pose for him, producing two versions over a two-week period, the second of which is shown here (the first version is in the Norton Simon Museum, Pasadena, California). Vincent sent a sketch to Theo, introducing it with a note: 'You'll shortly make the acquaintance of Mr Patience Escalier – a sort of man with a hoe, an old Camargue oxherd, who's now a gardener at a farmstead in the Crau.'[38] His invocation of a 'man with a hoe' is a reference to a picture of that title by Millet, which he had seen and admired in Paris (see p. 18). Regarding the colour in the portrait, Vincent added: 'I find that what I learned in Paris is fading, and that I'm returning to my ideas that came to me in the country before I knew the Impressionists . . . Because instead of trying to render exactly what I have before my eyes, I use colour more arbitrarily in order to express myself forcefully.'[39]

Patience Escalier glows in the tones of the sun and the earth: his yellow hat evokes a radiant sun; his weathered red-and-brown face and hands, the earth. As art historian Meyer Schapiro observed, 'his blue cape and the burnt orange background are an inversion of the Provençal sky and earth.'[40] His folded hands rest on a cane, much as Millet's peasant leans on his hoe, and the position of the hands, together with the imploring expression of his face and eyes, suggest prayer. Vincent had long sympathized with the common people, but unlike his potato eaters or Millet's man with a hoe, Patience Escalier does not verge on caricature but conveys dignity and piety in a work which is not constricted by natural appearances and employs colour for maximum effect.

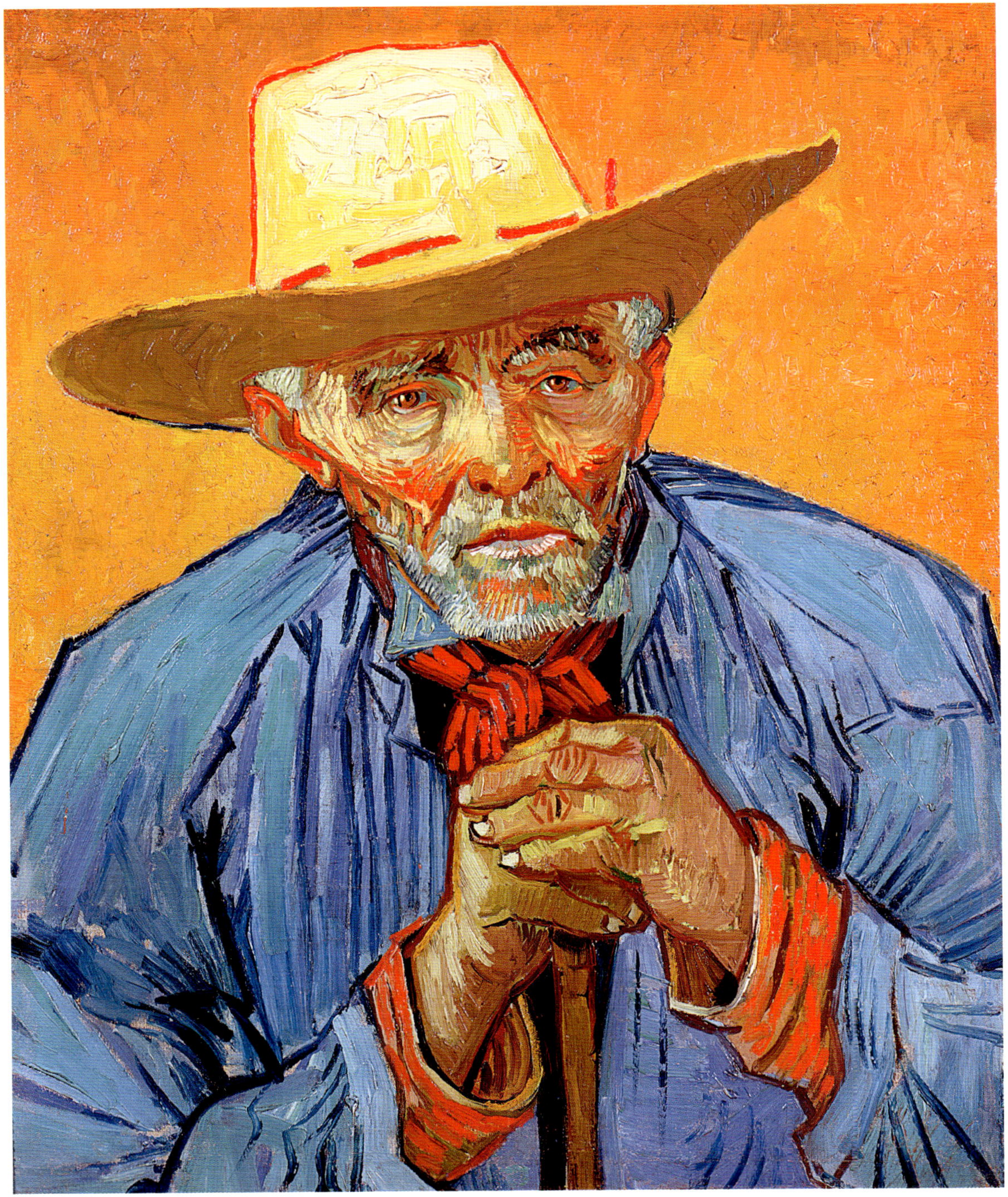

Late August
1888

SUNFLOWERS

National Gallery, London

Oil on canvas | 93 × 73cm (36⅝ × 29¾in)

In summer 1888 Vincent conceived the idea of decorating the walls of the Yellow House in Arles with still lifes of sunflowers, in order to create effects 'like those of stained-glass windows in Gothic churches'.[41] In the last week of August he created four sunflower paintings. 'I am hard at it, painting with the enthusiasm of a Marseillais eating bouillabaisse,' he reported to Theo. 'I'm working at it every morning from sunrise on, for the flowers fade so soon, and the thing is to do the whole in one rush.'[42]

The first three paintings in the series are based on colour contrasts of yellow and blue, with backgrounds ranging from pastel blue-green to deep royal blue.[43] With the fourth, shown here, Vincent employed what he called a 'light on light' technique, in which he reduced the gradations of light to dark.[44] The composition is painted in combinations of yellow and green, with yellow as the dominant colour. The textured light yellow background is contrasted with the smooth ochre surface on which the vase rests, while the upper and lower portions of the vase mimic, in mirror image, these contrasts of colour and texture. The flowers themselves, rendered in thick impasto and resting on rhythmically bending stems, are animated in their expressiveness. They range in their stages of development: some are in full bloom; some are past their prime; some are yet to emerge fully.

The yellows of the composition, and the sunflowers themselves (*les tournesols*, in French) are tributes to the sun of the Midi. The painting is an expression of joy, and the placement of Vincent's signature at the centre of the Provençal vase implies his identification with the flowers.

Albert Aurier (1865–92), who himself led a tragically brief life, was the only critic who wrote a detailed appreciation of Vincent in the artist's lifetime. In an article for *Mercure de France*, Aurier made the case for Vincent as a Symbolist: 'If we refuse to acknowledge … idealistic tendencies beneath this naturist art … how would one explain … that obsessive passion for the solar disc, … and … for that other sun, that vegetable-star, that sumptuous sunflower, that he repeats tirelessly, monomaniacally?'[45] In response, Vincent wrote a lengthy, appreciative letter to the critic, in which he declared that his sunflowers symbolize 'gratitude'.[46]

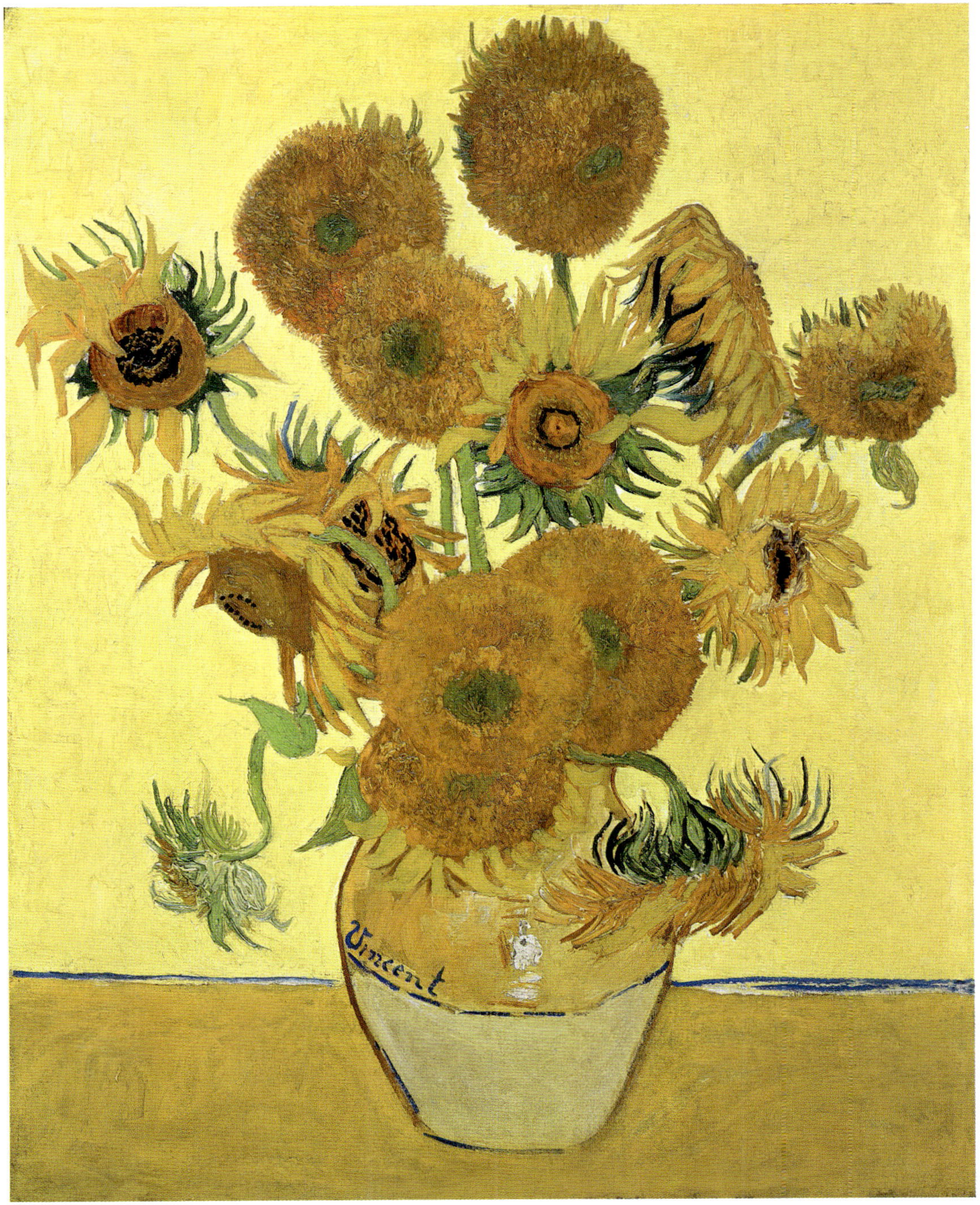
Vincent

Early September
1888

THE NIGHT CAFÉ

Yale University Art Gallery, New Haven

Oil on canvas | 72.4 × 92.1cm (28½ × 36¼in)

In spring 1888, while awaiting funds to furnish the rooms he had rented in the Yellow House at Place Lamartine in Arles, Vincent had found temporary quarters on the same street, in a room above the Café de la Gare. The café, run by Joseph Ginoux and his wife Marie, remained open throughout the night, when it would frequently be inhabited by those whom Vincent called 'night prowlers' – pimps, prostitutes, drunkards, the poor and the homeless.[47] In early September, for three consecutive nights, he set up his easel to paint this scene.

The room is depicted in nightmarish perspective: from an aerial viewpoint, the textured yellow floorboards recede to the upper left, where a curtained yellow open doorway, resembling a phantom, echoes the silhouette of the sole standing figure, the white-garbed proprietor, Monsieur Ginoux. At the perimeters of the room are five seated figures: on the right, two shabbily dressed men occupy a table, while on the left a solitary man, apparently asleep, shelters his face in his folded arms, and a man and woman, he gazing at her profile, share a table by the doorway. Three yellow and green gas lamps dangle from the ceiling, each emitting yellow-and-green circles of light, rendered with thick strokes of paint; to the right of the doorway, at the centre of the bar, is a vase with a cluster of flowers which evokes the ceiling lamps. Above the doorway, syncopated with the lamps and the vase, is a clock specifying the time: a quarter-hour past midnight.

In contrast with the lethargy of the figures, and corresponding to the jarring perspective of the room and the energetic luminosity of the light fixtures, are intense colour contrasts – notably, the expanse of red wall, the green ceiling, the green top of the billiard table, and a single red billiard ball. Contributing to the sense of anxiety reflected in the scene are images of absence and loneliness – the large, dark shadow cast by the billiard table and the vacant chairs in the left foreground.

Painting *The Night Café* was an opportunity for Vincent to present a dystopian vision: 'I have tried to express the terrible passions of humanity by means of red and green,' he wrote to Theo,[48] and added, the following day, 'The café is a place where one can ruin oneself, go mad, or commit a crime.'[49]

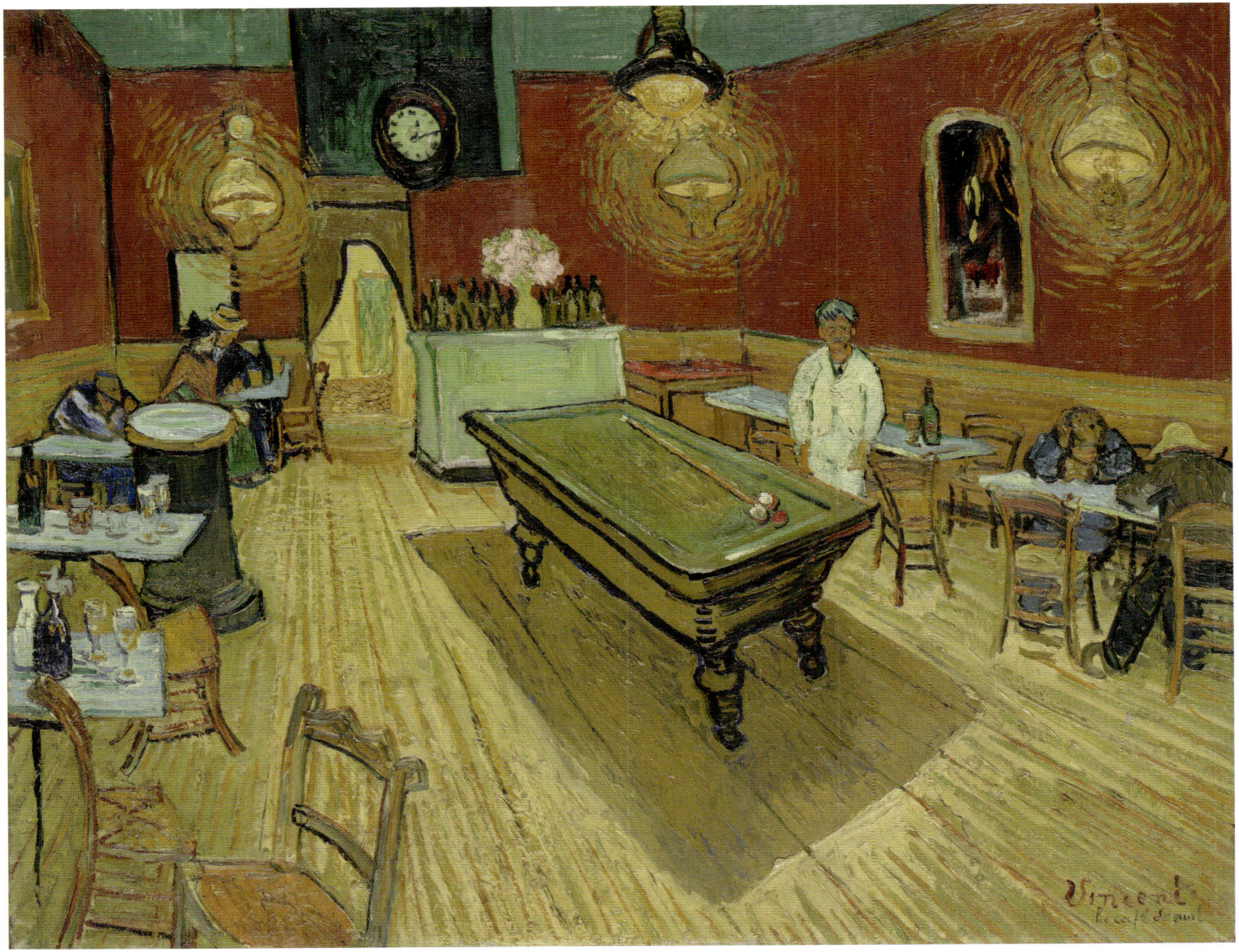
Vincent

Early September

1888

CAFÉ TERRACE AT NIGHT

Kröller-Müller Museum, Otterlo

Oil on canvas | 81 × 65.5cm (31⅞ × 26in)

On Place du Forum in Arles, beneath a yellow awning, guests enjoy a tranquil summer evening on the terrace of a café. A few people stroll along the cobblestoned street; a carriage approaches. The illuminated terrace emits a yellow glow, as do a display window across the road, the windows of houses, and the approaching carriage. In contrast to the yellow of the café and windows is the blue of the buildings at the left and right, while the blue and white of the starry sky above is a counterpart to the blue darkness and yellow glow on the street. As Meyer Schapiro has observed, the artist has created a visual correspondence between the town with its inhabitants and a benign universe: 'In the silhouette of the orange café floor and the adjoining window and doors, we discover the inverted shape of the blue sky; the scattered disks of the stars are matched in the elliptical table-tops below.'[50]

With this work, the night sky of Provence, which had so entranced Vincent upon his arrival in Arles, makes its first appearance in his painting. He would later devote landscapes to the subject (see *Starry Night over the Rhône* and *The Starry Night*, pp. 81 and 105), and include it in a portrait (*Eugène Boch*, 1888, Musée d'Orsay). He was likewise drawn to the nocturnal terrestrial world of Arles and painted *Café Terrace at Night* not from imagination but *in situ*, by artificial light. 'It often seems to me,' Vincent observed to Theo, 'that the night is much more alive and richly coloured than the day.'[51]

Café Terrace at Night was painted contemporaneously with *The Night Café* (see p. 77), a depiction of the interior of the Café de la Gare on Place Lamartine, which presents a diametrically opposite vision – an indication of the range of Vincent's emotional and creative life in Arles.

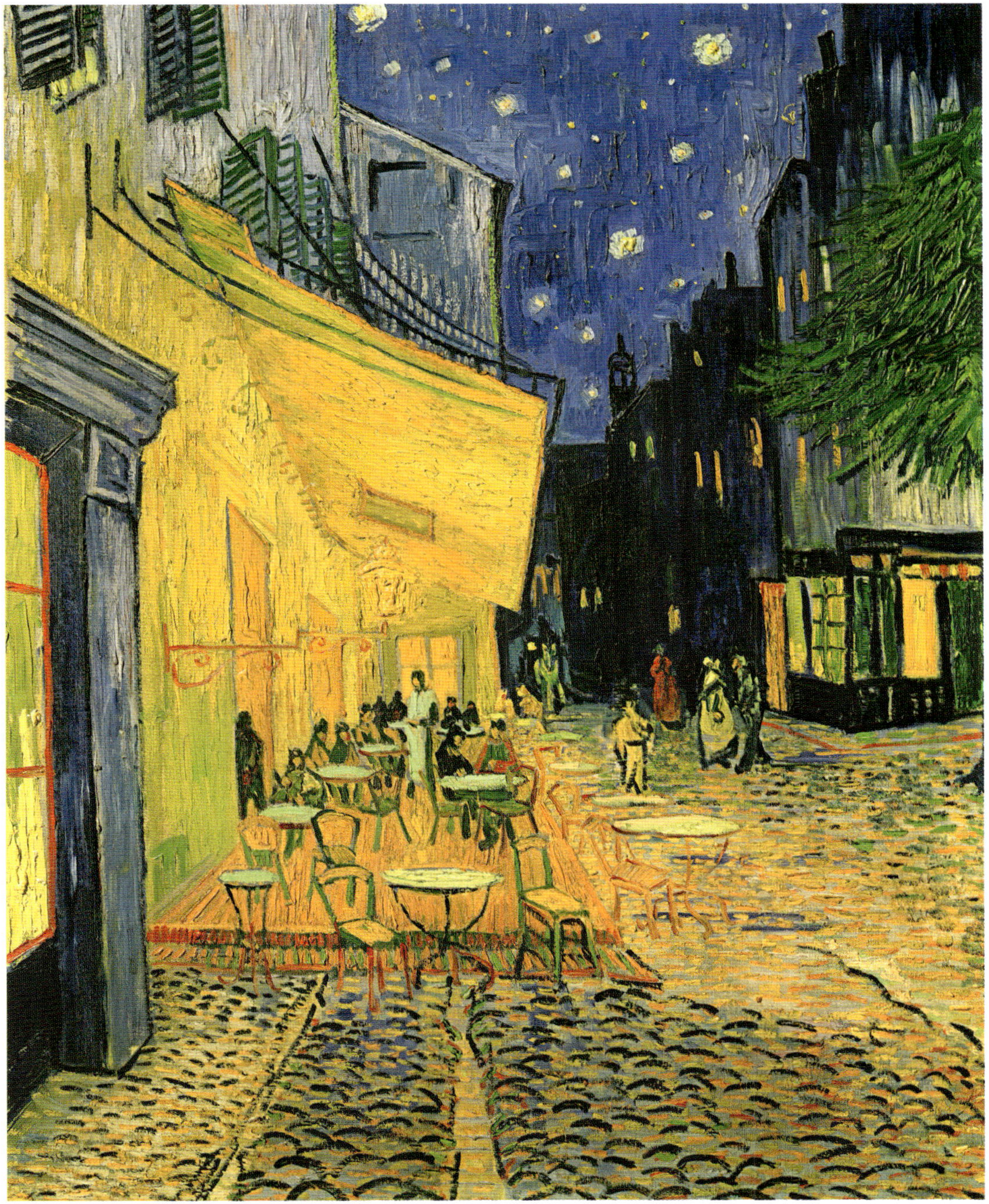

September
1888

STARRY NIGHT OVER THE RHÔNE

Musée d'Orsay, Paris

Oil on canvas | 72.5 × 92cm (28½ × 36⅕in)

Soon after Vincent's arrival in Arles in February 1888 he found himself as impressed by the night-time Provençal sky as by the brilliantly sunlit days. Well before he undertook *Starry Night over the Rhône* he contemplated painting a landscape with a star-filled sky. In April he wrote to Theo, 'I must … have a starry sky with cypresses, or perhaps above all, a field with ripe corn; there are some wonderful night skies here.'[52] Finally, in September, he informed his sister Wil, 'I definitely want to paint a starry sky now. It often seems to me that the night is even more richly coloured than the day … And arranging colours in a painting to make them shimmer and stand out through their contrasts, that's something like arranging jewels.'[53]

Starry Night over the Rhône was painted a short distance from the Yellow House on Place Lamartine. Vincent set up his easel under a gas lamp on the east bank of the Rhône, as the river bends south. Visible on the horizon on the left are silhouettes of the Romanesque churches of Saint-Julien and Saint-Trophime; the constellation known as the Big Dipper, a portion of Ursa Major, the Great Bear, is prominent in the sky. The sparkling stars interplay with the illumination of the gas-lit buildings of the town and their shimmering reflections in the Rhône, suggesting celestial and terrestrial harmony.

The composition is divided into three curved horizontal bands of earth, river and sky, each palpably different in texture and brushstroke. These bands employ muted colour harmonies of blue, green, white, yellow and black, allowing the luminous yellows of the stars, the gaslights and their reflections to command the viewer's attention. A pair of sailing boats are docked at the shore, counterparts of the two lovers on the quay, earthly embodiments of a harmonious universe.

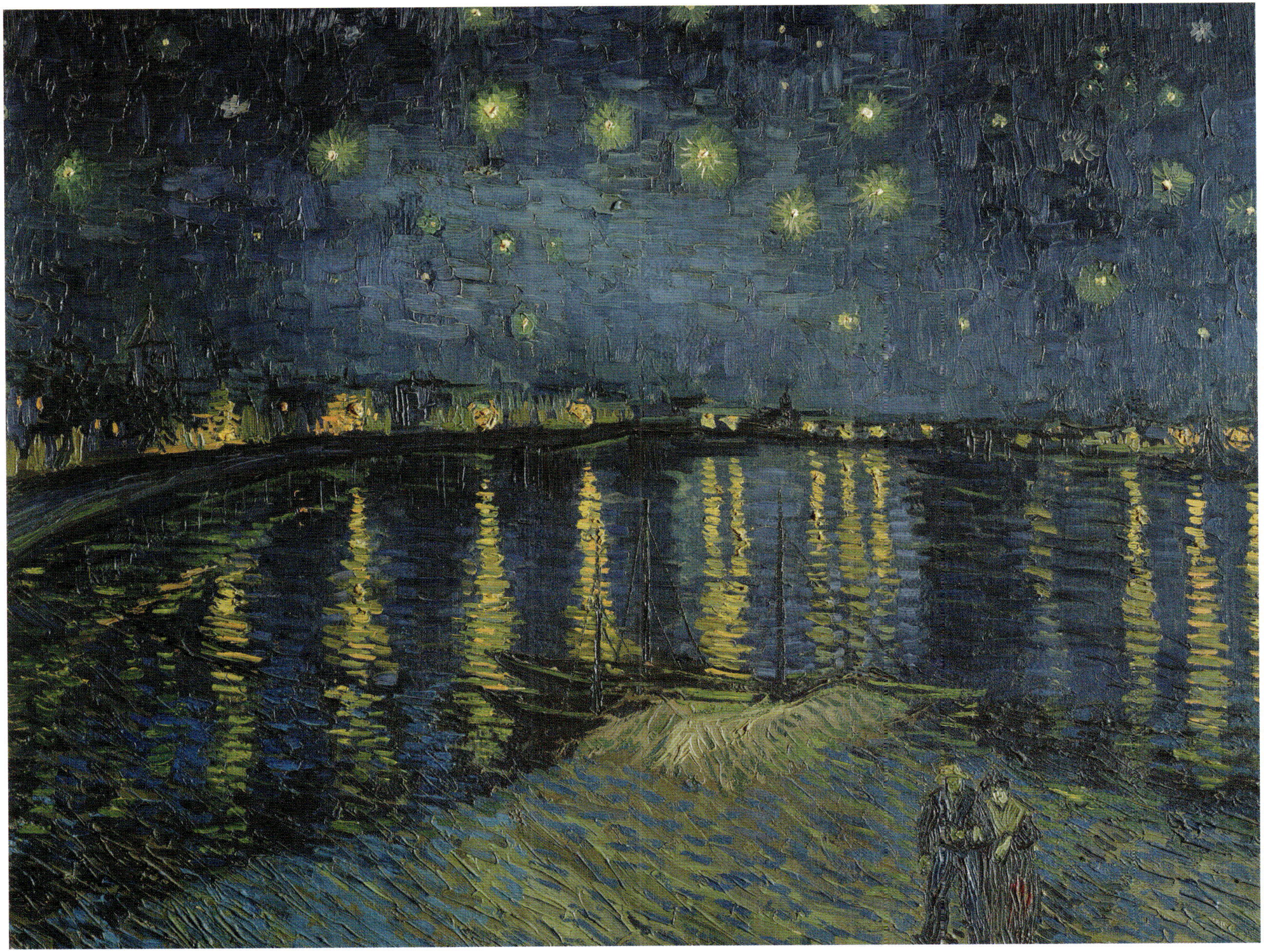

Mid-September
1888

SELF-PORTRAIT DEDICATED TO PAUL GAUGUIN

Fogg Museum, Cambridge, MA

Oil on canvas | 62 × 52cm (24⅜ × 20½in)

Vincent hoped to establish an artists' colony in Arles, and to that end he encouraged an exchange of self-portraits among his artist friends. After having received self-portraits from Gauguin and Bernard, he painted this work and sent it to Gauguin, inscribing it at the top of the canvas 'à mon ami Paul Gauguin' ('to my friend Paul Gauguin'). It was completed just before Vincent moved into the Yellow House, in mid-September 1888.

Vincent's hair and beard, shaved in the heat of summer, were beginning to grow back. Along with his gaunt appearance, the trimmed beard and coiffure gave him the air – at least in his own estimation – of a Buddhist monk. This was in keeping with his trope of the Midi as 'the equivalent of Japan',[54] and of his spiritual dedication to his art. In letters to Wil and Theo, he described the portrait: 'I've … done a new portrait of myself, as a study, in which I look like a Japanese';[55] 'a portrait of myself, *almost colorless*, in gray tones against a background of pale malachite'.[56] To Gauguin he wrote, 'I looked … for the character of a … simple worshipper of the eternal Buddha.'[57] Writing to Theo, he expounded on the metaphysical underpinnings of Japanese art: 'If we study Japanese art … we see a man, undoubtedly wise … who spends his time … [studying] a single blade of grass … I envy the Japanese the extreme clarity that everything in their work has … Their work is as simple as breathing.'[58]

In contrast with the self-portrait that Vincent painted in Paris on the eve of his departure for Arles (see *Self-Portrait as a Painter,* p. 49), he shows no indications of his profession. His gaze looks out towards infinity rather than at the viewer. The swirls of green behind him suggest not the wall of a studio, but a space without boundaries; nor is there any sign of an artist in his loose brown coat and waistcoat or in the medal on his shirtfront. His face is deeply modelled in pink-and-green light and shadow, emphasizing the sculptural qualities of his skull-shaped head. His high cheekbones are accentuated and, along with his slightly slanted eye sockets, suggest Asiatic features. Vincent is presenting himself not as a painter surveying the world, but as an individual soul contemplating the universe.

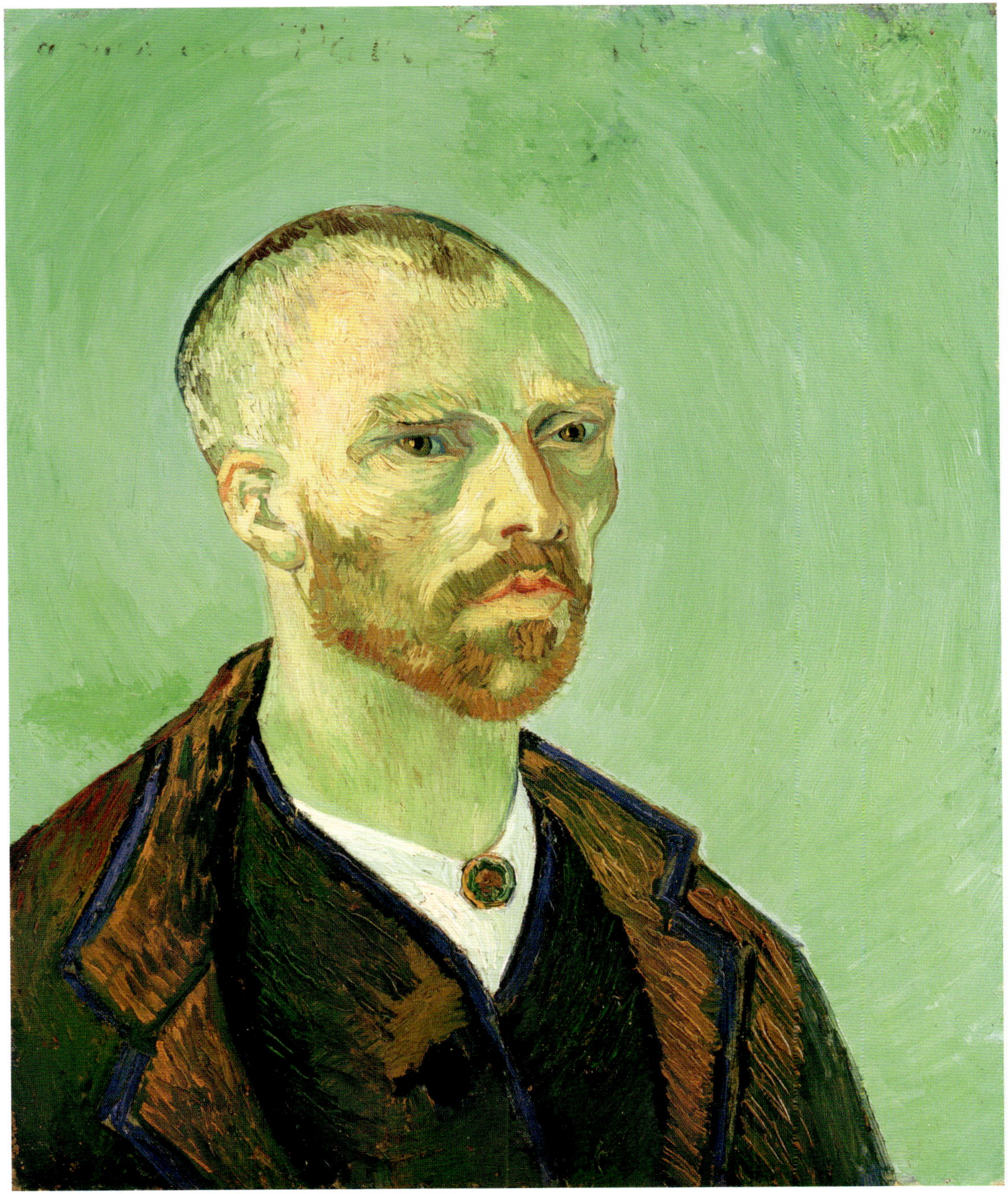

Late September **1888**

THE YELLOW HOUSE

Van Gogh Museum, Amsterdam

Oil on canvas | 76 × 94cm (29⅞ × 37in)

In May 1888 Vincent rented the east wing of a stucco-faced building on Place Lamartine, Arles, which he called 'the Yellow House'. In June he set up a studio on the ground floor, and in September, following the death of their Uncle Cent, Theo was able to provide funds for furniture. Vincent moved into a room on the upper storey, and furnished an adjoining guest room.

Vincent made a painting of the building and street and sent Theo a sketch with an accompanying description: the canvas shows 'the house and its surroundings under a sulphur sun, under a pure cobalt sky. That's a really difficult subject! But I want to conquer it for that very reason. Because it's tremendous, these yellow houses in the sunlight and then the incomparable freshness of the blue. All the ground's yellow, too.'[59]

For Vincent, the Yellow House held a significance beyond its role as his personal home and studio: he envisioned it as the headquarters of a future artists' colony in the Midi. Furthermore, yellow and its juxtaposition with blue was replete with spiritual meaning: blue is the colour of the sky; yellow, of the sun. Yellow and blue would dominate not only Vincent's diurnal paintings such as this one, but also nocturnal canvases such as *Café Terrace at Night* (see p. 79). Moreover, Vincent associated yellow with an artist whom he revered: the French Romantic painter Adolphe Monticelli. To his sister Wil he wrote: 'I think of Monticelli terribly often here … Monticelli is a painter who did the south all in yellow, all in orange, all in sulphur.'[60]

Vincent identified the juxtaposition of yellow and blue with another revered artist, one not associated with Provence. In September he wrote to Theo, ecstatically: 'I've never had such good fortune; nature here is *extraordinarily* beautiful. Everything and everywhere. The dome of the sky is a wonderful blue, the sun has a pale sulphur radiance, and it's soft and charming, like the combination of celestial blues and yellows in paintings by Vermeer of Delft.'[61]

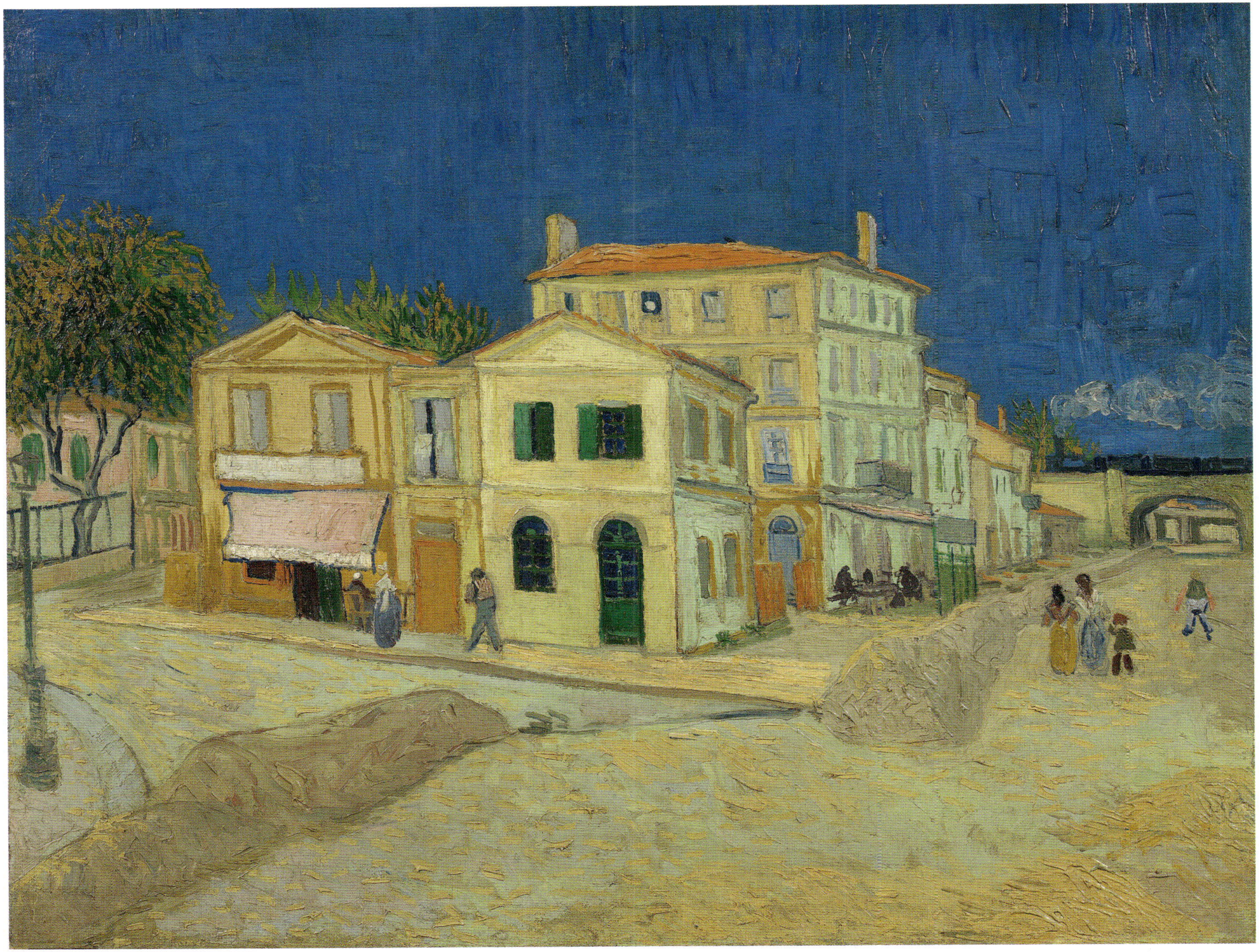

October
1888

BEDROOM IN ARLES

Van Gogh Museum, Amsterdam

Oil on canvas | 72 × 90cm (28⅓ × 36⅖in)

In October 1888, a month after completing *The Night Café* (see p. 77), Vincent made the first of three paintings of his bedroom at the Yellow House. (A year later he would recreate the painting twice: a work of similar dimensions is now at the Art Institute of Chicago, and a smaller version, made for his mother and sister, is at the Musée d'Orsay in Paris.) While the work was in progress, he sent a sketch to Theo, predicting 'It is going to be a contrast to … the night café.'[62] Whereas *The Night Café* expresses 'the terrible passions of humanity by means of red and green,'[63] looking at *Bedroom in Arles* 'ought to rest the brain, or rather the imagination', and its colour is meant to suggest 'rest or … sleep in general'. (In his letter to Theo, Vincent gives a detailed account of the colours of the painting; we know from his descriptions, and from microscopic studies made by conservators, that with the passage of time, there has been some deterioration of the colours, particularly of the red tones. For example, Vincent describes 'a floor of red tiles', 'pale violet' walls and 'scarlet' doors.)

The room is spare and uncluttered, 'cast shadows are suppressed', and the walls and floor are subdued in colour. Unlike the thick impasto that he frequently employs in other works, pigment is here applied 'in free flat tints like the Japanese prints.'[64] To the left of the window on the rear wall is a mirror; to its right is one of Vincent's landscapes; on the right-hand wall are, at the upper level, two of Vincent's portraits, and in the space beneath them are what appear to be Japanese prints. On the bed below is a crimson blanket, the most thickly painted and intensely coloured object in the room, and one that connotes deliverance from the troubles of the day. The orange wood footboard in the foreground, large in scale, dominates the composition.

Although very different in effect from *The Night Café*, the composition of *Bedroom in Arles* is surprisingly similar: a rising diagonal floor in deep perspective leads to an implied space beyond, on the other side of the room – in this case, visible through a window. Yet here the room conveys not an ominous portent, but a reassuring sense of shelter and protection from the exterior world.

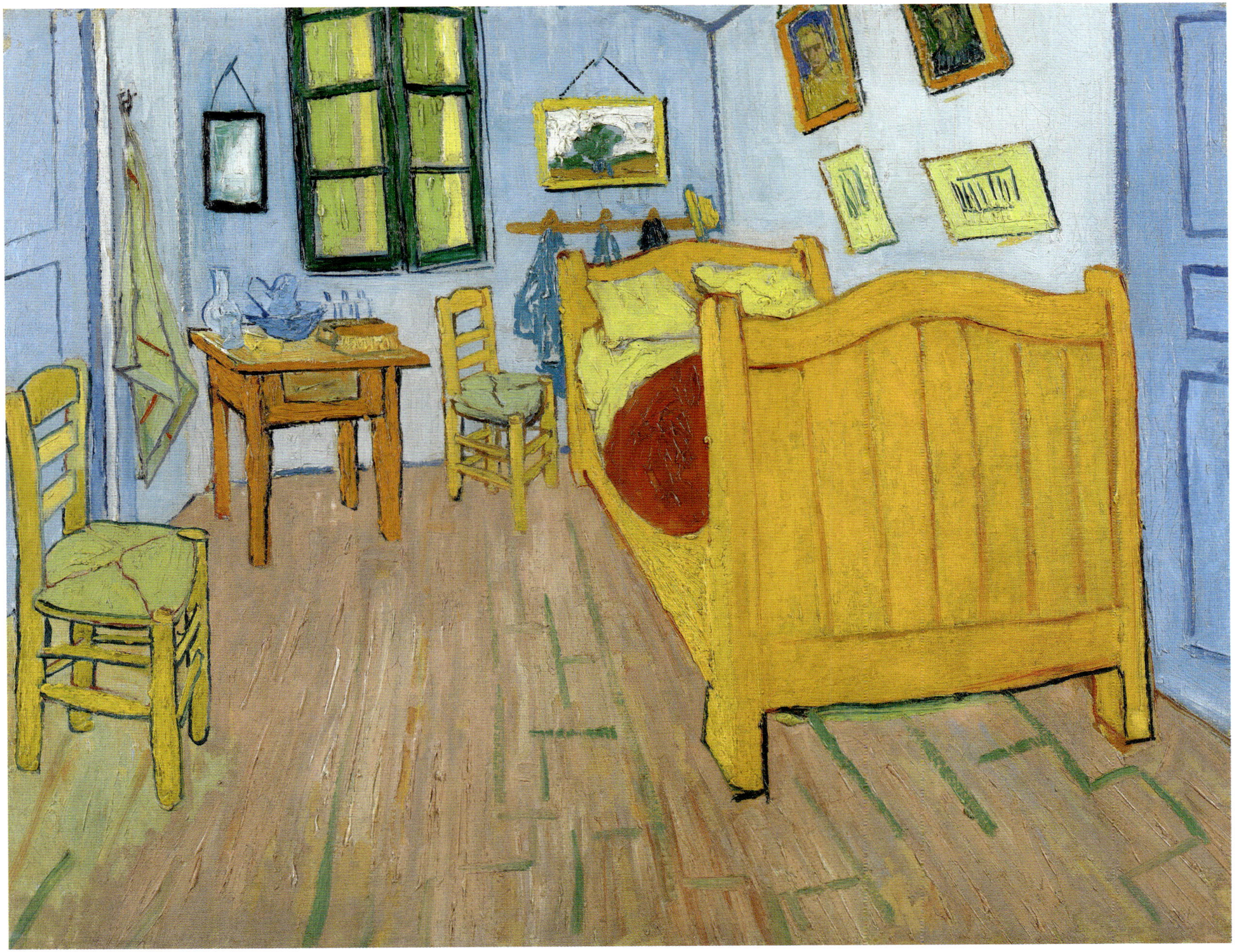

November

1888

VAN GOGH'S CHAIR

National Gallery, London

Oil on canvas | 93 × 73.5cm (36⅝ × 29⅛in)

In September 1888, in anticipation of Gauguin's arrival in Arles, Vincent reported to Theo on his plans for furnishing the Yellow House: 'For putting somebody up, there'll be the prettiest room upstairs, which I'll try to make as nice as possible, like a woman's boudoir, really artistic. Then there'll be my own bedroom, which I'd like to be exceedingly simple, but the furniture square and broad.'[65]

Gauguin arrived in Arles in late October, and by late November Vincent was able to report to Theo: 'It does me enormous good to have such intelligent company as Gauguin's, and to see him work.' Vincent sent his brother an inventory of his own recent output, including 'two studies … a wooden and straw *chair* all yellow on red tiles against a wall (*daytime*). Then Gauguin's armchair, red and green, night effect, on the seat two novels and a candle.'[66]

As Vincent indicates, the two paintings are pendants of one another, with *Gauguin's Chair* (see p. 21) a nocturnal counterpart of the diurnal *Van Gogh's Chair*, shown here. Although they belong to the genre of still life, they are in effect symbolic portraits, with each painting embodying characteristics of the chair's absent occupant. Gauguin's armchair, in flamboyant bentwood of red highlighted in violet, with a green-and-yellow striped seat that interacts with a multi-coloured patterned carpet, projects worldliness and self-confidence.

Vincent's chair is recognizable as one of two in *Bedroom in Arles* (see p. 87). It is an austere peasant's chair, of pale yellow unpolished wood, without armrests, on a floor of plain square tiles. Viewed from an elevated perspective, the grid of the chair's support engages in a visual dialogue with that of the floor below and of the adjacent blue door. On the seat are Vincent's omnipresent pipe and tobacco pouch, a contrast to the worldly books and phallic lighted candle of Gauguin's chair, attended by a lunar circular gas lamp. The two men were contrasts not only in personality but in approaches to art, and were engaged in a dialogue about painting. Van Gogh, like the Impressionists and the Dutch masters, tended to base his works on direct observation of nature, whereas Gauguin and his fellow artists of Pont-Aven tended to synthesize from nature. Vincent realized that he could learn from the Pont-Aven painters and hoped to use Gauguin's visit as an opportunity to pursue that dialogue.

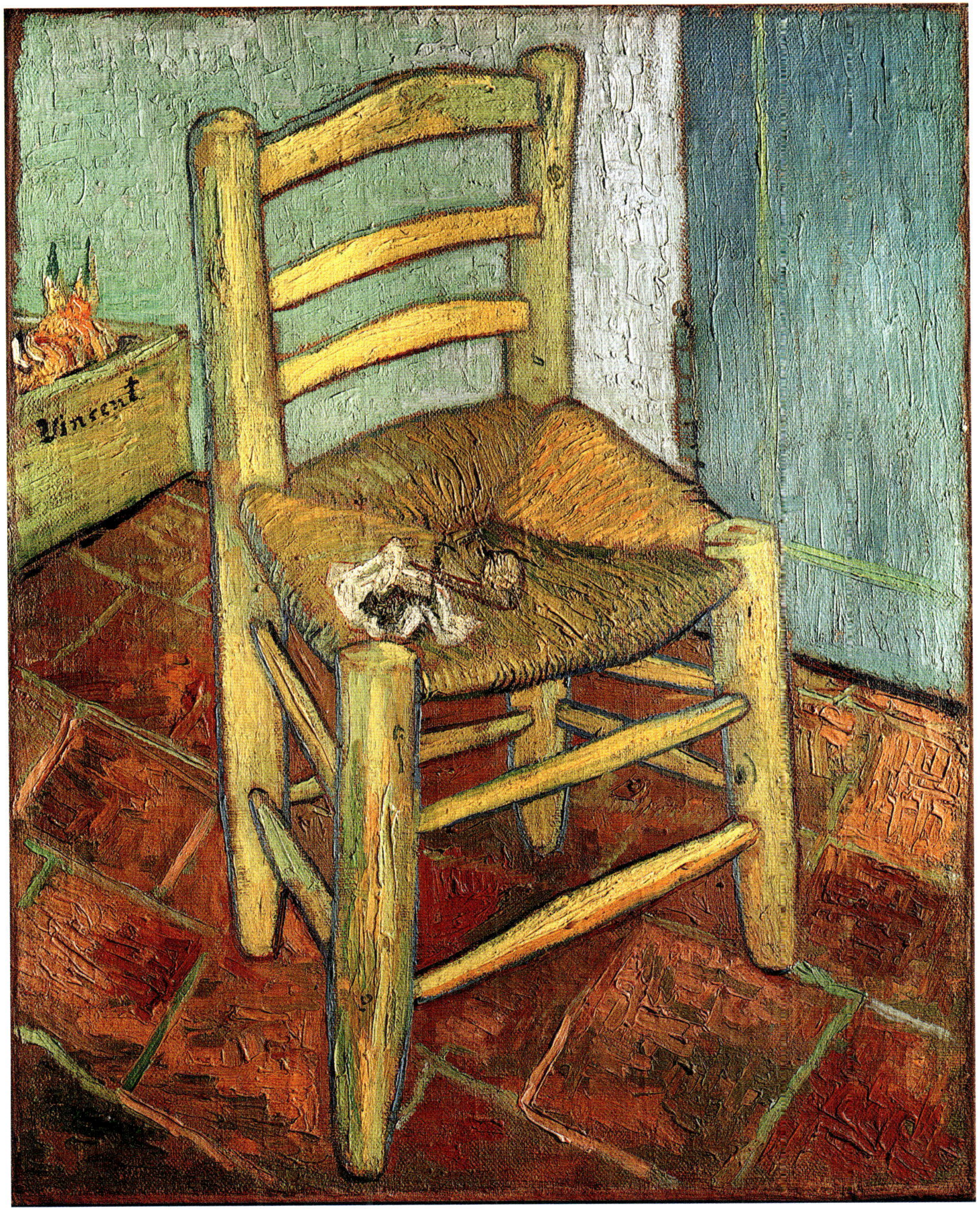
Vincent

December

1888

MADAME ROULIN AND HER BABY

The Metropolitan Museum of Art, New York

Oil on canvas | 63.5 × 51cm (25¼ × 20⅛in)

In the summer of 1888 Augustine Roulin, wife of the Arles postal worker Joseph Roulin, gave birth to their daughter Marcelle. Vincent wrote to his sister Wil, 'I am going to paint a baby in a cradle one of these days. The father … refused to have it baptized – he is an ardent revolutionary – and when the family grumbled, he told them that … he would baptize the child himself.'[67] Vincent's opportunity would come in December, while he was in the midst of a series of portraits of the whole family: Joseph, Augustine, sons Camille and Armand, and the infant Marcelle.

Marcelle is depicted not in a cradle, but in her mother's arms. Madame Roulin has a decidedly subsidiary role in the composition: her presence is cropped by the edge of the pictorial field; her face is depicted mostly in blurry outline, with its skin tone, in colour and texture, resembling the yellow-orange background. Her eyes meet neither the viewer's, nor those of her child. Her most prominent features are her large hands – ungainly at left, expressive at right – that lovingly support Marcelle, hold her upright, and display her for our contemplation.

Marcelle has not been idealized. Perhaps Vincent sees something of himself in the infant, displaying empathy for her awkwardness, and for her wide-eyed wonder at a world in which all things are new. Her head and upper arms are outlined in black, as if to steady the child, who in all likelihood would have held this position for only a few brief seconds. Her face, vividly modelled in white, red and green is, along with her mother's hands, the most three-dimensional feature of the painting. Her cap and garment, in white and pastel tones of green, is counterpart to her mother's deep green dress. The asymmetrical quality of her face is emphasized by its black outline and by the red-and-green complementaries of her cheeks. Her shoulders are raised, and each of her hands is diagonally posed in relation to one of her mother's. The relatively limited range of colour in the painting emphasizes harmonies of orange and green, with the child brought into prominence by her white-and-green attire.

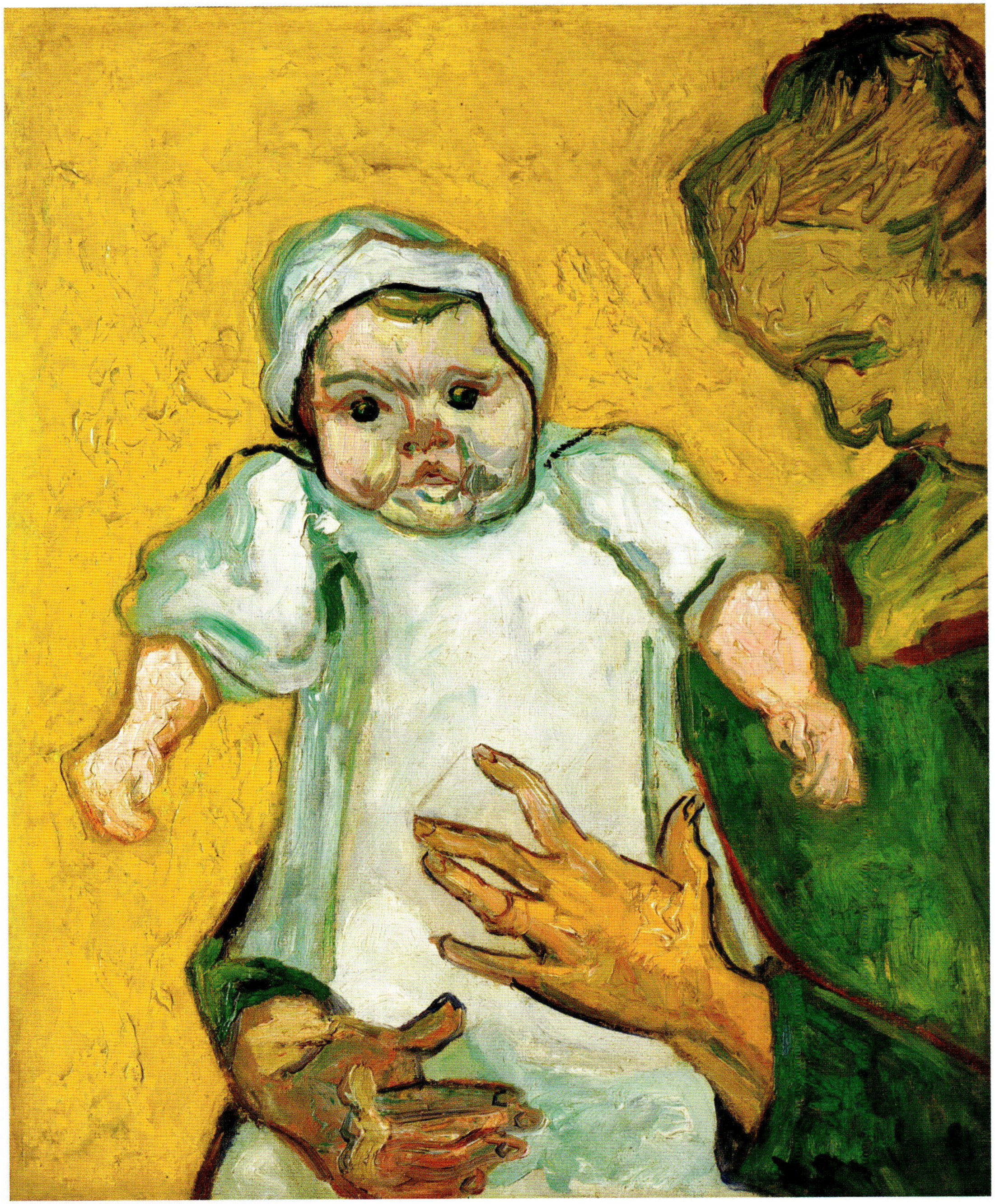

December
– January
1888-9

L'ARLÉSIENNE: MADAME JOSEPH-MICHEL GINOUX

The Metropolitan Museum of Art, New York

Oil on canvas | 90 × 72cm (35⅜ × 28⅜in)

In November 1888 Vincent wrote to Theo, 'I have an Arlésienne at last, a figure … knocked off in *one* hour, background pale lemon – the face grey – the clothing dark dark dark, just unmixed Prussian blue. She's leaning on a green table and is sitting in a wooden armchair – coloured orange.'[68] The Arlésienne was Marie Ginoux, wife of Joseph Ginoux, the proprietor of the Café de la Gare who appears in *The Night Café* (see p. 77) as a white-clad figure standing by the billiard table. Vincent was describing to Theo the first version of the portrait, now at the Musée d'Orsay in Paris. The second version, shown here, which was based on the original painting rather than on the sitter, was rendered with more deliberation and less spontaneity.[69] The Paris portrait also differs from its New York counterpart in that there are a pair of gloves and a folded umbrella on the table instead of an arrangement of books.

Both versions of Vincent's portrait of Mme Ginoux coincided with Gauguin's stay in Arles – indeed, in the course of his visit to the town, Gauguin would himself make several portraits of Mme Ginoux.[70] In works such as *L'Arlésienne*, he assimilated stylistic characteristics of the art of Gauguin, Bernard and their colleagues in Pont-Aven – sharp outlines, brilliant colours, and simplified, unmodelled forms. While he may have done so to attract the artists he wanted to join him, the evolution in his style benefited his own art.

Mme Ginoux is shown in a contemplative state, in three-quarter view, her cheek resting on her hand. There is an open book before her, but she does not look down; her gaze is directed inward, rather than outward. The crisply silhouetted figure, dressed and coiffed in deep blue, is set against a luminous yellow background. Pages of the books are of a light blue which matches the shawl, while the book covers are of a vermilion seen again in her shawl, face and chair. The intensity of colour contrasts and of light and dark tones suggest a depth of feeling beneath her tranquil demeanour.

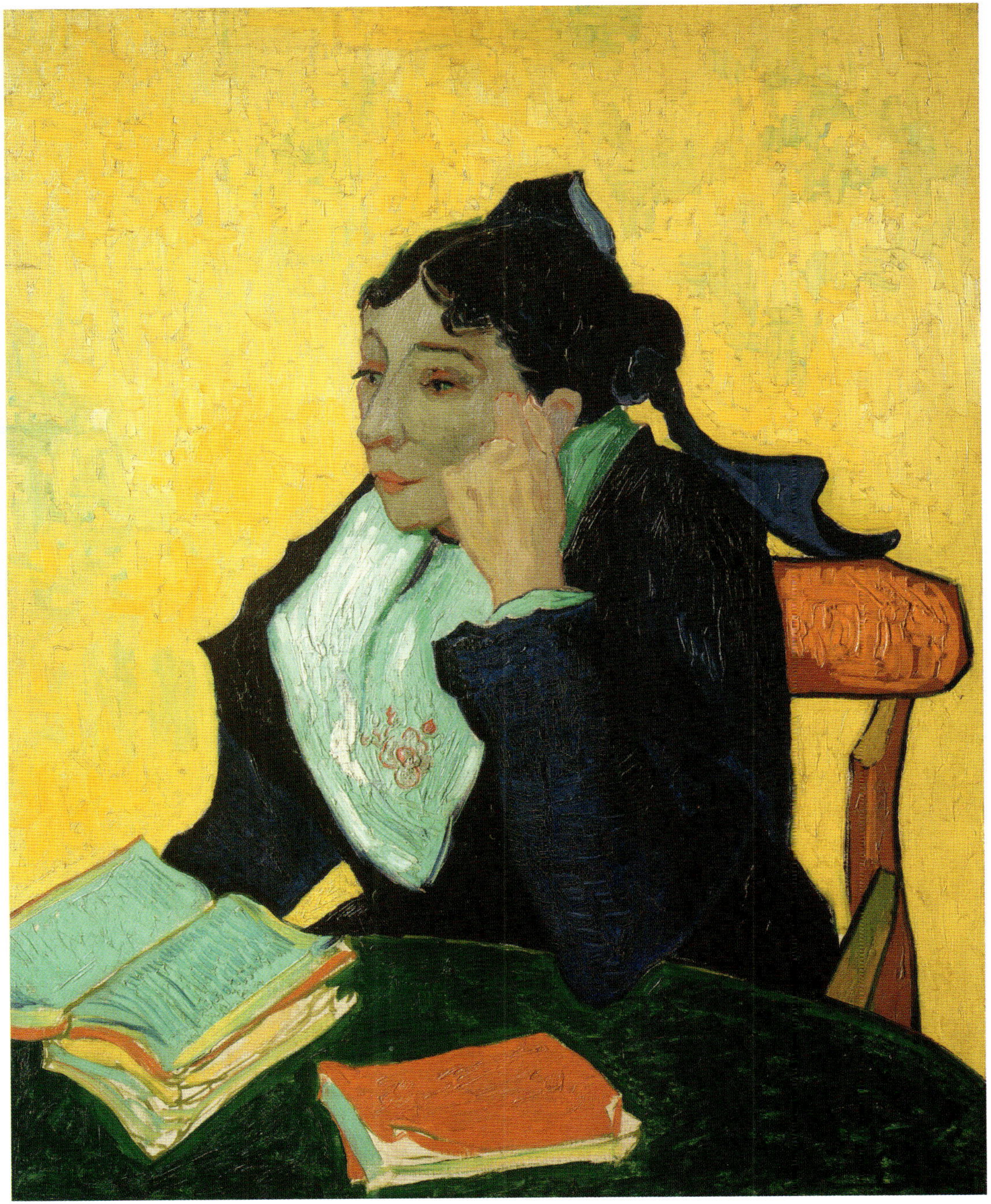

January
1889

SELF-PORTRAIT WITH BANDAGED EAR

Courtauld Gallery, London

Oil on canvas | 60 × 49cm (23⅝ × 19¼in)

Vincent's dreams of an artist's colony in Arles were shattered in December 1888. Following Gauguin's arrival on 23 October, he and Vincent lived and worked together for nine weeks. On 23 December, following a quarrel with Gauguin, Vincent underwent a violent and delusional episode in which he severed part of his own left ear. The following day he was hospitalized at the Hôtel Dieu in Arles, and although his condition was initially considered critical, by 7 January he was sufficiently recovered to return to the Yellow House. By that time Gauguin had summoned Theo to Arles, but both had departed for Paris on 26 December.

Vincent was soon back at work, where his output included two self-portraits.[71] In the painting shown here, the artist is presented in his studio, his face and upper body at three-quarter view, his gaze fixed outward. Although the bandage appears to cover his right ear, the artist has depicted himself in mirror image. The picture on the background wall, however – a Japanese woodblock print by Taiyensai Yoshimaru of geishas and a crane in a landscape before Mount Fuji (c.1870–80) – has not been reversed, although the arrangement of figures has been moved to the right in the print's composition in order to accommodate the contour of the artist's face. Vincent is bundled up for winter in a blue-and-black fur hat and green woollen overcoat, which suggests, along with his determined expression, rosy complexion, and clear blue eyes, a desire to return to physical and mental health.

Notwithstanding the tragic dimension of Vincent's current situation, the painting appears almost celebratory, its clear reds, greens and blues – unlike the muted, tragic colours of *The Night Café* (see p. 77) – evoking the holiday season. The composition is made up of interactions of rectangles and triangles, with an emphasis on upward motion: the rectangles of the studio door and its panels; the rectangular shapes of the Yoshimaru print at the right and of the blank canvas on the left; the triangles of the artist's head and of his upper body, of the easel at the left and of the mountain and fan of the print; the upward motion of the forklike shape of the easel; the upward gazes of the geishas; and the upward thrusts of their triangular group formation, of one geisha's fan and of Mount Fuji.

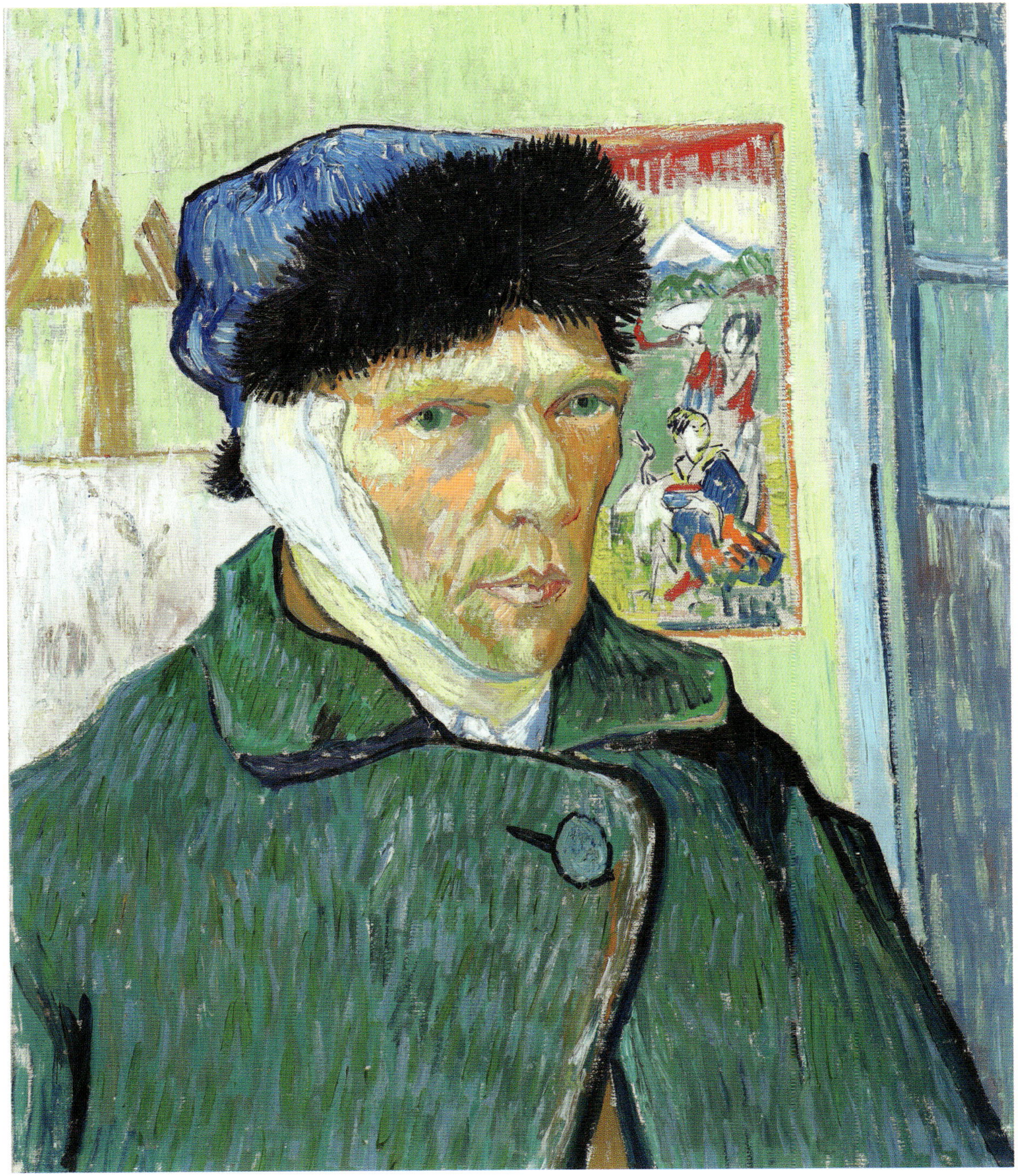

Late January
1889

PORTRAIT OF JOSEPH ROULIN

The Museum of Modern Art, New York

Oil on canvas | 64 × 54.5cm (25¼ × 21½in)

Between July 1888 and April 1889, Vincent painted six portraits of Joseph Roulin. He referred to Roulin as 'the postman', and invariably depicted him in uniform. Roulin was not in fact a letter carrier, but the *entreposeur des postes* – the official in charge of sorting the mail – at the Arles railway station.

'I am now at work with another model,' Vincent wrote to Theo in July, 'a postman in a blue uniform trimmed with gold, a big bearded face, very like Socrates. A violent republican, like Tanguy. A man more interesting than most.'[72] At this time he painted two portraits of Roulin: seated, at three-quarter length (Museum of Fine Arts, Boston), and a head-and-shoulders version (Detroit Institute of Arts), each set against a solid light blue background. In November and December he completed portraits of Roulin's family (see *Madame Roulin and Her Baby*, p. 91), including a third portrait of the postman – also head and shoulders, but against a solid yellow background (Kunstmuseum Winterthur, Switzerland).

In late December, in the midst of his work on *La Berceuse,* a portrait of Augustine Roulin (see p. 99), Vincent had a mental breakdown that included the mutilation of his left ear. Roulin visited him at the local hospital, consulted with Theo, intervened with authorities on his behalf, and accompanied him back to the Yellow House upon his release. In late January, Roulin was transferred to Marseilles, returning to Arles intermittently. After his departure, Vincent completed three more portraits of him, copied from earlier portraits and done in tandem with the five versions of *La Berceuse*.[73]

In April Vincent wrote to Theo: 'Yesterday … Roulin came to see me … He often has to carry loads you would call very heavy, but … he has the strong constitution of the peasant … He … has a … tenderness for me such as an old soldier might have for a young one.'[74]

In the portrait shown here, the artist employs short brushstrokes of light-filled colour. The pink and yellow of the postman's face have their counterparts in the flowers of the wallpaper design in the background, the highlights of his beard, and the buttons of his coat. This benign, nurturing father figure is a counterpart to his wife, *La Berceuse*. The flowers, leaves and arabesques behind him – along with his dynamic, swirling beard – emit protective, natural energy.

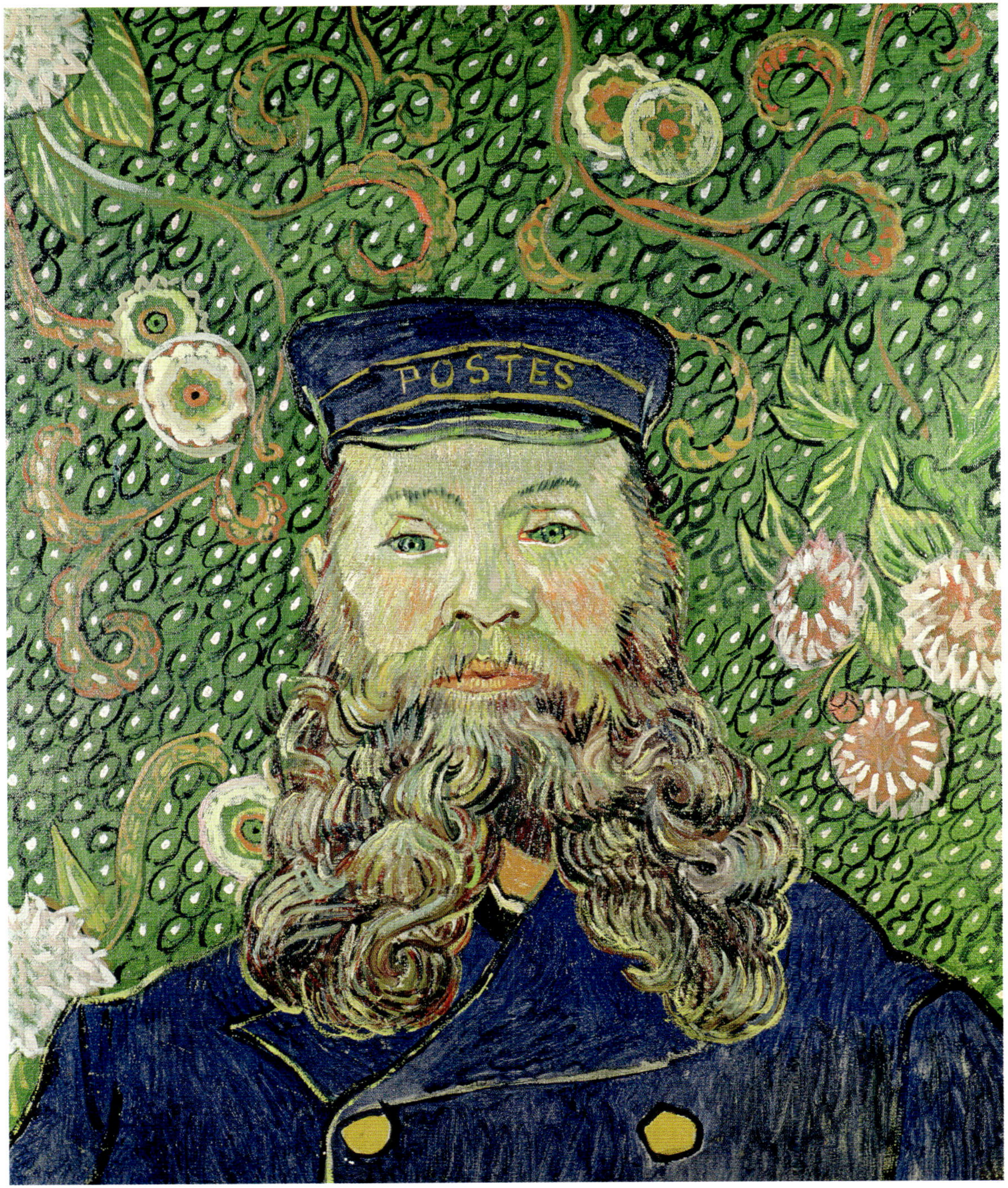
POSTES

January
– February
1889

LA BERCEUSE

The Metropolitan Museum of Art, New York

Oil on canvas | 92.7 × 73.7cm (36½ × 29in)

La Berceuse ('lullaby') is a portrait of Augustine Roulin, wife of the postman Joseph Roulin. The rope she holds leads to a cradle, unseen to the viewer, holding her infant child. Mme Roulin is attired in a dark green bodice and emerald-green skirt, which is set against a brilliant vermilion floor. In contrast to the flattened colour of her upper and lower body and of the lower background, her face and hair are modelled in visible brushstrokes of yellow, orange, red, green and blue. The dynamic wallpaper designs of flowers, leaves, stems, dots and arabesques play a symbolic role in the picture: they seem to radiate from Mme Roulin, embodying forces of fertility and vital energy.

Vincent did five versions of the painting.[75] The first of these was begun in December 1888; work on it was suspended during his mental breakdown. He resumed work on the painting in January 1889, and between January and February, during the course of his recovery, completed four additional versions. The one shown here, said to be his favourite,[76] was chosen by Augustine Roulin for her personal collection. On 25 May, Vincent sent a letter to Theo with a sketch of *La Berceuse*, depicting his conception of the painting as the central panel of a triptych, with panels of sunflowers on either side.[77] For Vincent, *La Berceuse* would provide comfort to troubled souls, as a lullaby soothes a child.

In a letter to Gauguin, Vincent described the colour in the picture: 'As an arrangement of colours: the reds moving through to pure oranges, intensifying even more in the flesh tones up to the chromes, passing into the pinks and marrying with the olive and Veronese greens.' Referencing Pierre Loti's novel *An Iceland Fisherman* (1886), Vincent added, 'If one placed this canvas … in a boat … of Icelandic fishermen … some … would feel the lullaby in it. Ah! my dear friend, to make of painting what the music of Berlioz and Wagner has been before us … a consolatory art for distressed hearts!'[78]

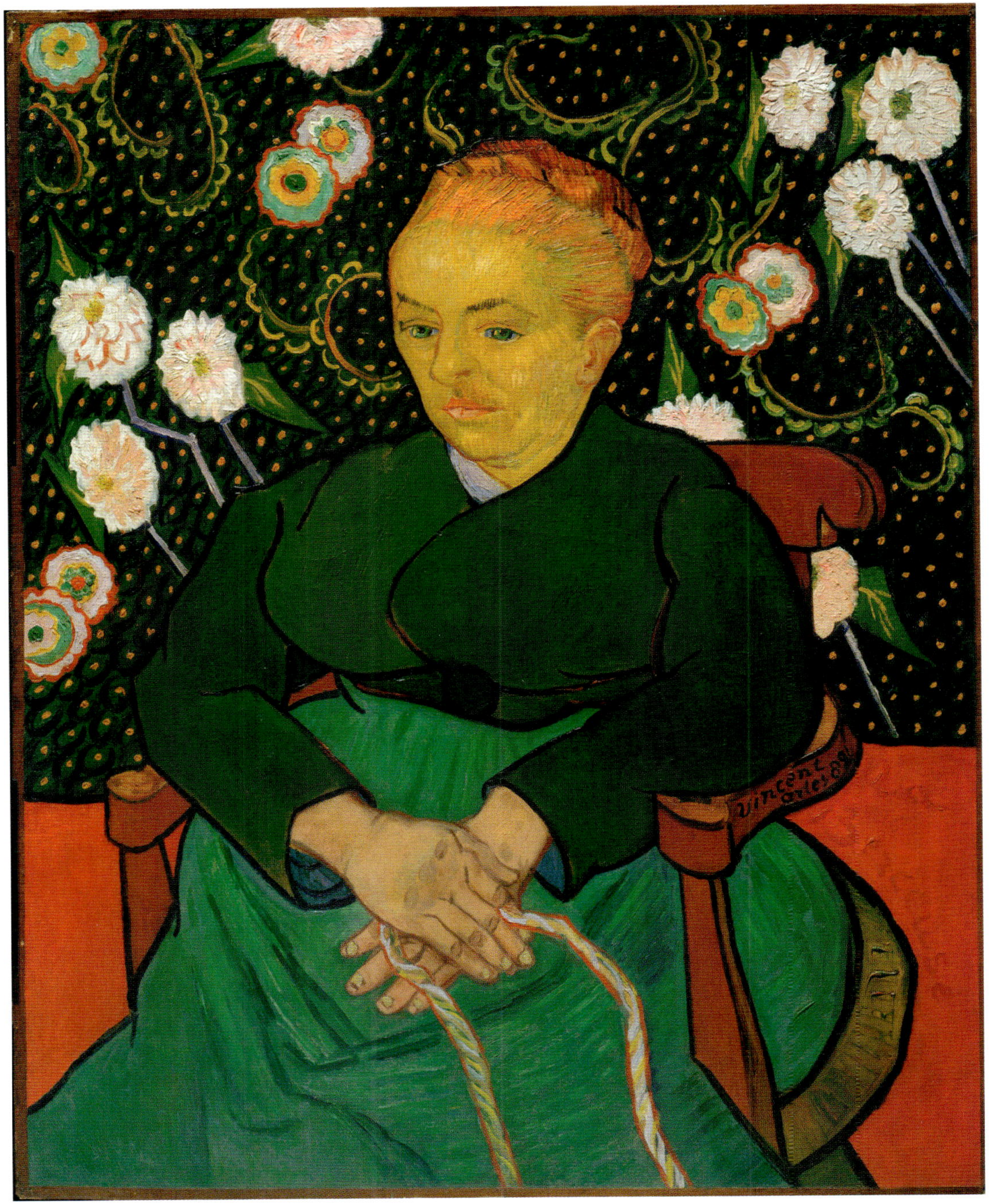

April
1889

PEACH TREES IN BLOSSOM

Courtauld Gallery, London

Oil on canvas | 65.5 × 81.5cm (26 × 32¼in)

For *Peach Trees in Blossom* of April 1889, Vincent returned to the plain of La Crau, which lies between the river Rhône and the Alpilles mountains; this had been the site of *The Harvest*, painted in June of the previous year (see p. 61). In a letter to Paul Signac, he included a sketch of the new painting, accompanied by a description of a 'countryside with little cottages, blue line of the Alpilles, white and blue sky. The foreground, enclosures with reed hedges where little peach trees are in blossom – everything there is *small*, the gardens, the fields … the trees, even those mountains, as in certain Japanese landscapes, that's why this subject attracted me.'[79]

As Cornelia Homburg notes, 'By characterizing the smallness of objects in his landscape as Japanese, Van Gogh alluded to the frequent descriptions of the delicate nature and miniature size of gardens in Japan and its art.'[80] The field of blossoming trees and the snow-capped mountain at the upper right of the composition evoke colour woodcuts such as those by Katsushika Hokusai (1760–1849).

The Japanese character of the landscape is enhanced by the oblique angle of vision, which emphasizes diagonals in the foreground and middle ground. By comparison, *The Harvest* is frontal and panoramic, in the mode of seventeenth-century Dutch landscapes. Whereas in *The Harvest* the blue wagon and the figure working in the field are central and prominent in the composition, giving emphasis to the fact that this is a working agricultural site, these elements are present but easily overlooked in *Peach Trees in Blossom*. Here, with a lower horizon, the sky – painted in broken Neo-Impressionist brushstrokes of white, blue and violet – plays a prominent role in the composition. The painting is composed of a series of bands, oblique and curving in the lower half, frontal and horizontal in the upper half. Beneath the sky is a register of more tactile mountains and Provençal houses in the manner of Cézanne; below them, clusters of flowering trees in atmospheric Impressionist brushstrokes; then a curving fence that echoes the blossom in its luminosity; and finally a green verge punctuated by a reddish-brown patch of earth, and a foreground of loose multi-coloured brushstrokes in blue, red, green and yellow.

Peach Trees in Blossom was among the last paintings that Vincent created in Arles. With the benefit of hindsight, it may be seen as a farewell to the 'New Japan' and the dream of a community of artists in the south.

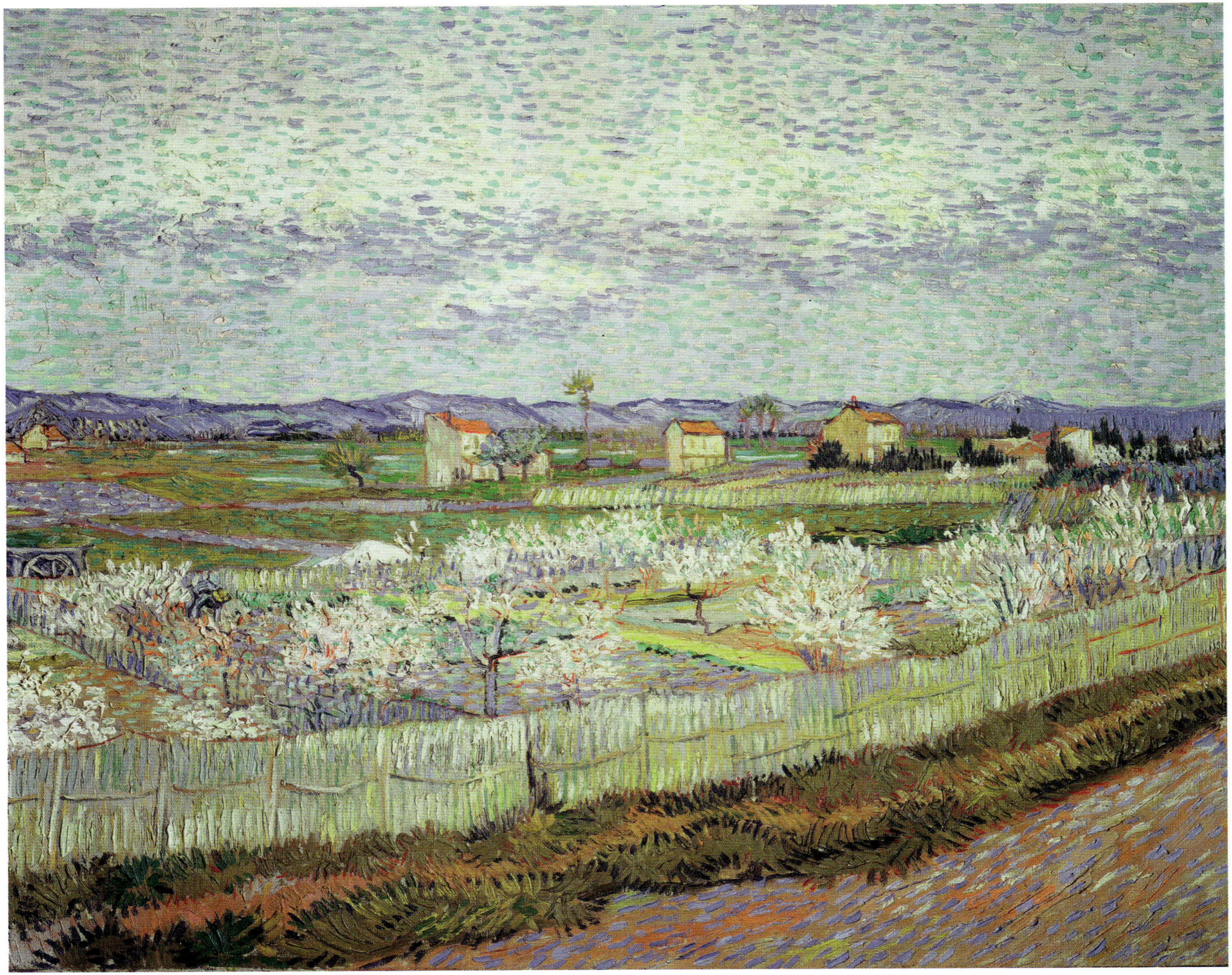

May

1889

IRISES

J. Paul Getty Museum, Los Angeles

Oil on canvas | 71 × 93cm (28 × 36⅝in)

In May 1889, within a week of his admission as a voluntary patient at the Saint-Paul de Mausole mental asylum in Saint-Rémy, Vincent was at work on a painting of irises from a garden in the hospital grounds. It embodies an interval in his life that is a calm before a storm. He was both taking advantage of a time of relative tranquillity in his emotional state, and by means of his diligence, hoping to forestall a future attack. As he would write to Theo: 'I am struggling with all my energy to master my work, thinking that if I succeed, that will be the best lightning-conductor for my illness.'[81]

Depicted from such a low vantage point that there is no visible horizon, the iris flowers, stems and leaves fill nearly the entire composition. The tapestry-like structure of the painting, and the animation of its surface pattern, anticipates the all-over compositions of works such as Claude Monet's *Water Lilies* and Jackson Pollock's Abstract Expressionist canvases.

The canvas is loosely but systematically divided into regions of colour: the animated, spiky green leaves at the centre are bordered above and below by joyously bursting violet and blue flowers; at the lower left is a wedge of textured red-orange ground, while at the upper left is a muted orange and green wedge of leaves and flowers. The painting combines this vivid, luminous colour with the animated linearity of Vincent's drawings. The iris flowers are described with individuality and specificity, with a single white iris in the upper left foreground standing out from all the others. The effect conveys not anxiety but radiance and joy.

There are no preparatory drawings for *Irises*, and Vincent seems to have regarded it as a study rather than a finished work. His brother Theo thought otherwise, and submitted it to the 1889 Salon des Indépendants, along with *Starry Night over the Rhône* (see p. 81). Both paintings were singled out for praise by the critic Félix Fénéon, who designated Vincent 'an amusing colorist' and perceptively noted that his irises 'violently slash into long strips their violet petals on sword-like leaves'.[82]

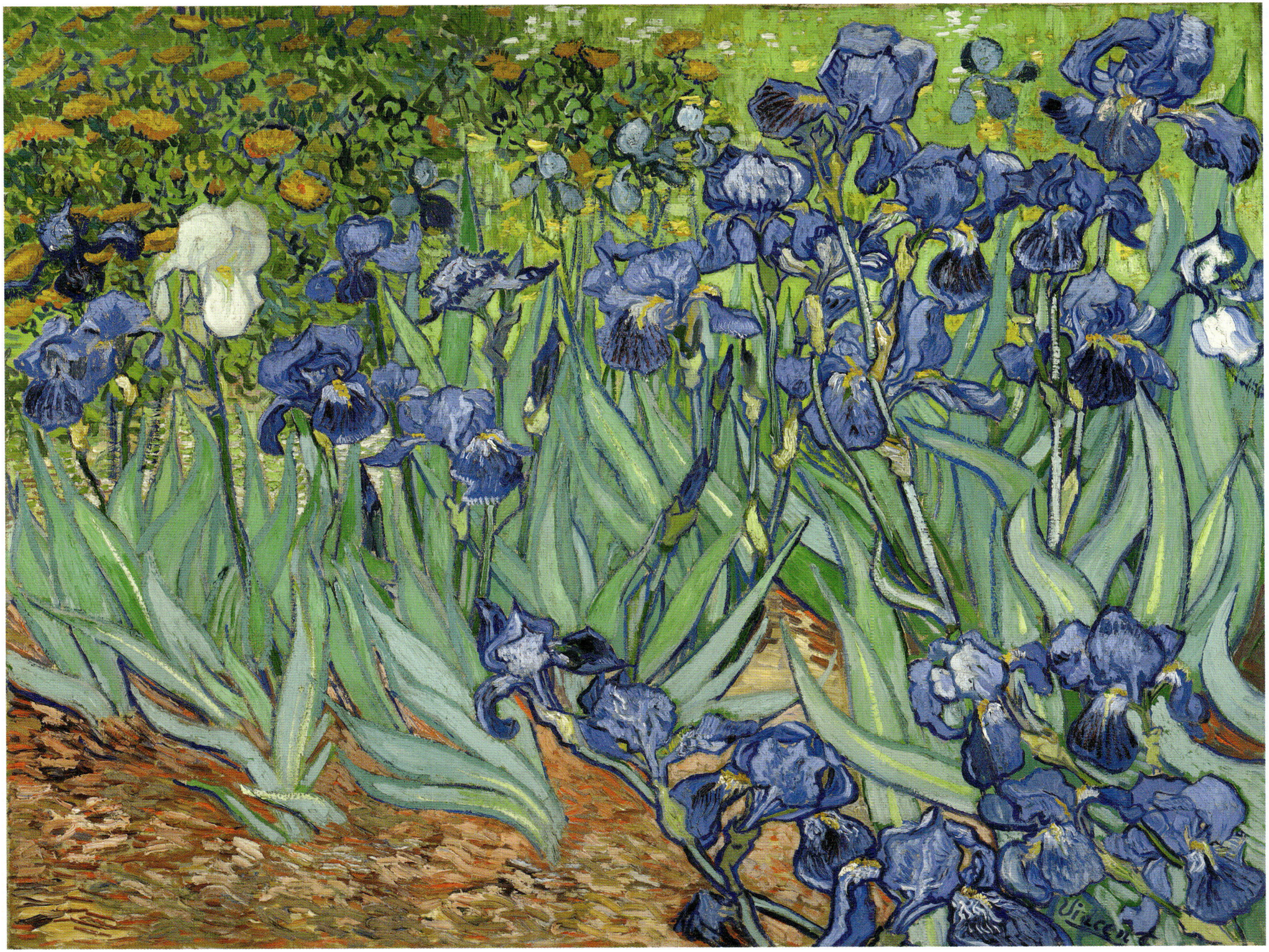

June
1889

THE STARRY NIGHT

The Museum of Modern Art, New York

Oil on canvas | 72.5 × 92cm (29 × 36¼in)

In June 1889, while Vincent was a patient at the asylum in Saint-Rémy, he painted a night landscape with a starry sky, returning to a theme he had explored in Arles in September 1888 (see *Starry Night over the Rhône*, p. 81). His mental and emotional state had changed drastically over the past year, accompanied by the increasing agitation of his pictorial style.

Even before he had created the earlier work, Vincent had told his brother Theo that he was eager to paint 'a starry sky with cypresses'.[83] At the left side of *The Starry Night*, the flame-like forms of cypresses spiral skyward, with the one at the far left seeming to scale the firmament. The night sky teems with cosmic energy: luminous stars of white, yellow and orange, like the waning moon, are surrounded by circles of light; spiralling swirls are echoed by the undulations of the Alpilles mountain range below. A church steeple, like the cypress tree, soars skyward, but the church itself and other buildings of the town, unlike the sky, mountains and trees, are stable and block-like. The town's architecture evokes that of Vincent's native Netherlands more than that of the Provençal town of Saint-Rémy.

The Starry Night is the nocturnal counterpart of *The Olive Trees* (see p. 107); the two works were both painted in June 1889. Both present an agitated, turbulent view of nature which reflected the artist's spiritual and emotional crisis at the time, but his methods in creating the two works were quite different. *The Olive Trees*, like *Starry Night over the Rhône* of the previous year, was painted *en plein air*, and based on direct observation, a method that Vincent had always favoured. *The Starry Night*, by necessity, was created via a more synthetic process. Vincent had a magnificent view of the night sky from the barred windows of his bedroom at the asylum, but he was not permitted to paint from his room, only to sketch. As a consequence, *The Starry Night* has more in common with paintings by his Post-Impressionist colleagues Paul Gauguin and Émile Bernard, who worked primarily from imagination, than with those of his Impressionist forebears.

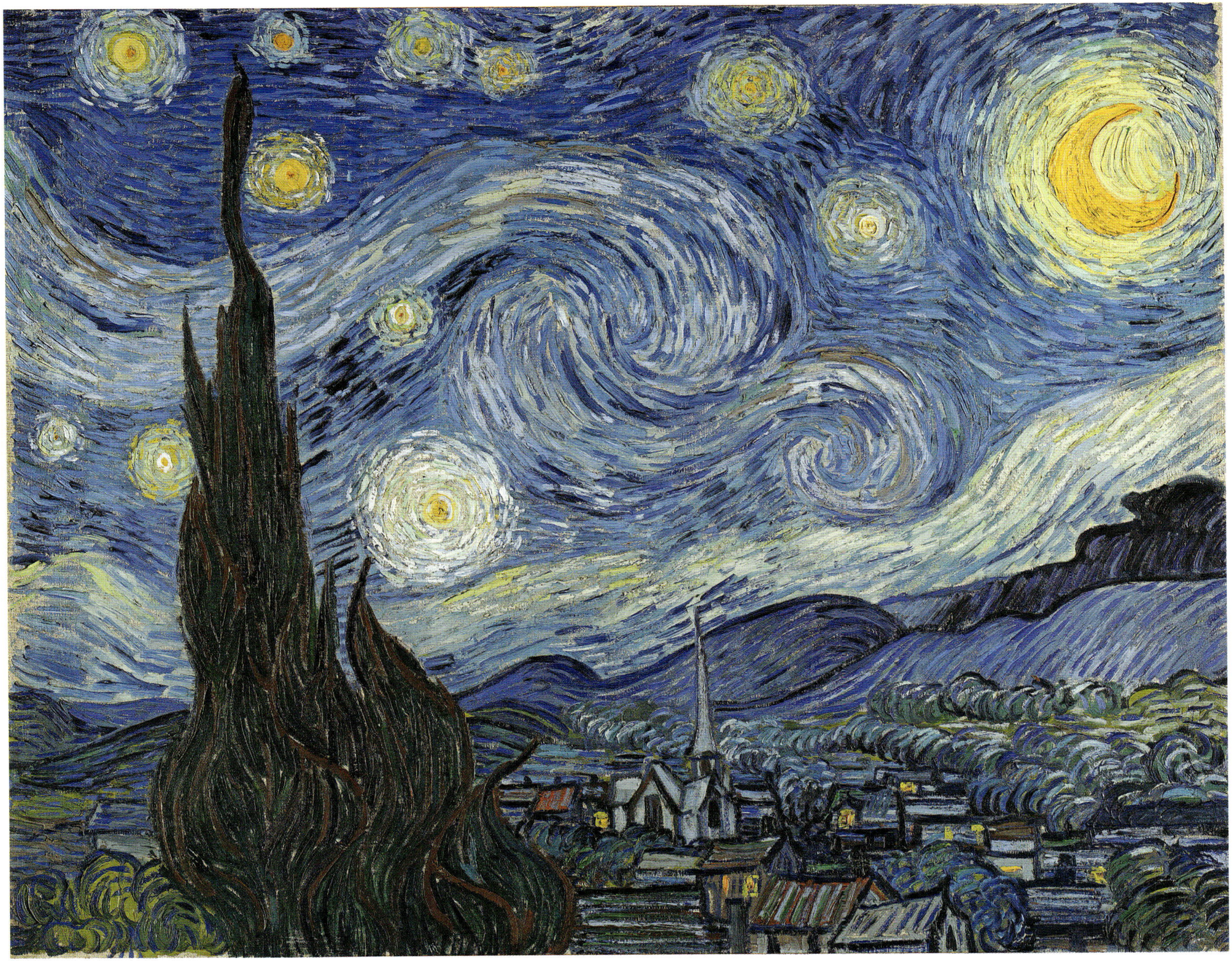

June
1889

THE OLIVE TREES

The Museum of Modern Art, New York

Oil on canvas | 72.6 × 91.4cm (28½ × 36in)

The critic Roger Fry would later comment on the increasing agitation of Van Gogh's paintings made during 1889, the first four months of which the artist spent in Arles before entering the Saint-Paul de Mausole mental asylum in Saint-Rémy, where he stayed for a year as a voluntary patient. On the occasion of a posthumous solo exhibition of his work in London in 1923, Fry observed: 'The rhythm becomes more rapid and more undulating, and all the forms tend to be swept together into a vortex of rapid brushstrokes.'[84] This is an apt description of two canvases Vincent executed in Saint-Rémy, which he seems to have conceived in tandem: *The Olive Trees* and its nocturnal counterpart *Starry Night* (see p. 105). In June 1889 Vincent reported to his brother Theo: 'At last I have a landscape with olive trees and also a new study of a starry sky.'[85] In September he informed Theo that both paintings 'are exaggerations from the point of view of the arrangement, their lines are contorted like those of the ancient woodcuts … [In *The Olive Trees*] I tried to express the time of day when one sees the green beetles and the cicadas flying in the heat.'[86]

The composition comprises four dynamic horizontal zones. The rolling arabesques of the Alpilles mountain range, in tones of blue and blue-black, are bracketed at left and right by the silhouettes of natural formations: at left, Les Deux Trous ('the two holes'); at right, Mont Gaussier. Beneath the hills are the vibrant trunks, branches and leaves of olive groves, in coils of light and dark green. The ground below, in swirling brushstrokes of blue, white, yellow and green, is as turbulent as a stormy sea. Above is a pale blue sky with a giant anthropomorphic maternal cloud, its contours visually rhyming with the mountain summits, presiding over all, including a smaller cloud in its wake. All of nature is in motion, and all of its elements reflect Vincent's intensified spiritual and emotional state.

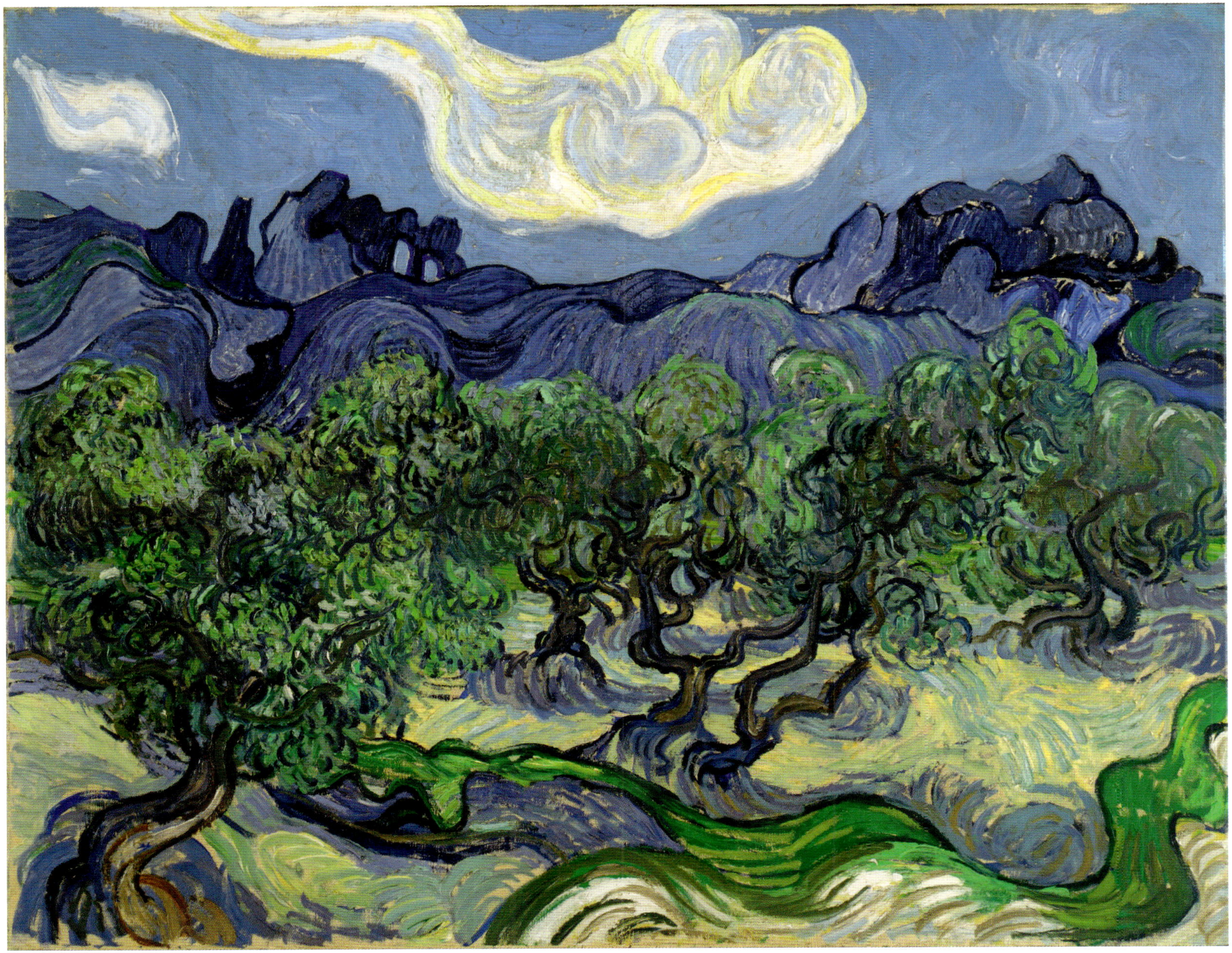

September
1889

A WHEATFIELD WITH CYPRESSES

National Gallery, London

Oil on canvas | 72.5 × 91.5cm (28½ × 36¼in)

Notwithstanding intervals of intense suffering and disorientation, Vincent's year at the Saint-Paul de Mausole asylum was a productive period in his life as an artist; during his confinement he completed more than 140 paintings, among them some of his greatest works. From the barred windows of his bedroom and studio he could look out over the vineyards, olive groves and wheatfields of the Provençal landscape, and he was allowed to paint within the asylum gardens; from time to time he could even go into the surrounding fields, provided he was accompanied by a member of the asylum staff.

In June 1889 Vincent wrote to his brother Theo: 'The cypresses are always occupying my thoughts … [They are] as beautiful in line and proportion as an Egyptian obelisk. And the green has a quality of such distinction. It is a splash of black in a sunny landscape.'[87] Between July and September he painted three versions of *A Wheatfield with Cypresses*. The first version (The Metropolitan Museum of Art, New York) was painted *en plein air* in July. In September, after an interval in which he suffered a mental breakdown, he painted the version illustrated here, based on the earlier painting. A third, smaller version, made as a gift for his mother and sister, is now in a private collection.

A Wheatfield with Cypresses is at once classic and dynamic. It is classical in the near symmetry of the composition, the rectangle of the painting bisected by the tilted arc of the horizon. It is dynamic in the turbulent energy of the landscape elements: the swirling, anthropomorphic clouds in tones of blue, white and grey; the rocky blue mountains of the Alpilles, which seem to mimic them; the olive grove at left, its trunks bent and its leaves fluttering in the wind; the contrapuntal field of wheat in luminous yellow, seeming to emanate heat; and the upright spiralling verticals of two adjoining cypresses of dark green, linking earth and sky. At the feet of the cypresses and at the lower right of the picture are beds of corn. The opposition of the cool blue sky and the hot yellow stalks of the wheat field is intensified by the application of paint, with both the sky and the field rendered in thick impasto.

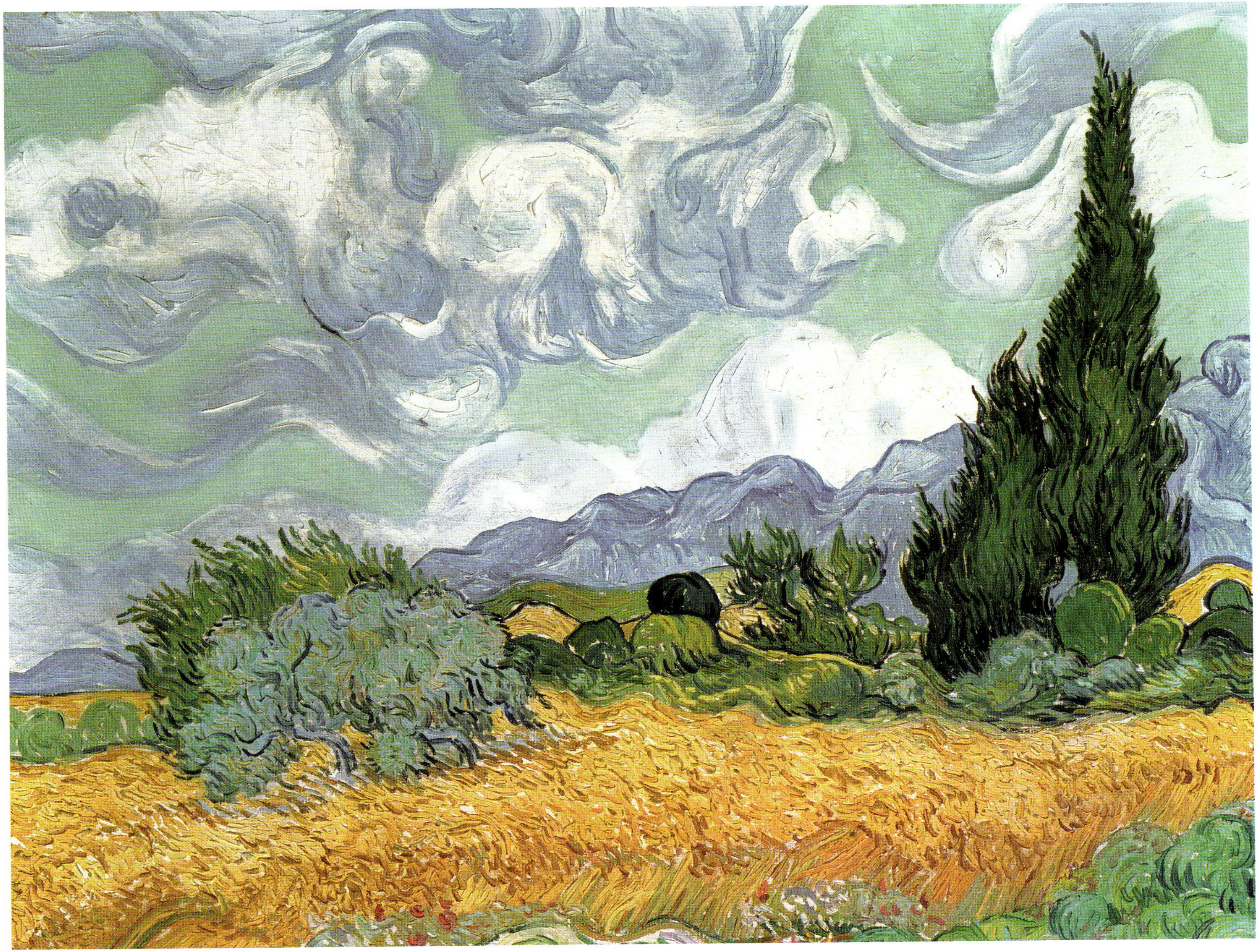

September
1889

SELF-PORTRAIT

Musée d'Orsay, Paris

Oil on canvas | 65 × 54cm (25⅝ × 21¼in)

The paintings and drawings that Vincent created during his year at the Saint-Paul de Mausole asylum frequently express an agitated, turbulent view of reality. The curvilinear rhythms that characterize landscapes such as *The Starry Night* and *The Olive Trees* (see pp. 105 and 107) can likewise be found in his portraits of this period.

From mid-July to late August 1889 Vincent suffered a series of debilitating mental attacks, described by the biographers Naifeh and Smith as 'spells of terrifying hallucinations … followed by faintness, vertigo … and then unconsciousness'.[88] In early September he wrote to Theo, 'I am working on two portraits of myself … One I began the day I got up; I was thin and pale as a ghost … But since then I have begun another one, three-quarter length on a light background.'[89]

In the second self-portrait, shown here, Vincent portrays himself against an abstract background of pale green, white and blue in swirling, undulating patterns comparable to those of the sky in *The Starry Night*. He is attired in his Sunday best, in a white collarless shirt with a pale green shadow, and a jacket and vest rendered in colours and brushstrokes that mimic the background.[90] His hair, beard and eyebrows are depicted in complementary orange, with the brushstrokes of his complexion and coiffure echoing the dynamic surroundings.

The portrait is remarkable for the controlled way with which the artist presents turmoil. He brilliantly conveys his determination to take advantage of his periods of lucidity to do disciplined work as a painter. He is the calm in the eye of the storm: notwithstanding the chaos that surrounds him, he is clear-eyed and focused, his facial expression resolute. 'Now my brain is working in an orderly fashion and I feel perfectly normal,' he reported to Theo, 'I think over my condition now with the hope of … having between the attacks … periods of lucidity and activity … I tell myself that I must not get too used to the idea of being an invalid.'[91]

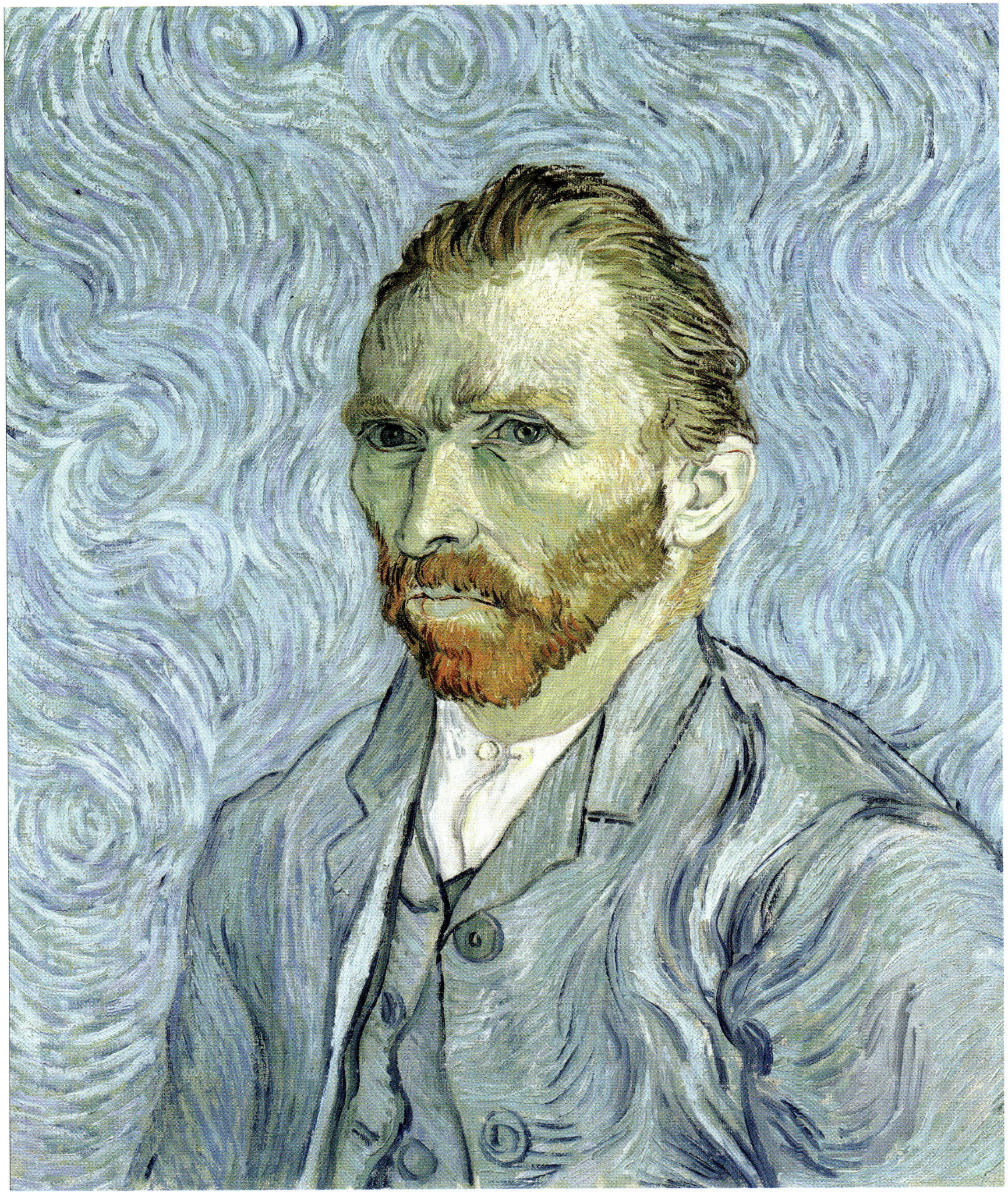

September
1889

NOON: REST FROM WORK (AFTER MILLET)

Musée d'Orsay, Paris

Oil on canvas | 73 × 91cm (28¾ × 35⅞in)

While at the asylum Vincent frequently made copies of works by artists he admired, particularly Delacroix and Millet. This was in part a consequence of his limited opportunities to paint the human figure within the confines of the asylum but was also a function of the spiritual solace he derived from communing with his artistic heroes. His method was to copy black-and-white reproductions of works by established artists and to recreate them in the colours and brushstrokes he had developed in Paris and Arles. He justified this approach by likening himself to a musician who performs not only his own original works but also those of fellow composers.

'We painters are always asked to *compose* ourselves and *be nothing but composers*,' he wrote to Theo. 'But in music it isn't so – and if such a person plays some Beethoven he'll add his personal interpretation to it … and it isn't a hard and fast rule that only the composer plays his own compositions.' Vincent then added, 'Since I'm above all ill at present, I'm trying to do something to console myself, for my own pleasure.'[92]

Noon: Rest from Work is one of a series, *Four Hours of the Day*, which Vincent based on a set of engravings after four pastel drawings by Millet depicting the work cycle of peasants in the fields (see p. 24).[93] Here a couple take a nap after an arduous morning of labour, partly shielded from the noonday sun by a large stack of grain. The man has removed his wooden shoes, which are now in the foreground right, next to a pair of sickles. This still life, as Robert Rosenblum has noted, is an 'emblem of work and rest and of a human pairing that must have been balm to Van Gogh's lonely and troubled spirit'.[94] The couple and the stack of grain in the foreground are likewise paired on the horizon, in full sunlight, with a stack, a wagon and pair of cattle, an arrangement that signifies the tasks awaiting them.

The colour scheme of the painting is based on intense contrasts of blue and complementary yellow-orange. In addition to the saturated blue of the sky there is a range of blues in the garments of the peasants. In contrast to the luminous yellow of the field and stack in the background, the shaded yellow-orange of the foreground is permeated with swirling green and black brushstrokes; the blue sky is similarly animated with pulsating energy. This environmental energy is apparent even in the couple's attire. It is evident that their reprieve from arduous work is only temporary.

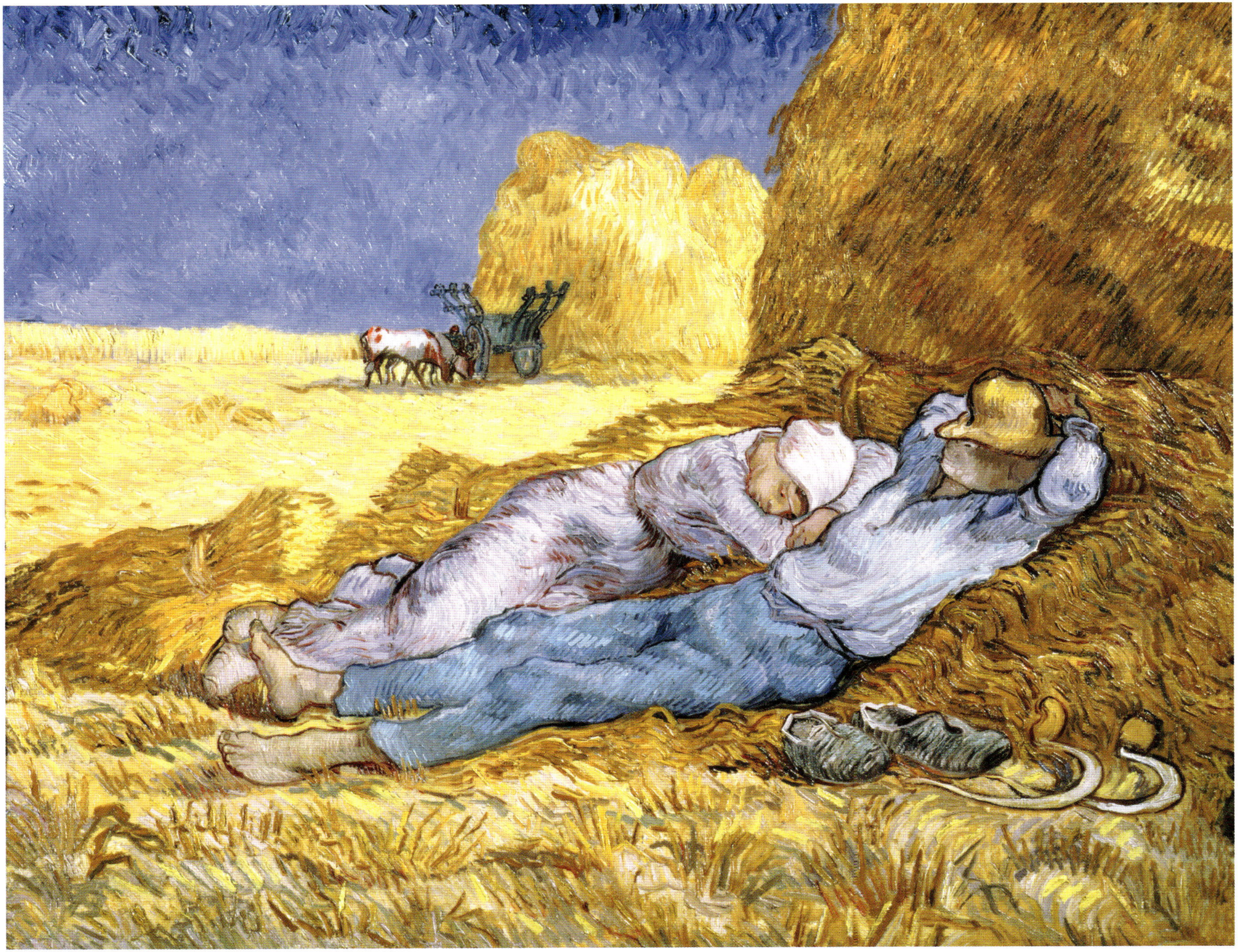

September – October **1889**

CORRIDOR IN THE ASYLUM

The Metropolitan Museum of Art, New York

Oil and black chalk on pink paper | 65 × 49cm (25⅝ × 19¼in)

Soon after Vincent was admitted to the asylum, Theo wrote to him, expressing concern: 'I hope that your stay will only be for a short length of time, for having these mad people as your neighbours can't be agreeable.'[95] 'The *fear* of madness is leaving me to a great extent,' Vincent replied, stoically. 'I see at close quarters those who are affected by it … There's someone here who has been shouting … for a fortnight, he thinks he hears voices and words in the echo of the corridors.'[96]

Corridor in the Asylum is one in a series of three works on paper depicting interiors of the hospital in Saint-Rémy.[83] Vincent does not mention them in his correspondence, and scholars have differed as to their medium and their dates of execution. Although in the earlier literature they were usually described as gouaches, recent scientific examination has established that they were executed with black chalk and thinly applied oil paint. The fact that they were painted in oil rather than gouache lends credence to the theory that they were made in September–October 1889, rather than in May–June as has been suggested; Vincent complained to Theo in October that he had run out of canvas, making painting on paper a necessity, rather than a choice.[98] In these weeks, having just suffered a violent mental attack, Vincent was reluctant to leave the hospital grounds – hence this series.

Although the picture is a fairly accurate description of the ground-floor passageway of the asylum (as is confirmed by photographs), the vision it conveys is of an endless labyrinth from which there is no escape. Colour is rhythmically repeated, with pale blue Romanesque arches, the yellow vault and the red floors, heavily textured with bold brushstrokes; in some places the pink of the paper is allowed to show through. In the background a running man is fleeing, though his flight is clearly doomed to failure. The vision conveyed is of hopelessness and endless despair, personified by the architecture itself.

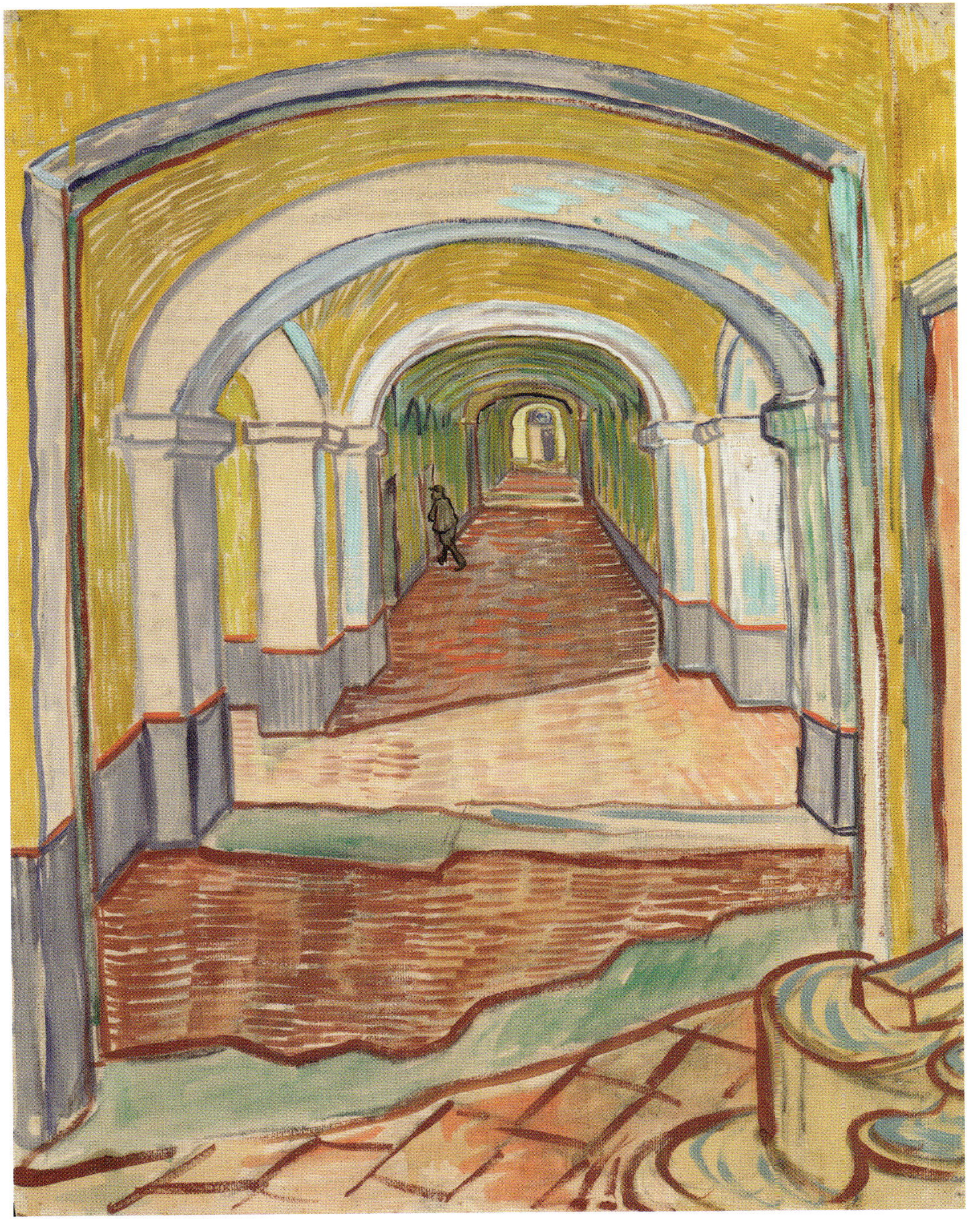

February
1890

ALMOND BLOSSOM

Van Gogh Museum, Amsterdam

Oil on canvas | 73 × 92cm (28¾ × 36¾in)

On 31 January 1890, in Paris, Theo's wife Johanna gave birth to a son. Theo wrote to Vincent in Saint-Rémy: 'How happy I'd be if in a while, when Jo's well again, you'll be able to come and see her and see our little one! As we told you, we'll name him after you, and I'm making the wish that he may be as determined and as courageous as you.'[99]

Vincent, who was just recovering from a mental breakdown, went to work on a large painting that would celebrate the birth of his nephew and namesake. The subject would be rebirth – an almond tree, the first blossom of the season. He described the work in nearly identical terms to both his mother Anna and his sister Wil: 'Large branches of white almond blossom against a blue sky.'[100]

Vincent depicts, in meticulous close-up detail, the upper portion of the tree; the trunk is not shown. The painting appears to have been based on a living tree, not on a still-life arrangement of cut almond blossoms. The artist 'looked up into the tree', as Van Gogh scholar Ronald Pickvance notes. 'This seems confirmed by the gnarled lower horizontal branch that is seen from below.'[101] Each branch and flower is closely observed and depicted in its individuality. The branches are represented three-dimensionally, modelled in light and shadow; they are set against a luminous blue sky, modulated, as Pickvance observes, 'by using two different blues and varying the size and direction of the brushstrokes'.

For this celebratory work, Vincent returned to the optimistic style of the first paintings he made in Provence, 'the Japan of the south'. It evokes Japanese woodcuts in its subject of almond blossom, its rendering of the flowers within firm outlines, and its positioning of them against the picture plane. This affinity with Japanese woodcuts can be seen by comparing the painting with a work from Vincent's collection, now in the Van Gogh Museum, Amsterdam: *Portrait of a Woman* by Utagawa Kunisada (1786–1865), the left wing of the triptych *Three Beauties* (see p. 27). The blossoming branches in the upper region of the print may have been a direct inspiration for Vincent's painting.

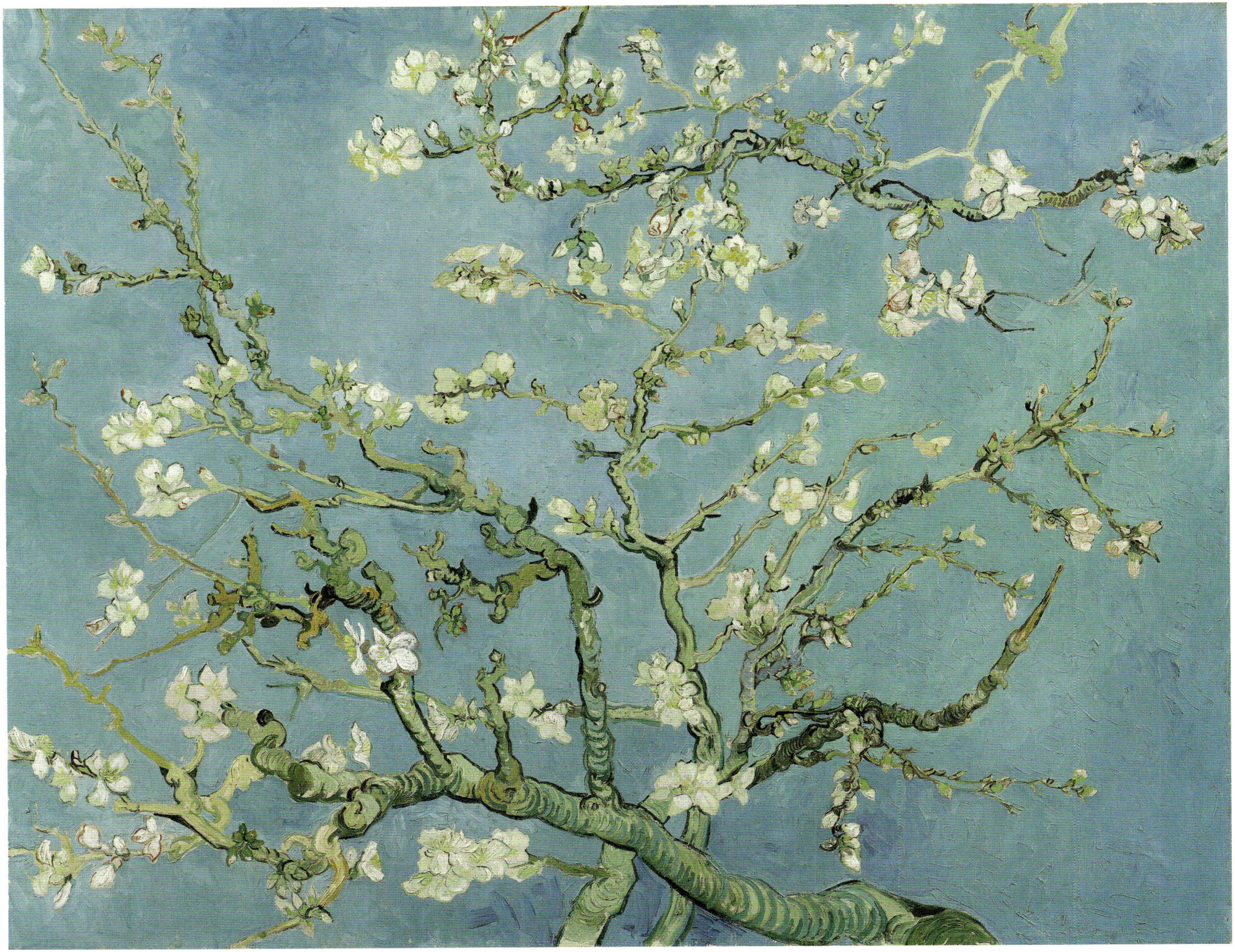

May
1890

SORROWING OLD MAN (AT ETERNITY'S GATE)

Kröller-Müller Museum, Otterlo

Oil on canvas | 81 × 65cm (31⅞ × 25⅝in)

In late February 1890, having temporarily left the hospital grounds for a visit to Arles, Vincent suffered a severe attack of mental illness. He was brought back to the asylum, where it took him two months to recover. Even during this crisis he was able to produce a number of small works – images of Holland – which provided him with some consolation. Finally, in late April, he wrote to Theo: 'What am I to say about these two last months? Things didn't go well at all. I'm sadder and more wretched than I can say … While I was ill I nevertheless still did some little canvases from memory which you will see later, memories of the North.'[102] He requested that Theo send some of his old figure studies, earlier 'memories of the North' for him to copy.

One of the images sent must have been a lithograph that Vincent had made in Holland in 1882, based on his own drawing of the same year, *Worn Out* (see p. 7). The model who had posed for the drawing was a resident of an almshouse in The Hague. A print of the lithograph is inscribed, in English, *At Eternity's Gate,* a title inspired by John Bunyan's seventeenth-century prose allegory *The Pilgrim's Progress,* which invokes a pilgrimage to the Gate of the Celestial City awaiting the poor and the oppressed.[103]

The contours of the painting are relatively faithful to the composition of the lithograph. Forms, however, are more rounded, less angular; space around the figure is enlarged, with the seated old man more distant from the viewer; receding floorboards are introduced. The cobalt blue of his attire is highlighted in light blue and white, and outlined in dark blue contours. His flesh is rendered in yellow-green, as are the chair and floorboards; complementary highlights of red brushstrokes animate the floor, chair and the flames of the fireplace; the background wall is of pale green and complementary violet.

Vincent rarely produced figure paintings and portraits while a resident of the asylum in Saint-Rémy. Given his state of mind when he made this painting – in his words, 'sadder and more wretched than I can say' – it does not take a leap of imagination to see why he chose to recreate this image; yet he seems to allow for redemption at the Gate of the Celestial City. The work may be regarded as a spiritual self-portrait.

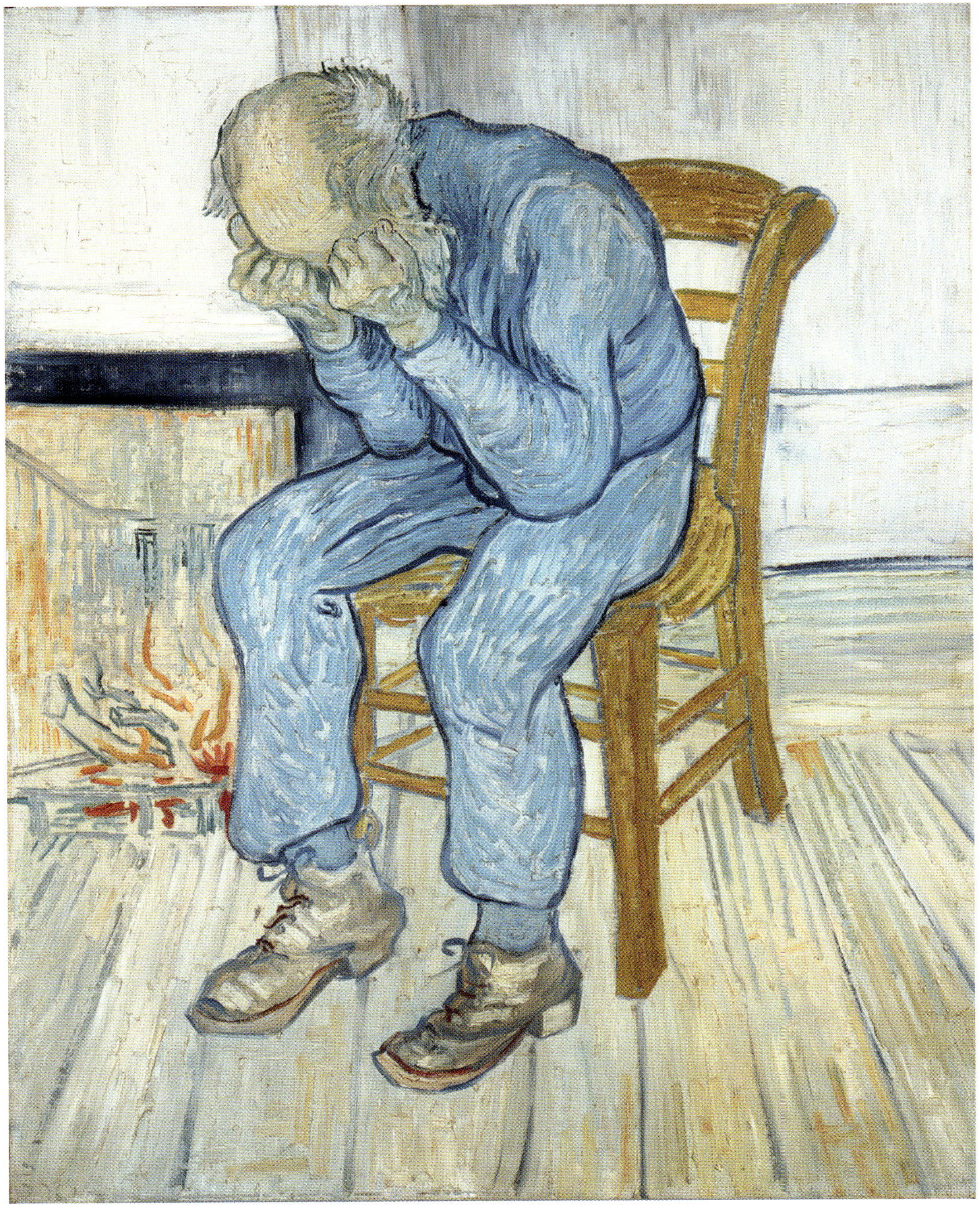

Mid-May
1890

LONG GRASS WITH BUTTERFLIES

National Gallery, London

Oil on canvas | 64.5 × 81cm (25½ × 31⅞in)

In early May 1890, during his final days of confinement in the asylum at Saint-Rémy, Vincent was desperate to leave. 'My surroundings here begin to weigh on me more than I can say,' he lamented to Theo. 'My word, I have been patient for more than a year – I need air, I feel overwhelmed with boredom and grief.'[104]

Work was his salvation. He painted a view of the asylum garden. 'As soon as I got into the park,' he reported, 'I got back all my lucidity for work; I have more ideas in my head than I could ever carry out, but without it clouding my mind. The brush strokes come like clockwork.'[105]

Vincent had first encountered the garden a year earlier, soon after his arrival in the asylum, and was immediately drawn to it. 'Since I have been here,' he had reported to Theo, 'the deserted garden, planted with large pines beneath which the grass grows tall and unkempt and mixed with various weeds, has sufficed for my work, and I have not yet gone outside.'[106] Perhaps the paradox of the walled garden – free, yet confined – was part of its initial attraction: it reflected Vincent's ambivalence about art-making under the restricted conditions of the asylum of Saint-Paul de Mausole.

As Martin Bailey observes, the composition of *Long Grass with Butterflies* 'has a claustrophobic feel'. This is somewhat mitigated, Bailey concedes, by the path in the upper left corner and the row of tree trunks to its right, details which 'succeed in giving a sense of three-dimensional space to the picture'.[107]

The artist is looking down on a sea of grass of light and dark green, highlighted in short brushstrokes of white, yellow and ochre, with floral touches in orange and violet, and punctuated with fluttering white butterflies. In a series of paintings in Arles and Saint-Rémy, with works such as this, as well as *Irises* and *Almond Blossom* (see pp. 103 and 117), and culminating in *Tree Roots* (see p. 133), Vincent was developing a visual language of all-over composition which anticipates tendencies in the abstract art of the twentieth century.

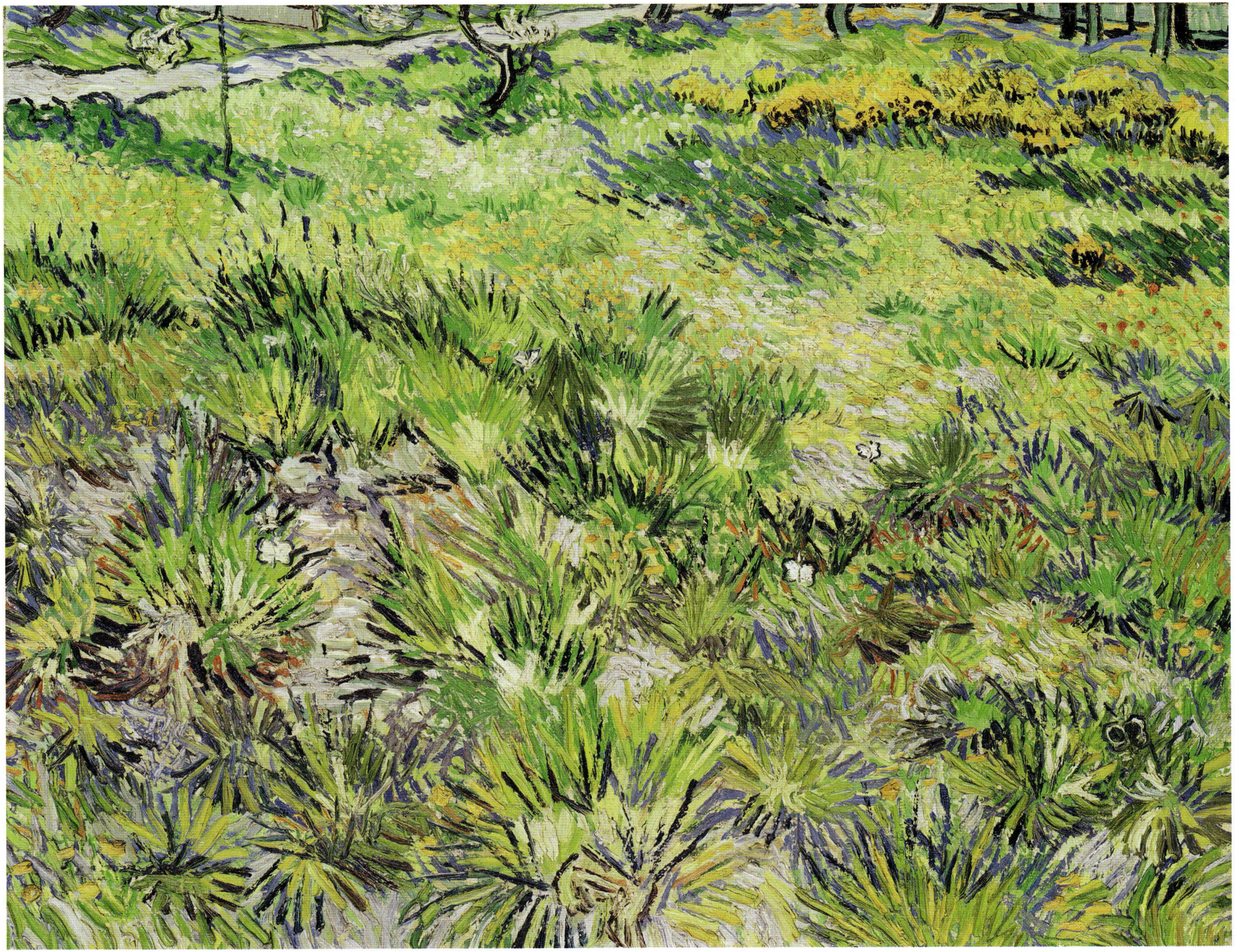

Late May
1890

PORTRAIT OF DR GACHET

Musée d'Orsay, Paris

Oil on canvas | 68 × 57cm (26¾ × 22½in)

In March 1890, Theo wrote to Vincent at the asylum in Saint-Rémy to say that he had met Dr Paul Gachet, a physician of whom Pissaro had spoken, and a consultation with him could be arranged as soon as Vincent arrived in Paris. Dr Gachet had experience of treating psychiatric patients and Theo had gained the impression from him that he was 'a man of understanding'.[108]

On 16 May Vincent left the asylum and took the train to Paris, where he was reunited with his brother, met Theo's wife Johanna and their infant child, saw artist friends, and visited Père Tanguy's shop. After three days he left Paris for the north-western suburb of Auvers-sur-Oise, where he would spend his remaining days, continuing his work as an artist under the benign supervision of Dr Gachet (1828–1909). When they met, Gachet was just short of his sixty-second birthday; Vincent was thirty-seven. Gachet, himself an amateur painter and engraver, was an art collector who had known numerous artists and writers, among them Courbet, Victor Hugo, Manet, Pissarro, Renoir and Cézanne.

Vincent found in Dr Gachet a kindred spirit. In a letter to Gauguin, he wrote, 'I have a portrait of Dr Gachet with the heart-broken expression of our time.'[109] He made two versions; the good doctor was so enamoured of the first that the artist painted a second, shown here, which he presented to him as a gift.[110] Gachet's facial expression is sorrowful, while his eyes register kindness and compassion. His pose – arm bent at the elbow, head resting on hand – is one traditionally associated with melancholy, as in Albrecht Dürer's engraving *Melencolia* (1514). On the table is a foxglove plant, a source of the drug digitalis, which is used as a homeopathic remedy, and is hence an attribute of Dr Gachet, who practised homeopathic medicine.

The emotional effects of the painting are imparted by both line and colour. The artist employs the complementary colours of green/red and blue/orange, punctuated by the smaller white areas of hat, collar and cuffs. The serpentine forms of the bent arms are echoed by the swirls of blue-and-white brushstrokes of Gachet's coat, and of the blue brushstrokes of the lower background behind his figure. Gachet had expressed great admiration for Vincent's *Self-Portrait* from Saint-Rémy (see p. 111), and Vincent sought to impart some of its dynamic qualities in his portrait of the doctor.

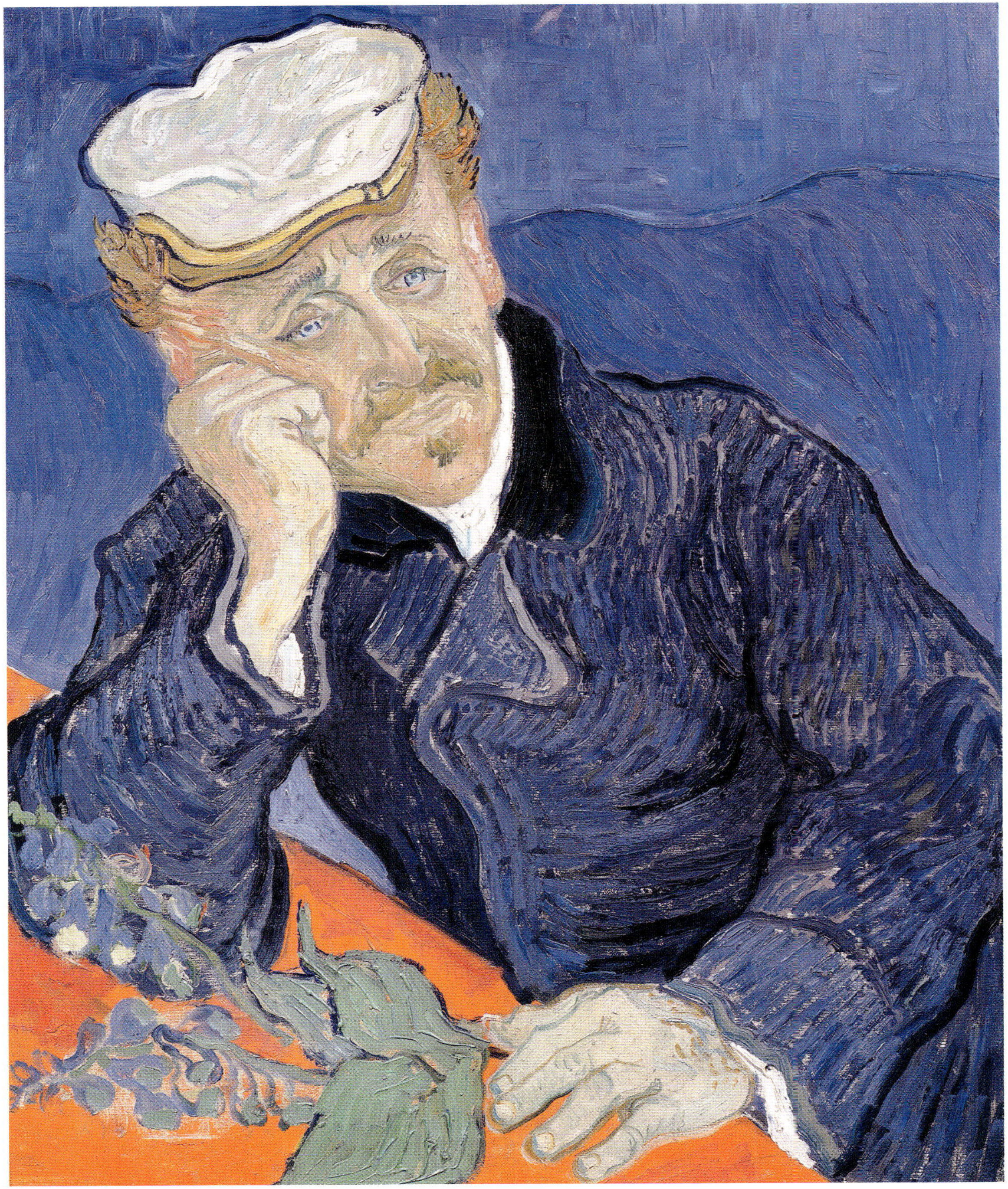

Early June

1890

THE CHURCH AT AUVERS

Musée d'Orsay, Paris

Oil on canvas | 94 × 74cm (37 × 29⅛in)

During his final days as a patient at the asylum in Saint-Rémy, Vincent felt nostalgic for the north. In April 1890 he wrote to Theo, asking his brother to send him some of his figure drawings from Nuenen, so that he could recreate some of the paintings. 'Then, if you like,' he added, 'I'll redo the old tower.'[111] Vincent was referring to a twelfth-century Romanesque church in Nuenen, surrounded by a graveyard, of which he had made eleven drawings and paintings in 1884–5.

In May, when Vincent arrived at Auvers-sur-Oise, the town evoked in him memories of his native Netherlands: 'Auvers is very beautiful … a lot of old thatched roofs, which are getting rare … it is the real country, characteristic and picturesque.'[112] In early June he made a painting of the town's church, and sent his sister Wil a detailed description: 'The building [is] violet-hued against a sky of … pure cobalt; the stained-glass windows appear as ultramarine blotches, the roof is violet and partly orange … It is nearly the same thing as [my] studies … in Nuenen of the old tower and … cemetery, only … now the color is more expressive, more sumptuous.'[113]

The Church of Notre-Dame-de-l'Assomption was built in the thirteenth century in the early Gothic style with adjoining Romanesque chapels, on a hill overlooking the centre of the town. Vincent painted it from the east, where the apse is located, rather than its entrance on the west. A luminous yellow path leads up to the eastern wall, then diverges. The figure walking along the path on the left, in traditional bonnet and peasant skirt, resembles a Dutch woman. The path and part of the lawn are illuminated by sunlight, but the church is largely in shadow; the position of the shadow on the path indicates early to mid afternoon. By depicting the building from the east, rather than displaying its façade, the artist emphasizes its function as a town landmark rather than its sacred symbolism. He has depicted the church in the naturalistic manner of seventeenth-century Dutch painting, while enhancing the work with brilliant colour and Post-Impressionist brushstrokes, especially in the sky, paths and lawn, and in the orange roof on the right.

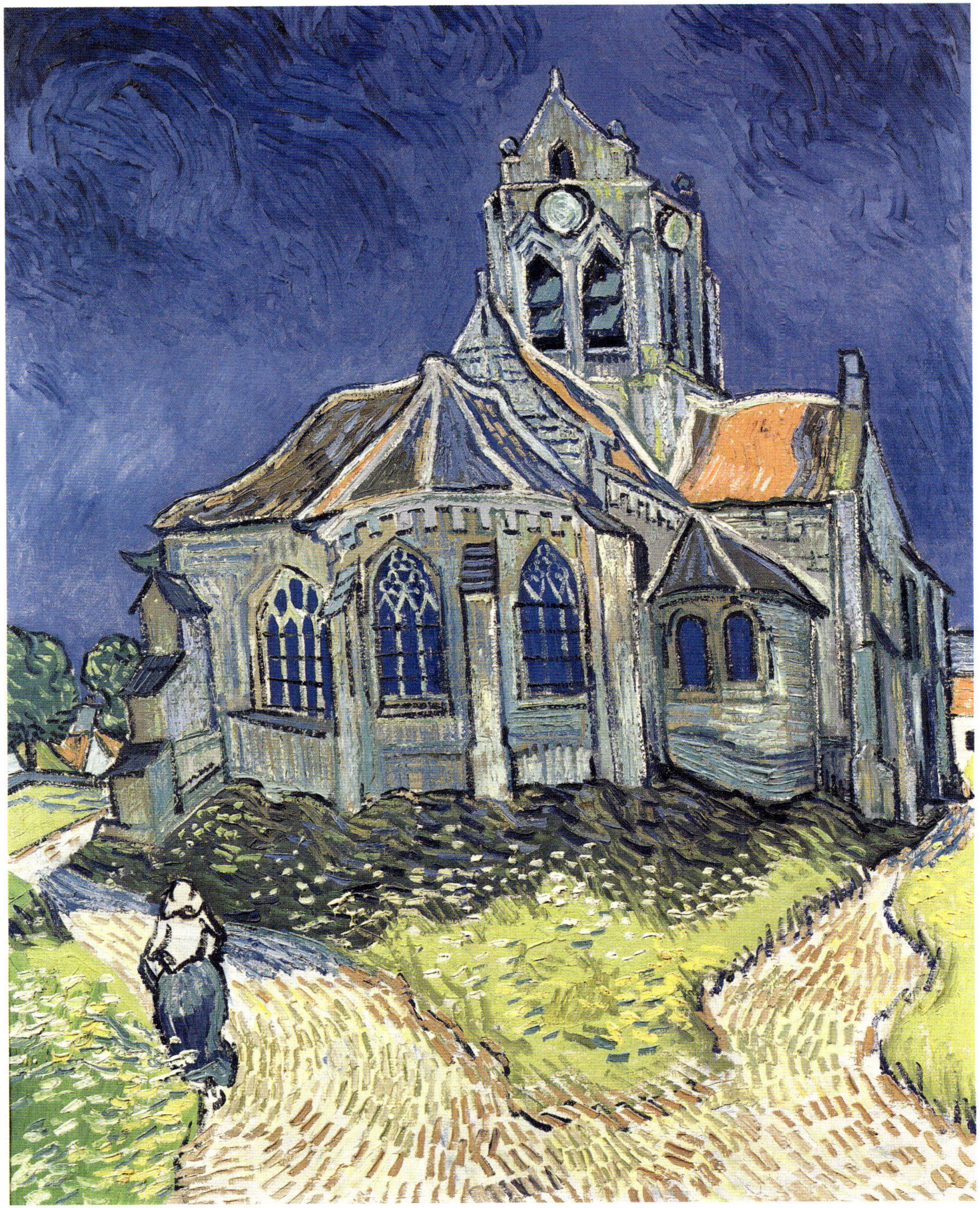

June

1890

STAIRWAY AT AUVERS

Saint Louis Art Museum

Oil on canvas | 51 × 71cm (20⅛ × 28in)

With this painting Vincent depicts the Rue de la Sansonne, a street adjacent to his residence at the Auberge Ravoux on the Place de la Mairie in Auvers. The nearly symmetrical composition is made up of sinuous, waving lines which converge at the centre. It conveys not the tempestuous anxiety of Saint-Rémy landscapes such as *The Starry Night* or *The Olive Trees* (see pp. 105 and 107), but a benign, picturesque view of village life. The focus of the painting is terrestrial, with almost no visible sky. The five figures – two young women along the road at the left, two mature women on the road in the centre, and an elderly man with a walking-stick on the stairway – suggest three stages of human existence.

Space in the painting is flattened; colour is predominantly pastel tones of green, blue, orange and yellow. Undulating forms are present in multiple variations: in the curvatures of the road and its adjoining greenery, in the stairway and its adjacent green arabesques, and in the curvilinearity of the five strolling figures. The houses at the top of the stairway act as a stabilizing force, with their horizontals and verticals and intense red roofs; they are echoed by rectilinear structures on either side of the road. Syncopated repetition of colour is used throughout: the yellow doorway and stairway and the yellow hats of the young women; the white dresses, white hat and the white building façade; the black windows and doorway at the top of the hill and the black skirts of the older women. At the upper left is a cluster of flowers and vegetation which approaches abstraction, including a downward swooping anthropomorphic form, like a guardian angel watching over the town.

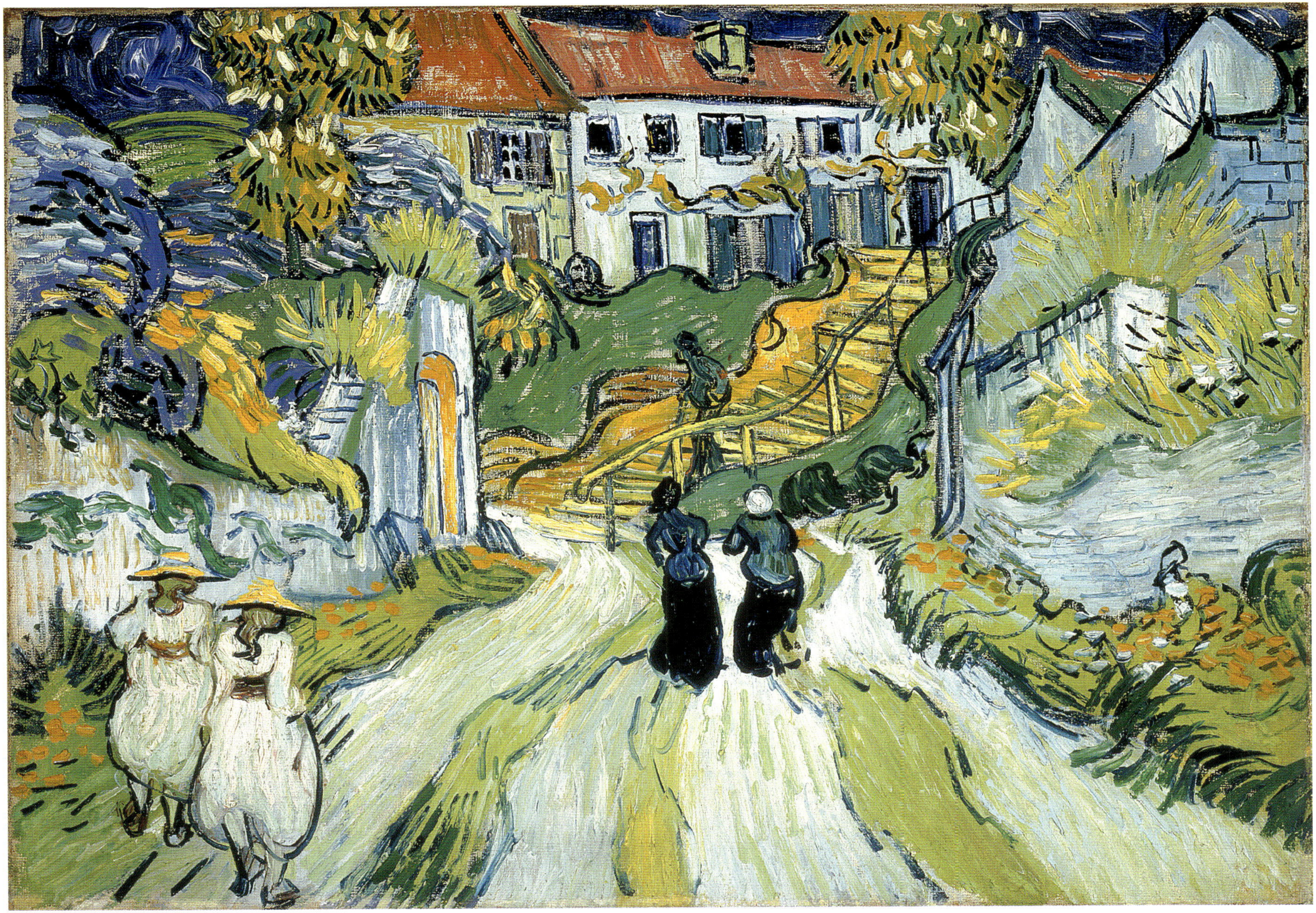

Mid-July
1890

WHEATFIELD WITH CROWS

Van Gogh Museum, Amsterdam

Oil on canvas | 50.5 × 100.5cm (20⅛ × 39¾in)

In early July 1890, Vincent travelled to Paris and saw Theo and his family for the last time. Theo's wife Jo later recalled that 'those were days of much worry and anxiety', which included concerns about their baby's health, Theo's possible plans to leave Boussod, Valadon and set up his own art dealership, and Vincent's unhappiness with the storage of his pictures. The critic Aurier and the painter Toulouse-Lautrec came to visit; the Impressionist painter Guillaumin was also expected, but, as Jo reported, 'Vincent … did not wait for this visit but hurried back to Auvers – overtired and excited, as his last letters and pictures show, in which the threatened catastrophe seems approaching, like the ominous black birds that dart through the storm over the wheatfields.'[114]

Vincent's fear of another attack of mental illness was now compounded by uncertainty about Theo's future financial support, along with intensified feelings of his own isolation. Back in Auvers, he reported to Theo and Jo that he was at work on two paintings depicting 'immense stretches of wheatfields under turbulent skies, and I made a point of trying to express sadness, extreme loneliness.'[115]

Wheatfield with Crows is disquieting to the viewer. Within the double-square rectilinear format, there are no verticals. Under a sky of swirling white and blue-black brushstrokes that evoke the tempest of *The Starry Night* (see p. 105), a flock of black crows swarms toward the picture plane. The arrangement of the field of wheat reverses the spectator's expectations: rather than receding toward the horizon, the two yellow wedges of windswept grain form their apexes in the foreground. The three red paths bordered by complementary green untrodden grass, rather than converging at the horizon, diverge at the foreground.

Despite these disturbing features, the painting is almost symmetrical. The white cloud at the centre nearly bisects the sky. The red-and-green paths are balanced at the centre, left and right, and the two wedges of wheatfield are nearly identical in their dimensions. Vincent seemed to be acknowledging this paradox when, in his letter to Theo and Jo, he added: 'I'd almost believe that these canvases will tell you what I can't say in words, what I consider healthy and fortifying about the countryside.'[116] Notwithstanding his despair, Vincent held out the hope that there were therapeutic forces in nature that could heal his mental illness.

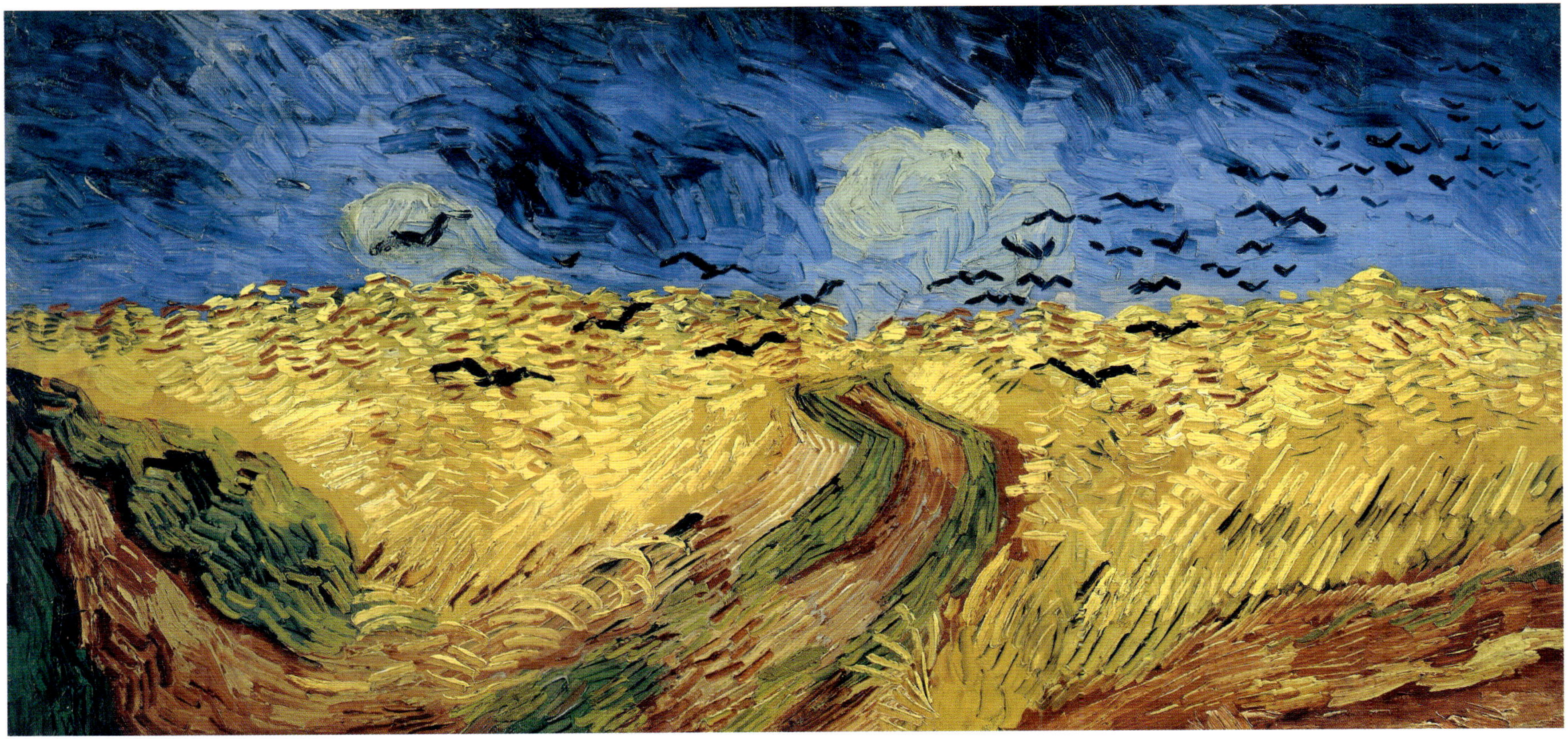

Late July
1890

FARMS NEAR AUVERS

Tate Gallery, London

Oil on canvas | 50 × 100cm (19⅝ × 39⅜in)

Upon his arrival in Auvers, Vincent had reported to Theo and sister-in-law Jo, 'Auvers is decidedly very beautiful. … There is a great deal of color here … there are such pretty middle-class country houses.'[117] To his sister Wil, he wrote: 'Here there are moss-covered thatched roofs which are superb, and which I am certainly going to do something with.'[118]

In Auvers, where Vincent spent the last three months of his life, he painted a series of landscapes featuring houses with thatched roofs, revisiting a subject he had frequently explored in Holland during the previous decade. His final work of the series, and the second-to-last painting of his life, was *Farms near Auvers*, depicted in the double-square frieze format of many of his Auvers landscapes (see *Wheatfield with Crows* and *Tree Roots*, pp. 129 and 133).[119] Like *Tree Roots*, it was still unfinished at the time of his death.

Farms near Auvers, which, as Ronald Pickvance notes, 'shows the most extensive view of thatched cottages in all of Van Gogh's Auvers canvases', was painted 'in the western extremity of the village … where … most of the remaining thatched houses were to be found'.[120] The yellow fields of ripened wheat in the background confirm a July date for the work. Unlike *Wheatfield with Crows*, there are no ominous signs present; the viewer is shown a benign vision of country life, depicted in the yellows, browns and greens of nature. The rolling cobalt blue mountains are echoed by the coiling greenery of the lush trees and the light blue walls of houses in the foreground, while the impastoed hatchings of the thatched roofs rhythmically repeat the patterns of the wheatfields. The four sunflowers at the foreground left, outsize in scale compared to the rest of the picture, are, as in other renderings of this flower in Van Gogh paintings (see p. 75) symbols of joy. It is as if the artist is presenting a Utopian vision of country life as shelter from the storm that he fears is approaching.

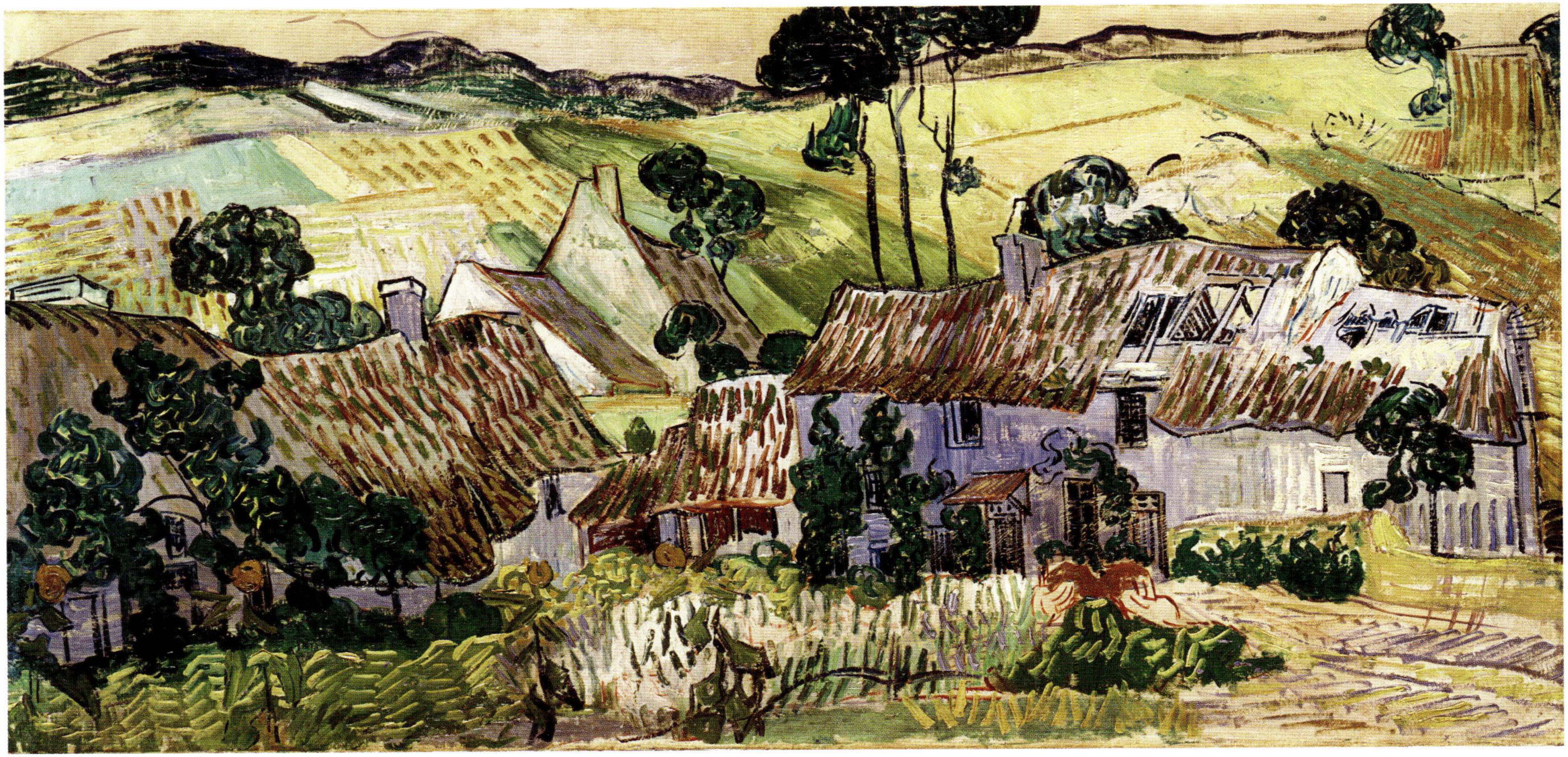

Late July
1890

TREE ROOTS

Van Gogh Museum, Amsterdam

Oil on canvas | 50.5 × 100.5cm (20⅛ × 39¾in)

Tree Roots – still unfinished at the time of his death – was Vincent's final painting. With this work, he was returning to a theme he had explored eight years earlier. In May 1882, from The Hague, he reported to Theo that he had just finished a large drawing of 'tree roots on sandy ground', having sought to imbue the landscape with the feeling of the 'passionate clinging to the earth, and yet being half torn up by the storm. I wanted to express … the struggle for life … in the black, gnarled and knotty roots. Or rather, because I tried to be faithful to nature as I saw it … something of that great struggle is shown.'[121]

Rendered in the double-square, horizontal frieze format that Vincent had used in a number of Auvers paintings, among them *Farms near Auvers* and *Wheatfield with Crows* (see pp. 131 and 129), *Tree Roots* is a fundamentally ambiguous painting. Though it is based on direct observation of nature, not every form can be clearly identified, and the painting verges on pure abstraction. There is, however, a subject depicted: gnarled roots, trunks, branches and leaves growing from chalky soil in a quarry on a steep limestone slope. Sunlight shines from left to right, from behind the artist's back, with the upper left of the composition in shadow. Scholars have differed as to whether there is very little horizon or no horizon at all; Ronald Pickvance asserts that there is 'no sky to determine background from foreground', whereas for Bert Maes and Louis van Tilborgh, 'the blue passage in the top left corner … can only be blue sky'.[122]

The painting raises the inevitable question – given that he would take his own life later that day – as to whether the artist's return to the earthbound subject of tree roots signifies a premonition of his own death. Vincent had long been aware that he was engaged in a struggle for life against his own destructive internal forces. Could the green serpentine forms swooping in from the left in the composition suggest this menace?

Notwithstanding its ambiguities of representation, *Tree Roots* is a structured, organized work. Its rhythmic, all-over composition, to a greater degree than any of Vincent's preceding paintings, anticipates the mid-twentieth-century canvases of Abstract Expressionists such as Jackson Pollock. It is perhaps appropriate that Vincent's final painting was a work in progress, and that it was a precursor of the Expressionism and abstraction of the century to follow.

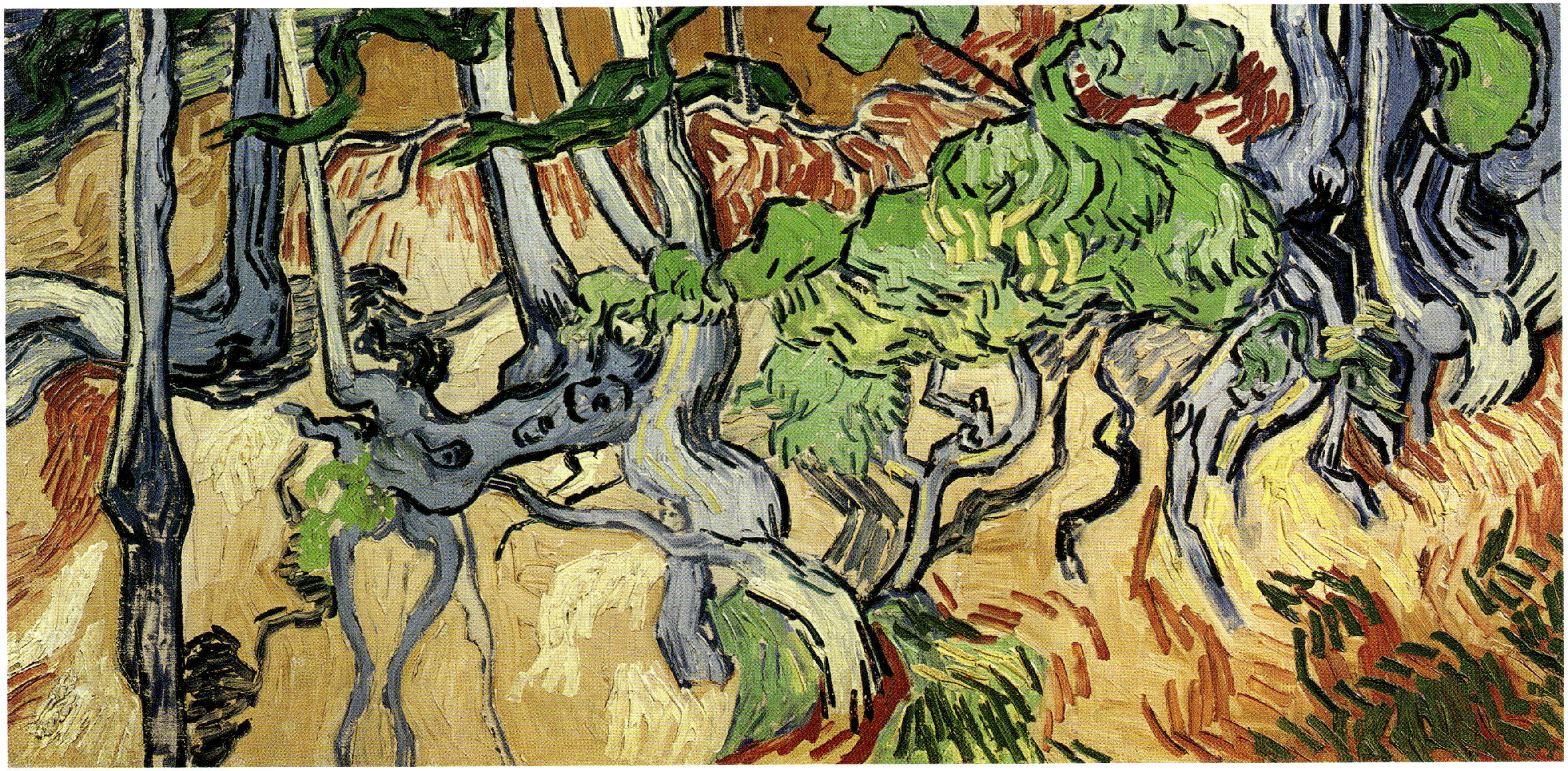

NOTES ON WORKS

INTRODUCTION

VvG = Vincent van Gogh
TvG = Theo van Gogh
JvGB = Jo Van Gogh-Bonger
WvG = Wilhelmina van Gogh

1 Van Gogh-Bonger 2000, letter 531, vol. III, p. 25.
2 There is no extant correspondence containing Theo's suggestion, or Vincent's reply. However, in a letter to Theo written two years later, Vincent made reference to 'the time when you spoke of my becoming a painter', noting that at first 'I considered it very impractical'; VvG to TvG, on or about 2 April 1882, Van Gogh-Bonger 2000, vol. I, letter no. 184, p. 331.
3 VvG to TvG, 8 December 1883, Van Gogh-Bonger 2000, letter no. 345a, vol. II, p. 231.
4 VvG to TvG, mid-June 1884, Van Gogh-Bonger 2000 letter no. 371, vol. II, p. 295.
5 Victor Hageman, interviewed by Louis Piérard, 'Van Gogh in Antwerp', *Les Marges*, January 1914, in Stein 1986, pp. 69–70.
6 VvG to TvG, on or about 28 February 1886, Jansen, Luijten and Bakker 2009, letter no. 567.
7 VvG to TvG, 21 February 1888, Van Gogh-Bonger 2000, letter no. 463, vol. II, p. 525.
8 VvG to TvG, 1 May 1888, Jansen, Luijten and Bakker 2009, letter no. 602.
9 VvG to TvG, ca. 28 June 1888, Jansen, Luijten and Bakker 2009, letter no. 634.
10 VvG to TvG, 18 August 1888, in Jansen, Luijten and Bakker 2009, letter no. 663.
11 VvG to Émile Bernard, on or about 21 August 1888, Van Gogh-Bonger 2000, letter no. B15, vol. III, p. 511.
12 VvG to TvG, 8 September 1888, in Jansen, Luijten and Bakker 2009, letter no. 676.
13 VvG to Paul Gauguin, 3 October 1888, Jansen, Luijten and Bakker 2009, letter no. 695.
14 VvG to Paul Gauguin, 17 October 1888, in Van Gogh-Bonger 2000, letter no. B22, vol. III, p. 526.
15 VvG to TvG, on or about 25 October 1888, in Van Gogh-Bonger 2000, letter no. 557, vol. III, p. 92.
16 VvG to TvG, 10 November 1888, in Van Gogh-Bonger 2000, letter no. 561, vol. III, p. 104.
17 VvG to TvG, on or about 19 November 1888, in Jansen, Luijten and Bakker 2009, letter no. 721.
18 Paul Gauguin, 'Avant et Après', *Mercure de France*, October 1903, in Stein 1986, pp. 125–6.
19 'Memoir of Vincent van Gogh by His Sister-in-Law', Van Gogh-Bonger 2000, p. xlv.
20 Paul Gauguin, 'Avant et Après', op. cit., p. 126.
21 Ibid, p. 126.
22 Ibid, p. 126. Editor Susan Alyson Stein notes, in the margin: 'Six days after the incident, Gauguin described the details to Bernard, but made no mention of the razor.'
23 Ibid, p. 127.
24 'Local News', *Forum Républicain*, 30 December 1888, in Stein 1986, p. 131.
25 VvG to TvG, 7 January 1889, Van Gogh-Bonger 2000, letter no. 569, vol. III, p. 114.
26 Bell 2015, p. 123.
27 VvG to TvG, 22 August 1889, in Van Gogh-Bonger 2000, letter no. 601, vol. III, p. 194.
28 Jansen, Luijten and Bakker 2009, letter no. 797, n. 6.
29 VvG to TvG, 31 December 1889 or 1 January 1890, in Van Gogh-Bonger 2000, letter no. 620, vol. III, p. 241.
30 G. Albert Aurier, "The Isolated Ones: Vincent van Gogh', *Mercure de France*, January 1890, Stein 1986, p. 182.
31 TvG to VvG, 31 January 1890, Jansen, Luijten and Bakker 2009, letter no. 847.
32 TvG to VvG, 29 March 1890, Van Gogh-Bonger 2000, letter no. T31, vol. III, p. 567.
33 Pickvance 1986, p. 73.
34 'Memoir of Vincent van Gogh by His Sister-in-Law', Van Gogh-Bonger 2000, p. l.
35 VvG to TvG and JvGB, 20 May 1890, Jansen, Luijten and Bakker 2009, letter no. 873.
36 Rewald 1956, pp. 389–90.
37 See Maes and Van Tilborgh 2013, pp. 67–8.
38 VvG to TvG, 23 July 1890, letter no. 651, Van Gogh-Bonger 2000, vol. III, pp. 297, 299–302.
39 TvG to JvGB, 25 July 1890, Jansen, Luijten and Bakker 2009, letter no. 902, n. 2.
40 Maes and Van Tilborgh reject the interpretation of the painting as a premonition of the artist's death, at least as a conscious choice, given that Vincent was in the habit of making such an interpretation only as an afterthought. See op. cit., p. 68.
41 This account of the circumstances of Vincent's death is based on that given by Ronald Pickvance in Pickvance 1986, 'Chronology', pp. 215–17. This account is in turn based on Émile Bernard's letter to Albert Aurier of 1 August 1890, which, in Pickvance's opinion, is the most accurate contemporary narrative. Steven Naifeh and Gregory White Smith, in *Van Gogh: The Life* [Nafei and Smith 2001], pp. 856–61, and 'Appendix: A Note on Vincent's Fatal Wounding', pp. 869–79, resuscitate an old rumour that Vincent was murdered by local boys in Auvers. They cite art historian John Rewald (1912–4) as having discovered this rumour in Auvers in the 1930s. It must be noted, however, that Rewald, a pioneering scholar of Impressionism and Post-Impressionism, never gave credence to the rumour. In *Post-Impressionism from Van Gogh to Gauguin* [Rewald 1956], he states definitively that Vincent committed suicide in Auvers; he never stated otherwise, either publicly, or, as far as is known, privately. Nafeih and Smith's argument is exhaustively refuted in 'The Life and Death of Vincent van Gogh,' *Burlington Magazine,* 1565, no. 1324 (July 2013), pp. 456–62 by Louis van Tilborgh and Teio Meedendorp [Van Tilborgh and

Meedendorp 2013]. See also Julian Bell, who, in *A Power Seething* [Bell 2015], p. 163, n. 67, effectively distils one of Van Tilborgh and Meedendorp's key arguments.

42 'Memoir of Vincent van Gogh by Mrs J. van Gogh-Bonger', in Van Gogh-Bonger 2000, vol. I, pp. xv-lii.

43 For this brief summary of Vincent's posthumous reputation, I am indebted to John Rewald, in Rewald 1986.

THE PAINTINGS

1 VvG to TvG, on or about 3 February 1884, Van Gogh-Bonger 2000, letter no. 355, vol. II, p. 260.

2 Van Tilborgh and Vellekoop 1999, pp. 61–5.

3 VvG to TvG, 30 April 1885, in Jansen, Luijten and Bakker 2009, letter 497.

4 VvG to TvG, 2 May 1885, in Jansen, Luijten and Bakker 2009, letter 499. The quote about Millet, which Vincent found in Alfred Sensier, *La vie et l'ouvre de J.F. Millet*, comes from the poet and critic Théophile Gautier (1811–72).

5 VvG to TvG, 6 July 1885, Van Gogh-Bonger 2000, letter no. 418, vol. II, pp. 400–2.

6 Signac to Gustave Coquiot, in Coquiot, *Vincent van Gogh*, Paris: 1923, cited in Rewald 1956, p. 55 and p. 78, n. 57.

7 VvG to TvG, ca. 23–5 July 1887, in Van Gogh-Bonger 2000, letter no. 462, vol. II, p. 523.

8 Émile Bernard, 'Julien Tanguy, called Le Père Tanguy,' *Mercure de France*, November–December 1908, in Stein 1986, pp. 92–3.

9 VvG to WvG, 16 and 20 June 1888, Van Gogh-Bonger 2000, vol. III, letter no. W4, p. 437.

10 VvG to Émile Bernard, 18 March 1888, in Jansen, Luijten and Bakker 2009, letter no. 587.

11 VvG to Émile Bernard, on or about 22 May 1888, Van Gogh-Bonger 2000, letter no. B5, vol. III, p. 465.

12 VvG to TvG, 12 or 13 June 1888, Jansen, Luijten and Bakker 2009, letter no. 624.

13 VvG to TvG, 5 August 1882, in Jansen, Luijten and Bakker 2009, letter no. 253.

14 VvG to TvG, on or about 3 or 4 June 1888, in Van Gogh-Bonger 2000, letter no 499, vol. 2, p. 588.

15 VvG to TvG, on or about 28 June 1888, in Jansen, Luijten and Bakker 2009, letter no. 634. The likely influence of Delacroix's *Christ Asleep during the Tempest* on Van Gogh's *Seascape at Saintes-Maries* is proposed in Van Uitert, Van Tilborgh and Van Heugten 1990, p. 118.

16 VvG to TvG, on or about 5 June 1888, in Jansen, Luijten and Bakker 2009, letter no. 620.

17 VvG to Émile Bernard, second half of June 1888, in Van Gogh-Bonger 2000, letter no. B6, vol. III, p. 490.

18 Ibid, p. 490.

19 This interpretation is proposed by Colta Ives in Ives, Stein, Van Heugten and Vellekoop 2005, p. 186.

20 VvG to Émile Bernard, second half of June 1888, in Van Gogh-Bonger 2000, letter no. B6, vol. III, p. 490.

21 VvG to TvG, on or about 5 June 1888, Van Gogh-Bonger 2000, letter no. 500, vol. II, pp. 589–90.

22 VvG to Émile Bernard, between 17 and 20 July 1888, Van Gogh-Bonger 2000, letter no. B11, vol. III, p. 503.

23 VvG to TvG, 12 June 1888, Van Gogh-Bonger 2000, letter no. 496, vol. II, p. 582.

24 VvG to TvG, on or about 1 July 1888, Van Gogh-Bonger 2000, letter no. 505, p. 607.

25 In his letter to Theo of 12 June, cited in n. 24, above, Vincent wrote of this painting, 'It is exactly like a Salomon Konink [sic] – you know, the pupil of Rembrandt who painted vast level plains'. Vincent was conflating Salomon Koninck (1609–56) with his uncle, Philips de Koninck (1619–88). Both were followers of Rembrandt, though only Philips was a landscape painter, and neither was Rembrandt's pupil.

26 VvG to TvG, 12 or 13 June 1888, Jansen, Luijten and Bakker 2009, letter no. 624.

27 VvG to Émile Bernard, 19 June 1888, Jansen, Luijten and Bakker 2009, letter no. 628.

28 VvG to TvG, 13 April 1885, Van Gogh Bonger 2000, letter no. 400, vol. II, p. 363.

29 VvG to TvG, 21 June 1888, Jansen, Luijten and Bakker 2009, letter no. 629.

30 VvG to TvG, ca. 28 June 1888, Jansen, Luijten and Bakker 2009, letter no. 634. Although Vincent had not seen the original painting of *The Sower*, he was familiar with prints and Millet's pastel sketch.

31 VvG to TvG, on or about 18 March 1888, Van Gogh-Bonger 2000, letter no. 469, vol. II, p. 533.

32 VvG to TvG, 29 July 1888, Van Gogh Bonger 2000, letter no. 514, p. 620.

33 Pierre Loti, *Madame Chrysanthème Complete*, Chapter XLII. Pierre Loti, pen name of Louis Marie-Julien Viaud (1850–1923), was a French naval officer and author, known for his novels with exotic locales.

34 VvG to TvG, 28 April 1889, in Jansen, Luijten and Bakker 2009, letter no. 763.

35 VvG to TvG, 3 September 1888, in Van Gogh-Bonger 1978, letter no. 531, vol. III, p. 25.

36 VvG to TvG, 21 June 1888, in Jansen, Luijten and Bakker 2009, letter no. 629. In his letter of 8 August 1888, Vincent informs Theo, 'I've worked again on a figure of a Zouave, sitting on a bench against a white wall...', Jansen, Luijten and Bakker 2009, letter no. 657.

37 Schapiro 1983, p. 72.

38 La Camargue is a region south of Arles; La Crau is another region in Provence.

39 VvG to TvG, 18 August 1888 in Jansen, Luijten and Bakker 2009, letter no. 663.

40 Schapiro 1983, p. 75.

41 VvG to Émile Bernard, on or about 21 August 1888, Van Gogh-Bonger 2000, letter no. B15, vol. III, p. 511.

42 VvG to TvG, 21 or 22 August 1888, Van Gogh Bonger 2000, letter no. 526, vol. III, pp. 18–19.

43 The current locations of these versions of *Sunflowers* are Private Collection, United States, and Bayerische Staatsgemäldesammlungen, Munich. A third painting,

formerly in Yokohama, Japan, was destroyed by fire in World War II. In January 1889 Van Gogh painted three *répétitions* of the *Sunflowers* series, now located in Van Gogh Museum, Amsterdam; Philadelphia Museum of Art; and Sompo Museum of Art, Tokyo.

44 VvG to TvG, 21 or 22 August 1888, Van Gogh Bonger 2000, letter no. 526, vol. III, p. 18.

45 G.-Albert Aurier, 'The Isolated Ones: Vincent van Gogh,' *Mercure de France*, January 1890, in Stein 1986, p. 191.

46 VvG to G.-Albert Aurier, 9 or 10 February 1890, Van Gogh-Bonger 2000, letter no. 626a, vol. III, p. 257.

47 VvG to TvG, 6 August 1888, in Jansen, Luijten and Bakker 2009, letter 656.

48 VvG to TvG, 8 September 1888, in Rewald 1956, p. 234 and p. 240, n. 59.

49 VvG to TvG, 9 September 1888 in Van Gogh-Bonger 1978, letter 534.

50 Schapiro 1983, p. 80.

51 VvG to TvG, 8 September 1888, in Jansen, Luijten and Bakker 2009, letter no. 676.

52 VvG to TvG, 9 April 1888 in Van Gogh-Bonger 1978, letter 474, vol. 2, p. 541.

53 VvG to TvG, 9 and about 14 September 1888 in Jansen, Luijten and Bakker 2009, letter no. 678.

54 VvG to TvG, about 5 June 1888, Jansen, Luijten and Bakker 2009, letter no. 620.

55 VvG to WvG, 9 and about 14 September 1888, Jansen, Luijten and Bakker 2009, letter no. 678.

56 VvG to TvG, 16 September 1888, Van Gogh-Bonger 2000, vol. III, letter no. 537, p. 37.

57 VvG to Paul Gauguin, Jansen, Luijten and Bakker 2009, 3 October 1888, letter no. 695.

58 VvG to TvG, 23 or 24 September 1888, Jansen, Luijten and Bakker 2009, letter no. 686.

59 VvG to TvG, on or about 29 September 1888, Jansen, Luijten and Bakker 2009, letter no. 691. After he completed the painting, Vincent made a watercolour of *The Yellow House* (Van Gogh Museum, Amsterdam), which he sent to his brother on 9 or 10 October, so that Theo could 'form an idea of the colour' (letter no. 700).

60 VvG to WvG, on or about 26 August 1888, Van Gogh-Bonger 2000, vol. 3, pp. 445–6.

61 VvG to TvG, 15 September 1888, Jansen, Luijten and Bakker 2009, letter no. 683.

62 VvG to TvG, 17 October 1888, in Van Gogh-Bonger 1978, letter no. 554, vol. III, p. 86.

63 VvG to TvG, 8 September 1888, in Van Gogh-Bonger 1978, letter no. 533, vol. III, p. 28.

64 VvG to TvG, 17 October 1888, in Van Gogh-Bonger 1978, letter no. 554, vol. III, p. 86.

65 VvG to TvG, 9 September 1888, Jansen, Luijten and Bakker 2009, letter no. 677.

66 VvG to TvG, on or about 19 November 1888, Jansen, Luijten and Bakker 2009, letter no. 721. On 17 January 1889 Vincent informed Theo that he had just done some reworking of the painting of his own chair (ibid., letter no. 736).

67 VvG to WvG, 21 or 22 August 1888, Van Gogh-Bonger 2000, letter no. W6, vol. III, p. 442.

68 VvG to TvG, about 3 November 1888, Jansen, Luijten and Bakker 2009, letter no. 717.

69 Ronald Pickvance writes of the New York portrait: 'It could well be possible that Van Gogh painted it specially for Madame Ginoux just before he left Arles in May 1889'; see Pickvance 1984, p. 207.

70 Gauguin painted a portrait of Mme Ginoux in the foreground of his painting *Night Café in Arles* (Pushkin Museum, Moscow), and portraits of her by Gauguin, under the title *L'Arlésienne*, are at the Kröller-Müller Museum, Otterlo; the Galleria Nazionale d'Arte Moderna, Rome; and the São Paulo Museum of Art.

71 The second, *Self-Portrait with Bandaged Ear and Pipe*, is in a private collection.

72 VvG to TvG, 31 July 1888, Van Gogh-Bonger 2000, vol. II, letter no. 516, p. 623. 'Tanguy' refers to the paint seller and art dealer Julien Tanguy; see p. 46.

73 In addition to the portrait shown here, there are two other portraits of Roulin in this series, both frontal head-and-shoulders views with decorative backgrounds: one is in the Kröller-Müller Museum, Otterlo, and a second is in the Barnes Foundation, Philadelphia.

74 VvG to TvG, on or about 4 April 1888, Van Gogh-Bonger 2000, letter no. 583, vol. III, pp. 147–8. At this time Vincent was 35 years old; Roulin was 48.

75 The original painting, now at the Kröller-Müller Museum, Otterlo, differs from later versions in that the wallpaper patterns are denser and more detailed. Subsequent versions are the work here illustrated, which was formerly in the private collection of Walter Annenberg, and since 2002 has been in the Annenberg Collection of The Metropolitan Museum, New York; and versions in the Art Institute of Chicago; the Museum of Fine Arts, Boston; and the Stedelijk Museum, Amsterdam.

76 Rewald 1956, p. 315.

77 VvG to TvG, 25 May 1889, in Van Gogh-Bonger 2000, letter no. 592, vol. III, p. 171.

78 VvG to Paul Gauguin, 28 January 1889, in Jansen, Luijten and Bakker 2009, letter no. 743.

79 VvG to Paul Signac, 10 April 1889, Jansen, Luijten and Bakker 2009, letter no. 756.

80 Cornelia Homburg, 'Van Gogh's Japan: Embracing an Idea,' in Van Tilborgh, Bakker, Homburg, Kōdera and Uhlenbeck 2018, p. 93. As examples of writers who employed these descriptions, Homburg cites Théodore Duret, Pierre Loti and Victor Champier; see p. 179, n. 1.

81 VvG to TvG, 5–6 September 1889, Van Gogh-Bonger 2000, vol. III, letter no. 604, p. 204.

82 Félix Fénéon, 'The Fifth Exhibition of the Société des Artistes Indépendants.' *La Vogue*, September 1889, in Stein 1986, pp. 180–1.

83 VvG to TvG, 9 April 1888 in Van Gogh-Bonger 1978, letter 474, vol. 2, p. 541.

84 Roger Fry, 'Van Gogh', *The Burlington Magazine*, December 1923, in Stein 1986, p. 354.
85 VvG to TvG, on or about 18 June 1889 in Jansen, Luijten and Bakker 2009, letter no. 782.
86 Ibid., letter no. 805, on or about 20 September 1889.
87 VvG to TvG, 25 June 1889, in Van Gogh-Bonger 2000, letter no. 596, vol. III, p. 185.
88 Naifeh and Smith 2001, p. 772.
89 VvG to TvG, 5 and 6 September 1889, Van Gogh-Bonger 2000, vol. III, pp. 201–2. In the first self-portrait described (National Gallery, Washington, DC) he wears a dark blue painter's smock, set before a swirling dark blue background, and holds a palette and brushes.
90 In the shoulder at the left and the sleeve at the right there is a suggestion of violet. It can be inferred that this colour was originally more pronounced, but has faded with time; Vincent described the finished painting in a letter to his sister Wilhelmina: 'the blue is a fine southern blue and the suit is light lilac'. Vincent van Gogh to Wilhelmina Van Gogh, 5 June 1890, Jansen, Luijten and Bakker 2009, letter no. 879.
91 VvG to TvG, 5 and 6 September 1889, Van Gogh-Bonger 2000, vol. III, p. 202.
92 VvG to TvG, on or about 20 September 1889, Van Gogh-Bonger 2000, vol. III, p. 216.
93 The engravings were by Jacques-Adrien Laveille (1818–62). Vincent's other paintings in the series are: *Morning* (1890, Hermitage, St Petersburg), *The End of the Day* (1889, Menard Art Museum, Monaki, Japan), and *Evening* (1889, Van Gogh Museum, Amsterdam).
94 Rosenblum 1989, p. 482.
95 TvG to VvG, 21 May 1889, Jansen, Luijten and Bakker 2009, letter no. 774.
96 VvG to TvG, 23 May 1889, Van Gogh-Bonger 2000, letter no. 592, vol. III, pp. 173–5
97 The other two pictures in the series are *Window in the Studio* and *Vestibule of the Asylum*, both in the collection of the Van Gogh Museum, Amsterdam.
98 See Hulsker 1977, p. 416, and Marije Vellekoop in Ives, Stein, Van Heugten and Vellekoop 2005, pp. 322–6.
99 TvG to VvG, 31 January 1890, Jansen, Luijten and Bakker 2009, letter no. 847.
100 VvG to Anna van Gogh-Carbentus, 19 February 1890, Jansen, Luijten and Bakker 2009, letter no. 855. See also VvG to WvG, 19 February 1890, Ibid., letter no. 856.
101 Pickvance 1986, p. 178. Pickvance maintains that 'this painting was surely done out of doors'. I believe, however, given that the tree's upper portion appears to have been observed from close proximity, it is likely to have been viewed from a window of the artist's bedroom, rather than from the ground.
102 VvG to TvG, 29 April 1890, Van Gogh-Bonger 2000, letter no. 629, vol. III, p. 261.
103 Berge, Van Kooten and Rijnders 2003, p. 353.
104 VvG to TvG, 4 May 1890, Van Gogh-Bonger 2000, letter no. 631, vol. III, p. 267.
105 VvG to TvG, on or about 1 May 1890, Van Gogh-Bonger 2000, letter no. 630, vol. III, p. 264.
106 VvG to TvG, on or about 23 May 1889, Van Gogh-Bonger 2000, letter no. 593, vol. III., p. 173.
107 Bailey 2006: p. 94.
108 TvG to VvG, 29 March 1890, Van Gogh-Bonger 2000, letter no. T31, vol. III, p. 567.
109 VvG to Paul Gauguin, on or about 17 June 1890, Van Gogh-Bonger 2000, letter no. 643, vol. III, pp. 286–7.
110 The two works differ principally in their backgrounds, which in the first version (Private Collection) has some of the swirling quality of Vincent's *Self-Portrait*, 1889 (p. 111), and in the presence on the table in the second version, in addition to the foxglove plant, two books by the Brothers Goncourt, whose naturalistic writings embody the modern spirit.
111 VvG to TvG, 29 April 1890, Jansen, Luijten and Bakker 2009, letter no. 863.
112 VvG to TvG and JvGB, 20 May 1890, Van Gogh-Bonger 2000, letter no. 635, vol. III, p. 273.
113 VvG to WvG, 5 June 1890, Van Gogh-Bonger 2000, letter no. W22, vol. III, p. 470.
114 'Memoir of Vincent van Gogh by Mrs. J. van Gogh-Bonger', in Van Gogh-Bonger 2000, vol. I, p. lii.
115 In addition to *Wheatfield with Crows*, Vincent was referring to *Wheatfield under a Clouded Sky* (1890, Van Gogh Museum, Amsterdam).
116 VvG to TvG and JvGB, on or about 10 July 1890, Jansen, Luijten and Bakker 2009, letter no. 898.
117 VvG to TvG and JvGB, on or about 21 May 1890, Van Gogh-Bonger 2000, letter no. 636, vol. III, p. 274.
118 VvG to WvG, on or about 21 May 1890, Van Gogh-Bonger 2000, letter no. W21, vol. III, pp. 468–9.
119 For the attribution of *Farms near Auvers* as Van Gogh's second-to-last painting, see Maes and Van Tilborgh 2013, pp. 67–8.
120 Pickvance 1986, p. 269.
121 VvG to TvG, 1 May 1882, in Van Gogh-Bonger 2000, letter no. 195, vol. 1, p. 360. The drawing cited is *Study of a Tree* (1882, Kröller-Müller Museum, Otterlo).
122 Pickvance 1986, p. 282, and Maes and Van Tilborgh 2013, p. 59.

BIBLIOGRAPHY

Bailey 2006: Martin Bailey, *Van Gogh and Britain: Pioneer Collectors*, exh. cat. Edinburgh: National Galleries of Scotland, 2006.

Bell 2015: Julian Bell, *Van Gogh: A Power Seething*. Boston and New York: Icons Series, New Harvest, Houghton Mifflin Harcourt, 2015.

Berge, Van Kooten and Rijnders 2003: Jos ten Berge, Toos van Kooten and Mieke Rijnders, *The Paintings on Vincent van Gogh in the Collection of the Kröller-Müller Museum*. Otterlo: Kröller-Müller Museum, 2003.

Hulsker 1977: Jan Hulsker, *The Complete Van Gogh: Paintings, Drawings, Sketches*. New York: Harrison House/Harry N. Abrams, 1977.

Ives, Stein, Van Heugten and Vellekoop 2005: Colta Ives, Susan Alyson Stein, Sjraar van Heugten, and Marije Vellekoop, *Vincent van Gogh: The Drawings*, exh. cat., The Metropolitan Museum of Art, New York, and Van Gogh Museum, Amsterdam. New Haven and London: Yale University Press, 2005.

Jansen, Luijten and Bakker 2009: Leo Jansen, Hans Luijten and Nienke Bakker, eds., *Vincent van Gogh: The Letters*, Version: April 2017. Amsterdam & The Hague: Van Gogh Museum & Huygens ING, www.vangoghletters.org

Loti 2016: Pierre Loti, *Madame Chrysanthème Complete*. www.gutenberg.org/files/3995/3995-h/3995-h.htm

Maes and Van Tilborgh 2013: Bert Maes and Louis van Tilborgh, 'Van Gogh's *Tree Roots* up close', in Louis van Tilborgh, *Van Gogh: New Findings, Van Gogh Studies 4*. Zwolle and Amsterdam: WBooks and Van Gogh Museum, 2013.

Naifeh and Smith 2001: Steven Naifeh and Gregory White Smith, *Van Gogh: The Life*. New York: Random House, 2011.

Pickvance 1984: Ronald Pickvance, *Van Gogh in Arles*, exh. cat., The Metropolitan Museum of Art, New York. New York: Harry N. Abrams, 1984.

Pickvance 1986: Ronald Pickvance, *Van Gogh in Saint-Rémy and Auvers*, exh. cat., The Metropolitan Museum of Art, New York. New York: Harry N. Abrams, 1986.

Rewald 1956: John Rewald, *Post-Impressionism from Van Gogh to Gauguin*. New York: The Museum of Modern Art, 1956.

Rewald 1986: John Rewald, 'The Posthumous Fate of Vincent van Gogh', in *Studies in Post-Impressionism*. New York: Harry N. Abrams, 1986, pp. 244–54.

Rosenblum 1989: Robert Rosenblum, *Paintings in the Musée d'Orsay*. New York: Stewart, Tabori & Chang, 1989.

Schapiro 1983: Meyer Schapiro, *Vincent van Gogh*. New York: Harry N. Abrams, 1983.

Stein 1986: Susan Alyson Stein, *Van Gogh: A Retrospective*. New York: Park Lane, 1986.

Van Gogh-Bonger 2000: Johanna van Gogh-Bonger, ed., *The Complete Letters of Vincent van Gogh*, 3 vols., third edition. Boston, New York and London: Little, Brown and Company, 2000.

Van Tilborgh, Bakker, Homburg, Kōdera and Uhlenbeck 2018: Louis van Tilborgh, Nienke Bakker, Cornelia Homburg, Tsukasa Kōdera and Chris Ohlenbeck, *Van Gogh & Japan*, exh. cat., Van Gogh Museum, Amsterdam. Sapporo and Brussels: Hokkaidō Shimbun Press and Mercatorfonds; New Haven and London: Distributed by Yale University Press, 2018.

Van Tilborgh and Meedendorp 2013: Louis van Tilborgh and Teio Meedendorp, 'The Life and Death of Vincent van Gogh', *Burlington Magazine*, 1565, no. 1324 (July 2013), pp. 456–62.

Van Tilborgh and Vellekoop 1999: Louis van Tilborgh and Marije Vellekoop, *Vincent Van Gogh Paintings, Volume I: Dutch Period, 1881-1885, Van Gogh Museum, Amsterdam*. London: Lund Humphries, 1999.

Van Uitert, Van Tilborgh and Van Heugten 1990: Evert van Uitert, Louis van Tilborgh, and Sjraar van Heugten, *Vincent van Gogh*, exh. cat., Rijksmuseum Vincent van Gogh, Amsterdam and Rijksmuseum Kröller-Müller, Otterlo. Milan and Rome: Mondadori Arte and De Luca Edizioni d'Arte, 1990.

GLOSSARY

abstraction Art in which forms do not represent objects in external reality or nature.

Abstract Expressionism Also known as the New York School, American abstract art, c. 1945–60, as practised by such artists as Jackson Pollock, Willem de Kooning, Mark Rothko and Barnett Newman.

all-over composition A canvas covered in paint from edge to edge, in which each area of the composition is given equal attention and significance.

anthropomorphic Having human shape; often applied to non-human objects, such as trees or clouds.

arabesque Surface decoration of rhythmic, intertwined linear patterns of flowers, leaves or scrollwork.

architectonic Relating to the use of architectural principles as a fundamental element of design, such as linear and grid forms.

avant-garde Artistic movements characterized by innovative, experimental ideas.

Barbizon School A group of naturalist painters, primarily painters of landscape, who gathered in the village of Barbizon in north-central France from the 1830s to the 1860s. Prominent among them were Théodore Rousseau, Jean-Baptist Corot and Jean-François Millet.

caricature A representation of a person in which the features are exaggerated, usually for the purpose of humour or satire.

chiaroscuro A treatment of light and shade in which strongly contrasting tones are employed in a painting.

classical composition Composition that is based on balance, symmetry and order.

complementaries The colour spectrum comprises primary and secondary colours. The primary colours are red, blue and yellow; the secondary colours are green, orange and violet. Each primary colour has a complementary secondary colour; the complementaries are red/green, blue/orange and yellow/violet. When two complementaries are juxtaposed, they produce maximum colouristic intensity.

composition The organization of forms in a work of art to creating a pleasing whole, involving such elements as shapes, masses, tones and colour.

contrapuntal A musical term, the adjectival form of 'counterpoint'. In music, counterpoint is created when two or more melodies are played simultaneously. By analogy, counterpoint in visual art is formed when two or more visual themes are simultaneously present.

curvilinearity Characterized by a curved line or lines.

Divisionism See Neo-Impressionism.

expressive Art in which the emotions of the artist take precedence over faithful rendering from nature.

Expressionism Art movements in the twentieth century, often employing distorted forms and exaggerated colour, primarily in Germany and Austria, in which the emotions of the artist take precedence over faithful rendering from nature. Among its practitioners were Erich Heckel, Käthe Kollwitz, Max Pechstein, Karl Schmidt-Rotluff, Emil Nolde, Ernst Kirchner, Oskar Kokoschka and Egon Schiele.

en plein air 'In the open air'; for artists, the act of painting figures and landscapes outdoors.

engraving the process of printing multiples of an artwork by incising lines on a surface such as a metal plate, wood block or linoleum block. Examples of engraving processes include etching, lithograph, and woodcut.

Fauvism A style of painting in France c.1905–6, led by Matisse and practised by others including Derain, Vlaminck, Rouault, Braque, Dufy, Camoin, Manguin and Marquet. The style employed bold colour, distortions of form and loose brushwork. It was the first avant-garde artistic style of the twentieth century.

Gothic The last phase of medieval art, beginning in France c.1140 and spreading throughout Europe in subsequent centuries; the style preceding the Renaissance.

gouache Opaque pigment with a water base, usually applied to paper.

Hague School A group of artists in The Hague, Netherlands, working between 1860 and 1890, who were influenced by the naturalistic painters of the Barbizon School in France. They were predominantly painters of landscape, which they often rendered in sombre tones. Prominent among them was Anton Mauve, Vincent van Gogh's cousin by marriage.

highlight A bright area in a painting, often indicating an illumination or reflection.

impasto The technique of applying paint thickly so that it is raised from the surface and its texture is visible to the viewer.

Impressionism The culmination of nineteenth-century realism. The Impressionists first exhibited together as a group in 1874. Impressionism is characterized by subjects such as landscape and scenes of middle-class urban life rendered in brilliant colour with optical techniques that capture the momentary effects of light. The Impressionists included, among others, Claude

Monet, Camille Pissarro, Alfred Sisley, Pierre-Auguste Renoir, Edgar Degas and Berthe Morisot.

in situ Literally, 'on the site'; when a work is created on the site, rather than reconstructed in the studio.

iridescence Of colour which is lustrous or changes according to the angle of view.

Japonism The influence of Japanese art and design on western art, beginning in the mid-nineteenth century.

luminosity The degree to which an object appears to radiate light.

mistral A strong, northwesterly wind that blows through the Rhône valley and southern France into the Mediterranean.

Neo-Impressionism Founded by Georges Seurat and Paul Signac and also known as Divisionism or Pointillism, Neo-Impressionism was an outgrowth of Impressionism. More systematic than its parent style, it broke down colour into small dots or points, separated on the canvas surface but intended to blend in the viewer's eye to recreate the effects of the brilliant colours of nature.

pétit boulevard Van Gogh's name for the Boulevard de Clichy in Montmartre. He used the term 'artists of the *pétit boulevard*' to refer to younger avant-garde artists in Paris, including himself, Paul Gauguin, Émile Bernard and Henri de Toulouse-Lautrec, who would later be known as Post-Impressionists.

Pointillism See Neo-Impressionism.

Pont-Aven School: An artists' colony which emerged in the 1850s in Pont-Aven. a town in Brittany in northwestern France. Leading artists in the group included Paul Gauguin, Émile Bernard and Paul Sérusier; see Synthetism.

Post-Impressionism The late nineteenth-century style that followed Impressionism, as practised by such artists as Cézanne, Gauguin and Van Gogh. These artists employed the brilliant colours of Impressionists, but sought in various ways to create artworks that were at once more subjective and more structurally permanent. The term was first employed in 1910, two decades after Van Gogh's death, by the English critic Roger Fry.

rectilinear Characterized by a straight line or lines which meet at right angles.

répétition A term employed by Van Gogh for copies that he made of his own drawings or paintings.

representation As opposed to 'abstraction'; the depiction of forms and figures as they appear to the eye.

Romanesque The medieval style, beginning in France in the eleventh century and subsequently spreading throughout Europe, which preceded the Gothic style.

Romantic art A style prevalent in the first half of the nineteenth century in which the imagination played a central part. Prominent among the Romantic painters in France were Eugéne Delacroix and Théodore Géricault.

salon Annual juried exhibition of painting and sculpture in France. Beginning in 1863 with the Salon des Refusés, independent salons were also held, juried and non-juried, where avant-garde artists often showed their work.

Salon des Indépendants An annual non-juried exhibition of artists held in Paris in spring since 1884. Originally formed in response to the traditionalism of the government-sponsored official salon, it has been a showcase for avant-garde art.

scumble To apply a thin layer of opaque paint over another layer so that, seen together, the layers produce a softened effect.

still life A work of art that depicts inanimate objects, such as fruit, flowers, dead animals, skulls, plants, shells, books or vases.

Symbolism A movement in art and literature in the last three decades of the nineteenth century. Symbolism was a reaction against Realism, with a tendency to look inward, and with an interest in myth and mysticism. Among its literary practitioners were Stéphane Mallarmé, Charles Baudelaire and Edgar Allan Poe. Symbolist painters included Gustave Moreau, Odilon Redon and Pierre Puvis de Chavannes.

synthesize Literally, 'put together', in contrast to analyse, 'take apart'. A process of art-making not by copying nature alone, but by employing memory and the imagination.

Synthetism Artists associated with Paul Gauguin and Émile Bernard who reduced forms to essentials and applied colour in flat areas bounded by strong contours were known as Synthetists.

stained glass Glass given translucent colour by staining with metallic oxides and joined by metallic strips. Stained-glass compositions of religious subjects often decorate church windows.

syncopated A musical term which can be translated to painting; rhythmic in such a way that the rhythm is offbeat or unexpected.

tactile In painting, having the illusion of tangibility; stimulating the imagination to sense the weight, mass and texture of an object.

thatched Roofing of a building made of straw or a similar material.

triptych A painted or carved work of three panels, arranged side by side.

ukiyo-e Literally, 'pictures of a floating world'. Japanese paintings or woodblock prints which flourished from the seventeenth to the nineteenth centuries, featuring such subjects as actors, courtesans and landscapes.

unmodelled Rendered flatly, rather than with the illusion of three dimensions.

woodblock print A print made from a block of wood in which the parts not cut away form the design; also known as a woodcut.

INDEX

CREDITS

Every effort has been made to trace the copyright holders and obtain permission to reproduce this material. However, the publishers will be glad to rectify in future editions any inadvertent omissions brought to their attention.

The publisher would like to thank the following collections for their kind permission to reproduce the illustrations in this book:

Page 2, J. Paul Getty Museum, Los Angeles, USA / Bridgeman Images; 5, Van Gogh Museum, Amsterdam, The Netherlands / De Agostini Picture Library / Bridgeman Images; 7, Van Gogh Museum, Amsterdam (Vincent van Gogh Foundation); 9, Musee d'Orsay, Paris, France / Bridgeman Images; 11, The Art Institute of Chicago, IL, USA / Helen Birch Bartlett Memorial Collection / Bridgeman Images; 13, Collection Kröller-Müller Museum, Otterlo, the Netherlands; 14, Van Gogh Museum, Amsterdam, The Netherlands / Bridgeman Images; 15, Musee d'Orsay, Paris, France / Bridgeman Images; 16 top, Metropolitan Museum of Art, New York, USA / Bridgeman Images; 16 bottom, Private Collection / Photo © Christie's Images / Bridgeman Images; 17, Museum of Fine Arts, Boston, Massachusetts, USA / Gift of Quincy Adams Shaw / Bridgeman Images; 18, J. Paul Getty Museum, Los Angeles, USA / Bridgeman Images; 21, Van Gogh Museum, Amsterdam, The Netherlands / Bridgeman Images; 24, Museum of Fine Arts, Boston, Massachusetts, USA / Gift of Quincy Adams Shaw through Quincy Adams Shaw, Jr., and Mrs. Marian Shaw Haughton / Bridgeman Images; 27, Van Gogh Museum, Amsterdam (Vincent van Gogh Foundation); 30, World History Archive/Alamy Stock Photo; 35, Van Gogh Museum, Amsterdam (Vincent van Gogh Foundation); 37, Van Gogh Museum, Amsterdam, The Netherlands / Bridgeman Images; 39, The Henry Barber Trust, The Barber Institute of Fine Arts, University of Birmingham / Bridgeman Images; 41, Rijksmuseum Kröller-Müller, Otterlo, Netherlands / De Agostini Picture Library / Bridgeman Images; 43, Van Gogh Museum, Amsterdam, The Netherlands / Bridgeman Images; 45, Collection Stedelijk Museum Amsterdam; 47, Musée Rodin, Paris, France / Peter Willi / Bridgeman Images; 49, Van Gogh Museum, Amsterdam, The Netherlands / De Agostini Picture Library / Bridgeman Images; 51, Rijksmuseum Kröller-Müller , Otterlo, Netherlands / De Agostini Picture Library / Bridgeman Images; 53, Private Collection / Photo © Lefevre Fine Art Ltd., London / Bridgeman Images; 55, Pushkin Museum, Moscow, Russia / Bridgeman Images; 57, Van Gogh Museum, Amsterdam, The Netherlands / Bridgeman Images; 59, Photo: Joerg P. Anders.©2019. Photo Scala, Florence/bpk, Bildagentur fuer Kunst, Kultur und Geschichte, Berlin; 61, Van Gogh Museum, Amsterdam, The Netherlands / Bridgeman Images; 63, Photo: Joerg P. Anders.© 2019. Photo Scala, Florence/bpk, Bildagentur fuer Kunst, Kultur und Geschichte, Berlin; 65, Rijksmuseum Kröller-Müller , Otterlo, Netherlands / De Agostini Picture Library / Bridgeman Images; 67, National Gallery of Art, Washington DC, USA / Bridgeman Images; 69, Metropolitan Museum of Art, New York, USA / Bridgeman Images; 71, Private Collection / Photo © Lefevre Fine Art Ltd., London / Bridgeman Images; 73, Private Collection / Photo © Lefevre Fine Art Ltd., London / Bridgeman Images; 75, National Gallery, London, UK / Bridgeman Images; 77, Yale University Art Gallery, New Haven, CT, USA / Bridgeman Images; 79, Rijksmuseum Kröller-Müller , Otterlo, Netherlands / Bridgeman Images; 81, Musee d'Orsay, Paris, France / Bridgeman Images; 83, Fogg Art Museum, Harvard Art Museums, USA / Bequest from the Collection of Maurice Wertheim, Class 1906 / Bridgeman Images; 85, Van Gogh Museum, Amsterdam, The Netherlands / Bridgeman Images; 87, Van Gogh Museum, Amsterdam, The Netherlands / Bridgeman Images; 89, National Gallery, London, UK / Bridgeman Images; 91, Metropolitan Museum of Art, New York, USA / Bridgeman Images; 93, Metropolitan Museum of Art, New York, USA / Bridgeman Images; 95, Samuel Courtauld Trust, The Courtauld Gallery, London, UK / Bridgeman Images; 97, Museum of Modern Art, New York, USA / Bridgeman Images; 99, Metropolitan Museum of Art, New York, USA / Bridgeman Images; 101, Samuel Courtauld Trust, The Courtauld Gallery, London, UK / Bridgeman Images; 103, J. Paul Getty Museum, Los Angeles, USA / Bridgeman Images; 105, Museum of Modern Art, New York, USA / Bridgeman Images; 107, Museum of Modern Art, New York, USA / Bridgeman Images; 109, National Gallery, London, UK / Bridgeman Images; 111, Musée d'Orsay, Paris, France / Bridgeman Images; 113, Musee d'Orsay, Paris, France / Bridgeman Images; 115, Metropolitan Museum of Art, New York, USA / Bridgeman Images; 117, Van Gogh Museum, Amsterdam, The Netherlands / Bridgeman Images; 119, Rijksmuseum Kröller-Müller , Otterlo, Netherlands / Bridgeman Images; 121, National Gallery, London, UK / Bridgeman Images; 123, Musée d'Orsay, Paris, France / Bridgeman Images; 125, Musee d'Orsay, Paris, France / Bridgeman Images; 127, Saint Louis Art Museum, Missouri, USA / Museum Purchase / Bridgeman Images; 129, Van Gogh Museum, Amsterdam, The Netherlands / Bridgeman Images; 131, ©Tate, London, 2019; 133, Van Gogh Museum, Amsterdam, The Netherlands / Bridgeman Images.
Cover Photograph © National Gallery, London/Bridgeman Images, Sunflowers

ACKNOWLEDGEMENTS

This book was made possible by a legacy of Van Gogh research. Credit should be given to the pioneers of Van Gogh scholarship, of which the following is an incomplete list: the late John Rewald; the late Jan Hulsker; the late Ronald Pickvance; the late Ingo F. Walther; Rainer Metzger; and Susan Alyson Stein. The original collection of Van Gogh's letters was edited by the artist's sister-in-law Johanna van Gogh-Bonger. A more recent collection of the letters, available both in print and online, was edited by Leo Jansen, Hans Luijten and Nienke Bakker. Advanced scholarship on Van Gogh's work continues today under the auspices of the Van Gogh Museum, Amsterdam.

I thank my friend, art historian Francis Naumann, for his moral support and editorial suggestions while this book was in progress.

Finally, I thank the management and staff of Pavilion Books, London: Polly Powell, publisher, who first suggested *Van Gogh in 50 Works*; my editor, Bella Cockrell; Michelle Mac, designer; Diana Vowles, copy editor and Emily Hedges, picture researcher.

Pavilion
An imprint of HarperCollinsPublishers Ltd
1 London Bridge Street
London SE1 9GF

www.harpercollins.co.uk

HarperCollinsPublishers
1st Floor, Watermarque Building, Ringsend Road
Dublin 4, Ireland

10 9 8 7 6 5 4 3 2

First published in Great Britain by Pavilion, 2019

John Cauman asserts the moral right to be identified as the author of this work. A catalogue record for this book is available from the British Library.

ISBN 978-1-911624-43-1

MIX
Paper | Supporting responsible forestry
FSC™ C007454

This book is produced from independently certified FSC™ paper to ensure responsible forest management.

For more information visit:
www.harpercollins.co.uk/green

Printed and bound in China